PATRIOTIC GAMES

SPORTS AND HISTORY
Peter Levine and Steven Tischler, General Editors

Sports and Freedom
    The Rise of Big-Time College Athletics
    Ronald A. Smith

Ellis Island to Ebbetts Field
    Sports and the American Jewish Experience
    Peter Levine

Brooklyn's Dodgers
    The Bums, The Borough, and the Best of Baseball
    Carl E. Prince

Patriotic Games
    Sporting Traditions in the American Imagination, 1876–1926
    S. W. Pope

PATRIOTIC GAMES

Sporting
Traditions
in the
American
Imagination,
1876–1926

S. W. POPE

New York   Oxford
Oxford University Press
1997

Oxford University Press

Oxford   New York
Athens   Auckland   Bangkok   Bogota   Bombay
Buenos Aires   Calcutta   Cape Town   Dar es Salaam
Delhi   Florence   Hong Kong   Istanbul   Karachi
Kuala Lumpur   Madras   Madrid   Melbourne
Mexico City   Nairobi   Paris   Singapore
Taipei   Tokyo   Toronto

and associated companies in
Berlin   Ibadan

Published by Oxford University Press, Inc.,
198 Madison Avenue, New York, New York 10016

Oxford is a registered trademark of Oxford University Press

Library of Congress Cataloging-in-Publication Data
Pope, Steven W. (Steven Wayne), 1962–
    Patriotic games : sporting traditions in the American imagination,
1876-1926 / S. W. Pope.
      p.   cm.
    Includes index.
    ISBN 0-19-509133-7
    1. Nationalism and sports—United States—History—19th century.
2. Nationalism and sports—United States—History—20th century.
3. Sports—United States—Sociological aspects—History—19th
century.   4. Sports—United States—sociological aspects—
History—20th century.   I. Title.
GV706.34.P67   1996
796'.0973—dc20   96-5506

9 8 7 6 5 4 3 2 1

Printed in the United States of America
on acid-free paper

For
    BILL,
        CATHY,
            JAMES,
                and
                    LORETTA

PREFACE

The most controversial issue in contemporary sports is the big money paid for athletic performances. Unlike any other occupation, professional athletes' salaries are so widely reported by the media that they have become household knowledge. Even people who have never attended a professional game are keenly aware of what certain well-publicized sports stars earn. During the 234-day major-league-baseball strike in 1994–95, fans and journalists alike heaped utter contempt on the players for their refusal to accept the owners' proposed salary caps. Defenders of free-market capitalism, joining hands with champions of workers' solidarity and collective bargaining, condemned the multimillion dollar salaries paid for "child's play."

Occasionally, the barbed criticisms abate during moments of heightened national significance—the Olympics are an obvious example. Since the 1960s, popular wisdom has been that American Olympians were "amateurs" who competed against the state-sponsored "professionals" of the Eastern bloc, in what journalists and television sports commentators described as grueling David-versus-Goliath contests. Just prior to the 1992 Barcelona Games, the world basketball-governing body, FIBA (International Amateur Basketball Federation) revised the eligibility requirements to enable professionals to participate. FIBA representatives wanted the basketball explosion to continue on the international level, and were willing to sacrifice their own teams' fate at Barcelona if the American superstars would agree to play.

When the official word came down that National Basketball Association (NBA) stars could compete, American sports fans rejoiced, and envisioned a "Dream Team" that would vindicate the nation's sporting culture, which had appeared threatened by the success of Eastern-bloc and Far East teams in recent Games. Without a Cold War to fight, many Americans were satisfied with the prospect of a proxy battle that would finally enable America's best to challenge the stable of professionals from other countries. To nobody's surprise, America's Dream Team trounced all its opponents by huge margins.[1]

A more apropos incident than the one that materialized before the medals ceremony could not have been invented to illuminate the transformation of sports over the past century. In their pursuit of mammon's gold, the United States Olympic Committee (USOC) sold the sponsoring rights to the athletes' medal-receiving warm-up outfits to Reebok, the athletic-footwear company—a deal that is merely part of an ambitious marketing scheme that currently nets the Olympic movement millions of dollars. Michael Jordan, superstar among the world's athletes, and, as Donald Katz characterized him, the symbol of "the great big marketplace-to-come in Barcelona,"[2] flatly refused to wear the Reebok-sponsored outfit at the medals ceremony. Teammate Charles Barkley followed Jordan's lead. The cause of their refusal was obvious: Both Jordan and Barkley are paid handsomely by a competitor, Nike, to wear and endorse its products. Katz discerns the irony of the dilemma:

> Here, after all, was a sports moment meant to reside above the marketplace, an event indicative of sport's traditional purity of purpose: the flag unfurled and the national anthem on the public-address system, the tears of young athletes glistening in the arc lights. And yet certain ostentatiously remunerated basketball players seemed willing to deny the nation this experience because of loyalty not to the flag, to the "glory of sport" or "honor of our teams," as the Olympic oath has it, but to a certain company in Oregon that markets their shoes.[3]

"These days," Barkley reflected, without shame, just after the Games, "you play a sport very well and that takes you to a certain level by itself." "But, Nike can take you way beyond that," he said, as if uttering a rehearsed commercial endorsement. Nike has helped me make a whole lot of money, and I'm not about to forget it."[4]

United States Olympic Committee officials announced that if Jordan, Barkley, David Robinson, John Stockton, Scottie Pippen, and Chris Mullen—the Nike endorsers comprising half of the American team (with the other players having Converse, Reebok, and Starter contracts)—did not wear the official awards-ceremony uniforms bearing the Reebok emblem, the basketball stars would not be allowed atop the medals stand when some 600 million television viewers in 193 countries heard *The Star-Spangled Banner*.[5]

The Nike guys capitulated, at least partially: They donned the Reebok uniforms. But Jordan and Barkley carefully arranged American flags around their necks so as to obstruct the Reebok emblem on their jackets. Jordan said later that he thought nobody would question his patriotism. But some did, and wrote letters to both Nike and the USOC headquarters complaining that wearing a flag was un-American! As Katz concludes, "Citizens who seemed unaware of the logo battle that had preceded the medals ceremony were offended by the flag being turned into clothing and associated with a mere game."[6]

One must strictly avoid castigating commercial "excesses," as *New York Times* journalist Robert Lipsyte, who proclaims that such episodes merely signal the fact that "sports are over because they no longer have any moral resonance." We must also reject the convenient myth that "sports no longer reflect the America of our dreams, and [that] stars of sports are no longer the idealized versions of ourselves." Nor should we caricature contemporary athletes, as Lipsyte does, as "prancing, steroid-bloated, coke-snorting, head-bangers" who appear to be "something short of men."[7] Rather, we should situate contemporary sports dilemmas within a proper historical framework. American fans have always been inherently suspicious about the commercialization of sports. "Once beyond adolescence," Stephen Fox writes, fans "often prefer an imagined golden age of the past, when athletes played the game for pure sport, the action on the field was cleaner and sharper, and star ballplayers in some more innocent era" were "heroic, straight-living 'role models.'"[8] None of that was ever true, but fans persist in yearning for a fantasized past.

How, then, can we explain the considerable staying power of the myth of amateurism and the deeply-rooted ambivalence toward professionalism? How, in the context of a commercially charged, mass-media-oriented culture can the viability of amateurism continue to be sustained? This book attempts to situate this controversy in a historical context that stretches back to the late nineteenth century, when an emergent generation of amateur bureaucrats clung tenaciously to a newly invented sporting ideology as a means of taking control of American athletics.

Pure amateurism never existed in the United States. The romanticized notions of "pure" sport played for "the love of the game" by athletes disinterested in profit were established in American sporting parlance only in the late nineteenth century, *after* institutional control over collegiate sports had begun to shift from the students to presidents and alumni (interested in publicity aimed at alumni donations and increased enrollments). Since then, colleges have hired professional athletic directors, coaches, trainers, scouts, and support staff and paid handsome salaries for their efforts. To mystify the seamier reality, the newly invented "amateur tradition" was quickly cast into moral and nationalistic terms. As I will argue in this book, the bureaucrats of amateurism made their case in the early twentieth century by linking their cause to Americanism—a vision that continues to be accepted as the given, natural, and purest form of sport today.

This arrangement indeed reigns supreme today because most people have been thoroughly indoctrinated and, thus, refuse to see amateur sports for what they really are—an industry that generates millions of dollars in profits for the mass media, corporate sponsors, amateur organizations, and universities. Despite its inherent intellectual dishonesty and dubious ethics, the problem with upholding amateurism, according to renowned sportswriter Leonard Koppett, is that it "guarantees daily indoctrination in false values."[9] For American society, the notion that athletic work should not be rewarded is a fundamental one. Although Americans rejected the old-world, privileged leisure class (that governed and played without pay) many years ago, many continue to tenaciously hold onto such values in relation to the world of sports—a contradiction to the central tenets of our society. "A more pervasive institutionalization of hypocrisy is hard to imagine," Koppett polemicizes passionately. "Almost all the harmful effects of the sports establishment can be traced to this misnamed 'ideal,' [and] poison," which have been pumped through American society for more than a century.[10] In short, Americans love their professionalized amateur sports, but are unwilling to admit the economic reality of these athletic spectacles. As a culture, we want to have our cake and eat it, too. I suggest that this act of national self-denial underlies contemporary popular contempt toward professional athletes.[11]

The resiliency of American amateurism illustrates how certain dominant notions about sport were established and institutionalized in the national imagination between the 1870s and the 1920s. This book attempts to address several other, related, questions: How did nationalism color the world of American sport between the late nineteenth and early twentieth centuries? How did a thriving sporting culture shape conceptions of America during the same period? How did American sports advocates legitimize the national identity by connecting their cause to American sensibilities? And, how did the invention of a vigorous, sporting culture inform America not only a century ago; but how, also, does it inform it today? I make no pretense whatsoever of fully answering these questions. Rather, I've tried to engage an ongoing debate about how our society came to be so thoroughly imbued with what several scholars have described as "the promise of American sport."

This book began as the doctoral dissertation I did at the University of Maine. I had never intended to write about sports until I worked as William Baker's teaching assistant in his popular "Sports in the Western World" course, during the fall of 1990. Under his tutelage, I became fascinated with the prospect of making sense of American nationalism through the study of sport. Bill prodded, challenged, and encouraged me in my work when neither of us had a clear idea of where the foray would lead. Baker shared his keen knowledge of sports and historical writing, and read subsequent drafts of my revised manuscript. I thank him for his patience, insight, wit, and generosity.

I am also deeply indebted to Stephen Hardy. Not only did Steve serve on my dissertation committee, but he encouraged me to develop more explicitly the amateurism theme that is now central to this book. His untiring guidance, conceptual suggestions, and thoughtful critique have shaped both this book and my understanding of sport and American culture.

I have also received timely encouragement and advice from colleagues, friends, and family. Sport scholars Doug Booth, Mark Dyreson, Elliott Gorn, Allen Guttmann, Peter Levine, Donald Mrozek, John Nauright, and Benjamin Rader have been in my corner for the past several years. Historians Richard Judd and David Smith read this manuscript in its initial dissertation form; their comments inspired me to recast several aspects. At Oxford, Sheldon Meyer championed the work and offered several valuable suggestions; Lisa Stallings and Barry Lenner gave thorough attention to the manuscript and thereby saved me from countless inconsistencies and embarrassments.

I thank my family—James, Loretta, and Eric Pope and Angela Harrington—for their love. I thank friends Pat Finn, Annette Langley, Janet Larkin, John Markward, Craig Stevens, David Tapley, Jack Warden, and Julia Warden for their unwavering moral support. I must also acknowledge a handful of musicians and songwriters: Charlie Parker, Miles Davis, Wes Montgomery, Thelonious Monk, George Gershwin, Cole Porter, B.B. King, Bob Wills, Hank Williams, Johnny Cash, and Ray Benson. Their artistry sustained my long, otherwise solitary, days in front of the computer screen as I prepared this work.

The final acknowledgement is to my best friend and true love, Cathy, who has supported me in countless ways throughout our ten years together. As one that has endured and assisted this project from the start, she has, truly, gone the distance. Without her, this book would not have been possible, and my life would be much less meaningful.

Portland, Maine   S.W.P.
May 1996

CONTENTS

AMERICANIZING SPORT FOR A NATIONAL CULTURE

ONE

SPORT AND AMERICAN IDENTITY

HISTORICAL CONTEXT

Between the 1876 centennial and the 1926 sesquicentennial, a national sporting culture was firmly established in the United States. During this era, which one sport scholar has characterized as the "cusp between America's Century of Work and its Century of Play,"[1] baseball became the acknowledged national pastime; basketball was invented; boxing exploded in popularity under new rules; football grew into a national, widely attended spectator sport; a recreation movement blossomed on the nation's playgrounds; and sports became central to the educational curriculum. In addition, tennis, golf, and bicycling swept through the middle class, while workers started their own semiprofessional and amateur leagues in a variety of team sports. Organizational and business structures arose to regulate and rationalize these new activities, which were enjoyed by professionals, college students, military personnel, industrial workers, African-Americans, Indians, town teams, and schoolchildren; games were played on sandlots, and in cow pastures, playgrounds, public parks, and modern stadiums.[2]

Moreover, between the opening of the transtlantic cable and the first play-by-play radio broadcast of major-league baseball, an American sporting audience and accompanying consciousness took shape.[3] As a result, the widespread popularity of institutionalized sports became the focus of daily conversations and helped promote an interlocking set of cultural ideas about America and its relationship with the world. More than mere amusement, sport both as metaphorical activity and class drama, helped define and display uniquely American visions through public discourse and through people's actual experiences on ballfields, in gymnasiums, and on playgrounds throughout the country.

By 1920, most Americans thought that organized sports provided the social glue for a nation of diverse classes, regions, ethnic groups and competing political loyalties. Walter Camp, one of the most influential shapers of modern American athletics, described sport as "the broad folk highway" of the nation. As calls for "Americanization" reached a crescendo after World War I, he illuminated the relationship between sport and the national life: "More people march together and contentedly and in democratic spirit along that highway," Camp maintained, "than along any other of the roads trod by humankind."[4] A whole host of cultural commentators concurred. Sport had indeed been transformed into one of the most influential activities involved in the production of a modern national identity.

Camp's characterization of sport as "the broad folk highway" of America would not have made sense in a country that was lacking a resilient national identity. Historical context was (and is) everything. But such an important precondition did not exist before the late nineteenth century. Although the American Revolution represented the first modern dramatization of an emergent nationalist ethos, political power, prior to the Civil War, continued to remain decentralized in local communities and regions; and the influence of the young nation-state was something that most citizens actually feared, that they thought should be strictly limited. Ordinary Americans occasionally marched through streets proclaiming that the nation-state was not necessarily a symbol of patriotic allegiance, but a vehicle for obtaining greater political equality and social justice. The colonies' separation from Britain stimulated the need for a cohesive national consciousness and American identity, but the Founding Fathers fostered this development primarily on an ideological terrain—liberty, equality, and republicanism. Whatever "reality" existed in American nationalism, David Waldstreicher writes, lay "not in any truly lasting political or ideological consensus among its followers, but in its practices"—celebratory events and the "reproduction of rhetoric and ritual in print."[5]

Consequently, pre–Civil War cultural activities and bodily practices were only rarely billed as exemplars of the national character. Sports were no exception. As early as 1858, the *Atlantic Monthly* referred to "our indigenous American game of baseball, whose briskness an unceasing activity are perhaps more congenial, after all, to our national character, than the comparative deliberation of cricket." In more dramatic fashion, in 1860, Irish-American boxer John Heenan challenged English champion Thomas Sayers for the supremacy of the boxing world. On this occasion, *Vanity Fair* published a satirical engraving—"The Two Champions"—depicting George Washington gripping the "Benicia Boy" in a headlock, while "Liberty" stood aside sighing for her country. Currier and Ives published cheap lithographs of both heroes, and the fight dominated the pages of not only the early sports journals, but of nationally circulated newspapers like the *New York Times* and even respectable middle-class magazines like *Harper's Weekly*. Boxing was indeed an ideal vehicle for rivalry among national symbols. Donning red, white, and blue shorts that featured the American eagle, Heenan emerged the victor after 42 rounds. The fight occurred when American nationhood was disturbingly tenuous; in 1860, the need for unifying national symbols was particularly acute. As Elliott Gorn notes in his study of early prizefighting, the Heenan–Sayers bout "deflect[ed] internal divisions onto an outside enemy" that allowed men to "experience a rush of patriotic fervor precisely when things were falling apart."[6]

The sport of boxing remained socially and culturally meaningless in America until the proper material conditions developed. In particular, Gorn points out, boxing depended on a large underclass of unattached men who had little to lose by entering the bloody ring. In the United States, labor remained scarce and relatively well compensated until the late 1860s. And unlike England, where prizefighting was patronized by influential men, America did not have a powerful aristocracy to counter the vehement opposition of the middle class to the immorality of "blood" sports. Wealthy sporting Americans might have followed boxing in sports journals like the *Spirit of the Times*, but most middle-class boxing fans did not yet fraternize with the principal social group to which boxing primarily appealed—the emergent working class— which remained isolated from the social forces that would transform American sports in the last decades of the nineteenth century.[7]

For all practical purposes, sports in pre–Civil War America remained segregated by class, and could not, therefore, claim a national following. Horse racing and cricket were restricted to eastern elites. Baseball was played primarily by the urban middle class and skilled craftsmen, and lacked a national organizational structure until the 1870s. Football did not take hold until the early 1870s, and for its first two decades was dominated by a small circle of elite private universities. Pedestrianism, or early commercialized track and field, was associated with workers and immigrants. And basketball was not invented until 1891. Thus, prior to the mid-1870s, America lacked both a dominant national identity and an established sporting tradition.

The Civil War reawakened the nationalist spirits of the revolutionary era and solidified the bonds between the Union and liberty. Between the mid-1860s and mid-1870s, sports proliferated, and were transformed from local and regional contests into nationally standardized and commercialized ones. Amateurism flourished in private clubs and in intercollegiate athletics, and open professionalism became an established sports feature as regional and national leagues were formed. Any residual doubts about the values or negative effects of sports were pushed aside by the "muscular Christianity" movement, which actively promoted athletics as healthy, socially beneficial activities. Competition became an interregional, intercity, national, and international phenomenon as individuals and teams from the United States, Britain, and Canada competed in games and contests—thus introducing the nexus between sports and nationalism.[8]

During the same period, a host of national organizations arose to regulate the burgeoning sporting culture. The dominant sport of the pre–Civil War era—horse racing—witnessed the birth of the National Association for the Promotion of the American Trotting Turf in 1870; the Grand Circuit opened in 1873; and in 1876, the National Association of Trotting Horse Breeders was organized. Pimlico, Belmont, Churchill Downs, and other tracks opened shortly thereafter, and summarily inaugurated major races (e.g., the Kentucky Derby) that became national spectacles.

In 1871, leaders of America's dominant post–Civil War sport organized the National Association of Professional Baseball Players. In addition to the several baseball minor leagues that emerged during the late 1870s and 1880s, the National League was established in 1876; and six years later, the American Base Ball Association (which later became the American League) initiated a rivalry that would last 21 years, until the two merged to become the major leagues. Further, yachting took on national as well as international proportions, with the commencement of the America's Cup Races of 1870, 1871, and 1876. And, the pre–Civil War professional sport of pedestrianism was eclipsed by the formation, in 1875, of an amateur track-and-field organization—the Intercollegiate Association of Amateur Athletes of America.

There were other significant organizational breakthroughs in amateur sports. Although football was limited to several eastern universities, the founding of an American Intercollegiate Football Association in 1876 helped eliminate differences in styles of play. Early collegiate athletics came to be more closely regulated in 1879, when the National Association of Amateur Athletes of America was formed (it was later reorganized as the National Collegiate Athletic Association, or NCAA). In 1888 the Amateur Athletic Union (AAU) emerged as the principal organizational rival of the NCAA. Athletics and physical education were stimulated by the founding, in 1885, of the International Training School of the YMCA (itself created in 1869) at Springfield, Massachusetts, and by the growth of the American Association for the Advancement of Physical Education.

Also, new national organizations were formed to regulate cycling, canoeing, skating, and croquet. Tennis was inaugurated on American turf in 1875, and by 1881, the sport was subsumed under the control of the United States Lawn Tennis Association; the prestigious Davis Cup championship was organized in 1900. Golf, imported from Scotland, was a new game that fascinated a leisure class of sportsmen at the early country clubs in the 1880s. They founded the United States Golf Association in 1894; its membership, four years later, numbered 103 clubs. By 1899, there were 887 golf clubs in the United States (154 were west of the Mississippi River), and by 1910, the National Golf Links of America sponsored 20 major tournaments.

Most Americans had no *direct* relationship with these early governing bodies. Nevertheless, they established the contests, rules, and ethos of modern sport, and popularized newly conceived sports traditions among the previously ambivalent population. In British historian Eric Hobsbawm's words, such contests provided "a public showcase for sport, as well as a mechanism for extending activities hitherto confined to the aristocracy and bourgeoisie to a widening range of 'middle classes.'"[9]

Many more Americans did, however, have direct access to the burgeoning print media, whose growth during this period paralleled the spread of organized sports and athletics. Prior to the Civil War, American magazines were marketed primarily to the educated middle- and upper-class audiences. From the 700 magazines published in 1865, the industry grew to 1,200 in 1870 and 3,300 by 1885. The magazines with the largest circulation figures were *Youth's Companion*, *Scribner's*, *Harper's*, *Century*, *The Ladies' Home Journal*, the *Delineator*, and the *National Police Gazette*. By century's end, circulation figures had spiraled to phenomenal levels, as magazines reached out to new, larger audiences beyond the upper-middle-class readers. Amid cutthroat competition, most magazines reduced prices from 35¢ to 15¢ to 10¢, and eventually to 5¢, consequently ushering in the mass-market phase of their evolution as shapers of American opinion.

Once the dust had settled, the *Literary Digest* (forerunner of *Time* and *Newsweek*) emerged as the leader, followed by *Collier's*. With its exceptional coverage of the Spanish-Amercan War, by the likes of Will Irwin, Richard Harding Davis, Finley Peter Dunne, and Ring Lardner—all of whom also wrote important articles on sports—the circulation of *Collier's* increased rapidly at the turn of the century. This reflected magazines' marketing strategy, aimed at a younger generation that did not identify with the Civil War, but did, instead, follow the exciting turmoil of expansionistic, imperialist America. Newspapers and sports journals also experienced similar growth during the post–Civil War period. After the establishment of A. G. Spalding & Brothers, in 1876, the *Spalding Guide* developed into the authority on rules of play, and the Spalding Athletic Library offered all sorts of sports handbooks. So did the *New York Clipper*, the *New York World*, the *New York Tribune*, the *Chicago Daily News*, the *Washington Post*, and the *National Police Gazette*. Moreover, in 1883 after he purchased the *New York World*, Joseph Pulitzer introduced the first sports department at a major newspaper; in 1886, the St. Louis weekly, the *Sporting News*, began publication; in 1895, William Randolph Hearst offered the first newspaper sports section; and by the mid-1890s, most major papers followed suit. Between 1890 and 1919, magazines and newspapers were unrivaled in capturing the imagination of American audiences; they were not only the only national communications media, but they also cultivated a captive audience for middle-class and elite voices.[10]

Infused with ritual, symbols, and Americanist rhetoric, sporting traditions were invented and perpetuated through the print media; national periodicals and journals of opinion; and books for popular markets. Waldstreicher demonstrates the parallel between rhetoric and ritual in the early newspapers' reporting of celebratory occasions in revolutionary America. "Rhetoric works like ritual in that it persuades through invocation of reliable, repeated movements," he writes, and "ritual, like rhetoric, brings us into communion with the performer and the performance."[11] In this sense, newspapers as printed rhetoric combined street theater and the act of reading. This relationship between journalism and performance explains the importance of the early sports media's effort to inform a growing public about athletics, while simultaneously reassuring the readers that such activities were commonplace throughout the country. As sport historian John Nauright explains, individuals and groups construct, revise, and reshape the interpretations of sports events that are subsequently digested by a wider audience. Sporting traditions are then presented to the public in a variety of ways, as part of a collective experience, to popularize and legitimize particular philosophies, products, and political ideologies.[12]

Although the Civil War stimulated patriotic fervor (especially in the North) and spawned national sports organizations, it was not until 1876, when they celebrated the nation's centennial and the end of Reconstruction, that most Americans thought of themselves as a nominally reunited nation. The exposition held in Philadelphia that year diverted attention from regional and racial problems; celebrated American achievements in industry, science, agriculture, and the arts; and announced that the United States had become a model by which all nations must measure progress. A growing social group of entrepreneurs and professionals nationalized the economy, expanded corporate power, and celebrated material progress. Nevertheless, as historian Alan Dawley argues, the bustling society and existing liberal state, designed a century earlier for a much different type of social system, grappled with the meaning of American values and ideals.[13]

The lower classes did not, however, passively accept such changes. Workers, farmers, immigrants, and other ordinary Americans drew on a long heritage of utopianism, radical abolitionism, and working-class activism to restore the republic to its original egalitarian principles—thus curtailing the ability of the ruling classes to enrich themselves through the state's machinery. Homegrown radicalism sought to broaden individual freedom, while resisting capitalist exploitation. Coinciding with proletarian revolts in Glasgow, Berlin, Turin, and Petrograd, millions of American workers synthesized these strands of proletarian experience and joined hands with comrades around the world in solidarity against capitalism; collectively, they posed a serious threat to the unified, nationalist thinking of the dominant social groups who sought to win tactical economic advantages at the expense of competing nation-states.[14] Seeking to preserve their power in the face of class conflicts, elites championed reform measures that, collectively, ushered in a state-regulated corporatist system in the early twentieth century. Such efforts materialized through compromise and accommodation among dominant sectors of the capitalist class and among smaller capitalists; and through other alliances and alignments that cut across class lines.[15]

Nevertheless, the business class's unrestrained drive for political and cultural power, and the powerful defense of local and vernacular interests that it provoked, ultimately created a willingness, on the part of many social groups, for some form of cooperation.[16] In varying degrees, all Americans experienced the transformative dislocations of industrial capitalism. Many, according to historian Robert Wiebe, experienced these changes as a crisis in their local communities. They became, Wiebe explains, a people under siege from seemingly hostile outside forces, especially from an invisible national market and an intangible national government.[17] By the 1890s, it became clear that national influence had achieved a new stability and permanency. Led by corporate elites whose fate was increasingly tied to the national market, a new political vision coalesced in American public culture. It emphasized the interest all social groups had in maintaining the growing national economy and the need for a more powerful nation-state that could mediate and regulate politics and culture. By the late nineteenth century, most groups within American society ultimately embraced a powerful, centralized nation-state as an ally in their myriad quests for moderating the unregulated change and competition of the era.

In an increasingly heterogeneous society, many Americans found it difficult to define the precise nature of their national identity: Was the nation defined by a shared culture of all the people, or by a political and economic apparatus that promoted the interests of the few over the many? During these late-nineteenth-century years of profound social crisis, what it meant to be an American, or to become an American, was the central question concerning national identity.[18]

Indeed, most Americans, as historian Nina Silber writes, devoted considerable attention to "understanding and articulating those common values or principles which seemed to capture the distinctive role and identity of the American nation"; many hoped to "construct a new, secular, and tangible focus for American national loyalty," which, Silber suggests, took the form of "a variety of self-conscious ruminations about nationalism and patriotism."[19] In the late nineteenth century, people of all classes formed national and international associations and identities. Community-based political campaigns and rallies declined as locales were overshadowed by activities initiated from distant offices. New problems, national in scope, and therefore virtually demanding the national, rather than the local or state, approach, included railway regulation, corporate trusts, currency matters, conservation, tariffs, control of political corruption, industrial safety and hygiene, poverty, and child labor. Under the auspices of hereditary societies and a multitude of patriotic organizations, Americans reflected on the meaning and lessons of the American experience, through strict observance of the symbols and rituals of the national experience. As Silber maintains, many people believed that patriotism would "unify the population around basic and time-honored values of manhood and womanhood, that workers and bosses, natives and immigrants would all come together as loyal American men and women."[20]

Paradoxically, the United States, one of the most clearly defined modern nations, faced a perplexing problem of national identity. In fact, the basic problem was one of assimilating a heterogeneous mass of people who were not Americans by birth.[21] Hobsbawm recognizes that the invented traditions around the turn of the century were designed to achieve this objective of Americanizing a diverse population. In particular, immigrants were strongly encouraged (and often forced) to accept the public rituals that commemorated the national holidays—especially the Fourth of July and Thanksgiving; and the educational system was transformed into a machine for political socialization, through the elevation of flag worship and of English as the compulsory language. Hobsbawm writes, "The concept of 'Americanism' as an act of *choice*—the decision to learn English, to apply for citizenship—and a choice of specific beliefs, acts and modes of behaviour implied the corresponding concept of 'un-Americanism.'"[22] Such a scenario threw doubt on a person's actual status as a member of the American nation.

As I will demonstrate in this examination of sport and American identity, nationalism provided the masses with something real, which strict class consciousness could not promise—a culture, notes British political scientist Tom Nairn, that, "however deplorable, was larger, more accessible, and more relevant to mass realities."[23] Nationalism appealed to psychological needs during a time when the community, family, church, and workplace were undermined by corporate capitalism. As the working-class culture itself became colonized by professionals, bureaucrats, and specialists—all of whom had an interest in opposing class warfare and promoting national unity—it embraced new symbols of community, re-created on the basis of the nation, not class. As Merle Curti explained, this new definition of nationalism celebrated the nation as the "highest form of human association" and effectively discounted arguments that individuals and locales had any right to break their ties to it.[24] The dominant vision of the newly transformed national identity was articulated by influential spokesmen like Theodore Roosevelt, who believed that there was room for but "one flag, the Stars and Stripes, . . . for but one loyalty, loyalty to the United States, [and] . . . for but one language, the language of the Declaration of Independence and the Gettysburg Address, the English language. . . . We must all of us be Americans, and nothing but Americans."[25] Nationalist sentiments traversed ideological lines as well. Edward Bellamy baptized his own form of socialism, calling it "nationalism," on the basis of his belief that "what Socialism desires to reach in a universal way for the world, nationalism desires to obtain within the limits of the nation."[26] On another occasion, Bellamy declared that the term *nationalism* seemed appropriate because "its purpose was to realize the idea of the nation with a grandeur and completeness never before conceived, not as an association of men for certain merely political functions, but as a family, a vital union, a common life, a mighty heaven-touching tree whose leaves are its people, fed from its veins, and feeding it in turn."[27]

Advocates of a national culture, did not however, issue a cohesive manifesto, as historian Michael Kammen has suggested, nor did they agree on a precise agenda. But collectively, Kammen shows, they agreed on the following notions: that a culture would not be parochial or sectional; that it would compensate for the excesses of American heterogeneity and provide some basis for cultural unification; would signify social maturity—a national coming of age; and reflect the belief that, by definition, a nation could not achieve greatness without manifestations of a national culture.[28]

All such hopes, dreams, and anxieties were refracted through the lens of sports. The rise of modern athletics provided the emergent middle class with new expressions of nationalism, through the choice and invention of nationally-specific sports. Central to the establishment of popular national sporting traditions was the need to affirm the nationally-specific character of particular sports. Between the 1870s and 1920s, considerable energies went into establishing the fact that baseball, a sport that had derived from various eighteenth- and nineteenth-century English games, was a uniquely American invention. Football, a sport that had existed since medieval times, was Americanized in the 1880s (i.e., transformed from its traditional rugby-soccer style to a regular scrimmage with set plays, passing, etc.). Track and field had existed since antiquity, but in the context of the revived modern Olympics, became the foremost American sport in international competitions. In fact, the only principal sport created in the United States, basketball, appeared late in the nineteenth century and did not become an important mass spectator attraction until after World War I. Organized mostly by middle-class men, institutionalized sports merged disparate social groups into a reasonably unified national community.

NATIONALISM: THEORY AND METHODOLOGY

My interest in nationalism predates my decision to write about American sport. As a doctoral student, I discovered that scholars had traditionally focused on the economic, political, and diplomatic factors in the origin and maintenance of modern nationalism, but that the nation no longer plays the starring role in historical scholarship that it once played. Indeed, from the mid-nineteenth century until the 1960s, the nation was the preeminent subject of American history, and the primary arena in which that history unfolded. But by the late 1960s and early 1970s, the dominant focus on political history was increasingly eclipsed within the profession by the new social and cultural history.[29] The pendulum has, however, recently swung back toward the study of larger structures and national communities, and toward what might be termed a social history of national politics.[30]

During my early forays into the study of national cultures, I was profoundly influenced by a coterie of British Marxist historians and political scientists associated with the *New Left Review*, who challenged the older leftist orthodox concept that nationalism was merely the battle cry of the capitalist class, mechanically imposed on society. Employing a more dialectical approach, Eric Hobsbawm, Stuart Hall, Raphael Samuel, Benedict Anderson, and Perry Anderson explained why nationalistic rhetoric and imagery sounded so persuasive not only to elites, but to the working classes as well. In so doing, they initiated the study of how national myths, symbols, and values have always been contested terrain, and pioneered a new set of premises, questions, and methods for a better understanding of this historical phenomenon.

My conceptual point of entry into the study of sport and national identity embraces the historical materialist approach, and is particularly informed by Antonio Gramsci's theoretical writings on cultural hegemony. Since the mid-1980s, *hegemony* has become an overused buzzword throughout many scholarly circles. The contemporary use of the term derives from the work of Gramsci, whose *Prison Notebooks* (written during the late 1920s and early 1930s) were not translated into English until 1971.[31]

Gramsci suggested that modern social groups rule mostly by persuasion, rather than by explicit coercion, and, most profoundly, within "civil society"; in fact, a fundamental class and its allies exercise "moral leadership" over the larger society through their control over the fundamental ideological institutions.[32] In short, a dominant class alliance becomes a hegemonic one when it has effectively articulated its version of social reality to the larger population, thus enabling it to become the universal class, expressing—in most cases—the "national interest." As cultural studies theorist Stuart Hall explains it: "The circle of dominant ideas does accumulate the symbolic power to map or classify the world for others; its classifications do acquire not only the constraining power of dominance over other modes of thought but also the inertial authority of habit and instinct. It becomes the horizon of the taken for granted; what the world is and how it works, for all practical purposes."[33] Such common-sense matters, however, must be continually renegotiated in specific historical situations involving conflict over cultural and socio-cultural resources. For the purposes of this study, such negotiations occurred within the realm of popular activities—including sports—which serve as a central site for the struggle over cultural hegemony.[34]

Echoing Marx's oft-quoted conviction that people make their own history, but not necessarily under conditions of their own choosing, Raymond Williams introduced "social practices" to emphasize how they continually re-create dominant ideas (and structures) through their own participation in a practice. At the same time, the preexisting conventions of the practice shape and constrain their behavior, and also provide the framework within which they interpret the practice in their own ways. Such an approach shifts the analysis from cause and effect to process. In terms of sports history, Stephen Hardy and Alan Ingham stress the need to explore the ways in which sport and leisure industries became embedded in the fabric of everyday life; the ways in which leisure practices are shaped by the participation of people, individually and collectively; and the ways in which multiple interests are expressed through these processes.[35]

Following Gramsci's emphasis on the role of "organic" intellectuals, this study scrutinizes those cultural leaders that articulated and popularized certain (ultimately) hegemonic ideas about sports and American identity. As Gramsci wrote, "every social group coming into existence creates its own organic intellectuals which give it homogeneity and an awareness of its own function, not only in the economic but also in the social and political fields."[36] Moreover, such "intellectuals" are distinguished "less by their profession than by their function in directing the ideas and aspirations of the class to which they belong."[37] Influenced by Gramscian theory, historians Hobsbawm and Williams have interpreted the vestiges of organic intellectuals' imaginative ideological labor—national myths, rituals, and metaphors—as "invented" or "selective" traditions. According to Hobsbawm, invented traditions are "symbolic responses to novel situations which take the form of reference to old situations."[38] Tradition is the clearest expression of the dominant and hegemonic pressures—the most powerful practical means of incorporation, which Williams suggested as "an intentionally selective version of a shaping past and a pre-shaped present, which is then powerfully operative in the process of social and cultural definition and identification."[39] From a whole possible range of past and present conditions in a particular culture, he argued, "certain meanings and practices are selected for emphasis and [other] meanings and practices are neglected and excluded."[40]

The historical process of inventing national traditions is, moreover, closely related to the problematical nature of public memory. Public memory represents a body of beliefs and ideas about the past (and includes the fundamental issues about the entire existence of a society—its organization, its structure of power, and the very meaning of its past and present); these help a society understand its past, present, and future, which are fashioned and legitimized in the public sphere. People use it as a cognitive device for mediating competing interpretations, and for privileging some explanations over others. Thus, the symbolic language of patriotism is central to public memory in the United States because it has the capacity to mediate both vernacular loyalties to local and familiar places and official loyalties to national and imagined structures.

Ultimately, national memory is shared by people who have never seen or heard of one another, yet who regard themselves, as Benedict Anderson has so persuasively argued, as having a common history. The parallel notions of identity and memory alert us to the fact that these terms are interdependent—neither is fixed and objective; both are representations, subjective constructions of reality, and not clearly bounded and demarcated, as we have thought. Each identity implies and, at the same time, masks a particular relationship. Thus, historians are obliged to decipher such constructions so as to expose and analyze the relationships they create and sustain.[41]

One clue here is that the process of inventing national traditions occurs most rapidly when fundamental transformations weaken or destroy the older patterns, and their carriers no longer prove to be compelling. Late in the nineteenth century, wrenching social transformations destroyed patterns for which old traditions and their institutional carriers were designed—dominant groups, particularly when challenged by movements that questioned their legitimacy, sought to maintain and reestablish the loyalty and cooperation of their subjects. As the quintessential patriotic social group, Hobsbawm demonstrates the middle class found it easier to establish a sense of belonging through external symbols, among which the nationalist traditions were most significant. As a result, the bourgeoisie, as a class in the making, invented new traditions which were rather unspecific and vague—revolving around patriotism, loyalty, duty, and "playing the game"—but which bolstered the fledgling nation-states of nineteenth-century Western society. Since the Industrial Revolution, invented nationalist traditions have been used to establish real or artificial communities, particular institutions and relationships of power, socializing value systems, and conventions of behavior.[42] As such, modern nations are, in the words of Anderson, "imagined communities," since "members of even the smallest nation will never know most of their fellow-members, meet them, or even hear of them, yet in the minds of each lives the image of their communion."[43] But the universal, invented folklore of modern nationalism is not entirely wrong, since if it were, it would be unable to function as myth. It is, Nairn argues, "a mechanism of adjustment and compensation, a way of living with the reality of those forms of historical development we label 'nationalism.' It supplies peoples and persons with an important commodity, 'identity.'"[44] Moreover, it "denotes the new and heightened significance accorded to factors of nationality, ethnic inheritance, customs and speech from the early nineteenth century onwards." This book will incorporate these theoretical assumptions and test the staying power of tradition as it applies to American sport.[45]

SCOPE AND ORGANIZATION OF THE BOOK

The study of sport offers a unique window into a larger historical process, in which men and women, social classes, and racial and ethnic groups struggle over different versions of how to live, how to work and play, and what to value. This process materializes in the "public culture"—a forum that historian Thomas Bender describes as the place "where power in its various forms is elaborated and made authoritative."[46] Sport sociologist Richard Gruneau alerts us to how, historically, the fundamental measures of power, manifested through sports, have had the capacity to establish selective traditions; to define "legitimate" sports forms and appropriate meanings connected with them; and to institutionalize such preferences in rules and organizations. These three critical measures of power in sport history inform this book.[47] Specifically, the ideological content of early-twentieth-century institutionalized sport becomes apparent when we consider some of the major polarities—amateurism versus professionalism; nationalism versus internationalism; individualism versus collectivism; class versus classlessness; masculinity versus femininity; and ethnicity (pluralism) versus Americanism. Moreover, a relative handful of rules committees and national experts have controlled the game forms played by most Americans, and relatively few manufacturers have supplied the goods used at all levels. For almost a century, this network of expert coaches, journalists, administrators, manufacturers, and dealers has largely shaped the boundaries of American sports. It is these essential themes and issues that this book will explore.[48]

This study makes no pretense of being a definitive social history of American sports during a critical period of their development. Individual sports are not covered in the conventional manner. Rather, I will discuss several important episodes in the making of a national sporting culture, and the ways in which such moments were given an Americanist ideological spin in the period between the nation's ultrapatriotic 1876 centennial and 1926 sesquicentennial extravaganzas. This period witnessed the unprecedented construction of nationalistic vestiges on both cultural and geographic landscapes.

On another, related level, this work contributes to our understanding of the staying power of amateurism. The book examines the creation of two dominant sporting ideologies—amateurism and professionalism. Prior to World War I, there was a profound ambiguity about the *preferred* ideology of sport among the American public. Chapter 2 suggests that the rising bureaucrats of amateurism sold their ideology to Americans and the world by playing to the nationalist sentiments of the era, and then briefly sketches how such notions were effectively incorporated into resilient, national athletic structures. While contemporaries and historians have long recognized the shallow and corrupt *material* aspects of amateurism, this book helps explain the attraction of its *ideal* aspects to so many twentieth-century Americans.

Amateurism is, in truth, an invented tradition that dates from only the end of the nineteenth century, and has been an important forum for the making of cultural hegemony in American society. Until 1896, amateurists developed a negative case against professional, commercialized sports. Then, after the revival of the modern Olympics, international contests gained national legitimacy. Thereafter, amateurists shifted to both a positive, and a less-negative, campaign. Indeed, as I argue in part II, leading amateurists ceased their attack on professionals after the tactical victory over professionalism, on the strength of the Olympics, which established an unshakable bond between amateurism and nationalism. Not until the 1960s could professional sport make serious inroads or boast the nationalist cause, since even baseball, the national pastime, was subject only to interracial debate (by the twentieth century, there was no more British-cricket bashing). I argue that Americans have tolerated the corrupt core of amateurism precisely because the progressive, nationalist, and military forces of the 1890s–1920s made it an American obligation. In the long history of American sports, there was nothing fundamentally new about this emergent ideology (muscular Christians and sports journalists had articulated similar views years earlier), but the forces of nationalism provided a powerful, renewed justification that completed the elevation of sports from a status of lower-class immorality and crass professionalism to one of middle-class respectability. In this sense, amateur sports perhaps carried the progressive mentality farther than any other progressive reform movement.[49]

Part III explores the ways in which sports came to be closely associated with the most conspicuous national rituals—the Thanksgiving and Fourth-of-July holiday celebrations. Both were important patriotic moments during which all classes, races, religions, and regions participated in the dramatization of the values and beliefs of American nationalism. Sports were the icing on the cake for these nationalistic rituals. Amid newly created traditions of fight songs, cheers, and postgame parties, football-playing colleges scheduled their major athletic rival for a "turkey day" contest and, in the process, helped transform the religious associations of the day into commercial, secular ones, and legitimized football as a bona fide American sport. The Fourth of July came to mean not only parades and patriotic speeches, but also baseball games, track

meets, and major boxing matches. Sports-filled Fourth-of-July celebrations bridged the transition from "spread-eagle" patriotism to more
subtle messages of class conciliation, ethnic assimilation, and the professional ethos. The struggle to define legitimate sporting traditions and
their meanings prompted bourgeois groups to oversee the ethnic and
working-class sports culture. Sporting traditions were invented to assimilate masses of immigrants into the American way of life. Those who
"played the game" embraced and affirmed their place in the American
community. Residual class and ethnic elements were sustained in one
form or another in established national sporting traditions, but ultimately the dominant cultural meanings prevailed—rationality, productivity, meritocracy, bureaucratic organization, corporate ownership, exchange principles, upward mobility, hero worship, fair play, patriotism,
and consensus.

American involvement in World War I provides the focus for part
IV. World-war-preparedness activities championed amateurism—and
safely ensconced the idea of sports for sports' sake, as the progressive
playground reformers had envisioned during the early part of the twentieth century. The U.S. entry in 1917 prompted vigorous debates about
national preparedness and stimulated federal, state, and local governments to fund sports and physical-fitness training. Military officials used
sports in soldiers' training and, as a result, did much to legitimize particular sports like boxing and football in the public's mind. The government attributed American military success to sports and the physical culture, and, after the war, supported a wide variety of programs and
public facilities designed to strengthen national physical prowess. By
the 1920s, big-time commercialized sports were a central component
of a burgeoning national consumer culture.

TWO

AMATEURISM

The Invention of an Athletic Tradition

Popular wisdom has it that amateurism is the original, pure state of sport. Every four years, during the Olympics, a bevy of sportswriters and cultural commentators credit the ancient Greeks for having initiated competitive athletics out of a deep, genuine love of sport for sport's sake, and as an appropriate activity for praising their gods. In stark contrast, contemporary labor-management disputes in American sports evoke diatribes about the "corrupting" influence of professionalism. For example, in 1995, the distinguished *New York Times* columnist Robert Lipsyte lamented that sports now "show us spoiled fools as role models, cities and colleges held hostage and games that exist only to hawk products."[1] Not only do athletes not "stand for anything beyond themselves," Lipsyte says, but the "connection between player and fan has been irrevocably destabilized." "Instead of sports," he writes, "we happily root for cartoons competing in athletic theme parks fueled without apology by violent thrills and endorsement dollars."[2] Although Lipsyte notes that Americans lost faith in the promise of sport during the late stages of the Vietnam War ("Vietnam punched out the lights of manhood," he says), such statements about the corrupting influence of commercialism and professionalism on sports are nothing new.[3]

Since the mid-nineteenth century, there has been a persistent debate about the preferred American sporting ethos, which has vacillated between the extremes of amateurism and professionalism. Over the years, the debate has been closely entwined with the national memory. As historian Warren Goldstein has argued in his history of the early period of professional baseball, sports exist on both a linear level and a cyclical one. The former charts the organizational and institutional developments; the latter revolves around the repetitive and generational relationships, which have remained remarkably consistent since the 1850s.

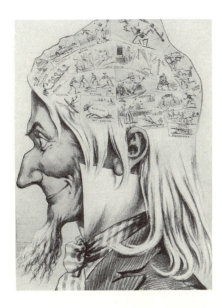

Entitled "Sports on the Brain," the British magazine *Puck* presented this "American Phrenological Chart" in an 1887 issue to lampoon the nation's sports craze.

Coaches carrying Princeton and Yale football players up Fifth Avenue to Manhattan Field prior to the 1893 Thanksgiving Day game. (From Parke Davis, *Football*)

Caspar Whitney was editor of the leading sports magazine *Outing* and America's most influential advocate of amateurism. c. 1904. (From *The Critic*, 1904)

The nostalgic "Where Base Ball Has Its Beginning" was the frontispiece of A. G. Spalding's 1911 history of the game that popularized the Doubleday myth.

William Howard Taft was the first American president to toss out a ball on opening day of the baseball season.

Jim Thorpe in the triumphant New York City
parade after returning from the 1912 Olympic
Games. (European Picture Service)

Printed amid debates about physical preparedness during World
War I, this 1915 *Life* cartoon "Training versus Muscle" has Uncle
Sam declaring "I see only two candidates that I can use." The
cartoon illuminates the backlash against the cult of big-time
collegiate athletics in favor of military training for the impending
wartime needs.

Y.M.C.A. war-work secretaries in training ca. 1917 (Y.M.C.A. of the U.S.A. Archives, University of Minnesota Libraries)

Soldiers playing Y.M.C.A-sponsored basketball at Camp Gordon (Atlanta, Georgia) ca. 1917. (Y.M.C.A of the U.S.A. Archives, University of Minnesota Libraries)

Soldiers playing Y.M.C.A -sponsored baseball in France during World War I.
(Y.M.C.A. of the U.S.A. Archives, University of Minnesota Libraries)

During the patriotically charged World War I years,
photographer Arthur Mole commanded 8,000
officers and enlisted men at Camp Wheeler, Georgia,
to march into position for this "living photograph"
of the Y.M.C.A. emblem. (From *Smithsonian*, January
1996)

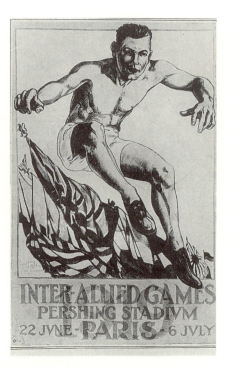

The official poster of the 1919 Inter-Allied Games held in France after the conclusion of World War I.

In the aftermath of World War I, a *Chicago Tribune* cartoonist satirizes the infatuation with fighting that captured the popular imagination in the 1919 Jack Dempsey–Jess Willard world heavyweight boxing bout staged on July Fourth.

A large Times Square crowd follows the 1919 World Series on a mechanical baseball diamond. (From Lawrence Ritter, *The Glory of Their Times*)

Boxing promoter George "Tex" Rickard with Gene Tunney, the ring's most celebrated star of the 1920s. Rickard, known as the King of Ballyhoo, raised the art of packaging sports events and figures to an unprecedented level. (Underwood & Underwood)

Basketball team
U.S.M.C. League Island
Navy Yard, Philadelphia,
Pennsylvania, 1923.
(Y.M.C,A. of the U.S.A.
Archives, University of
Minnesota Libraries)

Two of the greatest
sport celebrities of the 1920s,
Jack Dempsey and Babe Ruth,
strike a pose. (Charley Miller
Collection, University
of Maine at Orono)

"What Other Games Do You
Play?" asks Uncle Sam in this
1924 Columbus *Dispatch* cartoon
printed after the Olympic Games.
(Reprinted with permission from
the Columbus (Ohio) *Dispatch*.)

Every generation has its doomsayers. Consider how the following four random statements from 1868, 1915, 1927, and 1944 affirm Lipsyte's 1995 assessments:

> Somehow or other they don't play ball nowadays as they used to some eight or ten years ago. . . . I mean that they don't play with the same kinds of feelings or for the same objects they used to.
>
> The sordid element of baseball as a business has cast a shadow over the sport. [Players make too much money and become spoiled, one journalist thought; players are] parading about in their automobiles like princes, posing at cabarets and trotteries as little tin-gods.
>
> Today the players regard the game in a different light. . . . It is a means rather than the end. It has become a business with the boys, who play for the income.
>
> The player of today is too unwilling to exert himself. . . . [Once established, he] then falls into an indifferent pace. He somehow becomes very satisfied with himself and coasts along.[4]

Most people cling steadfastly to the notion that professional sports, as the latecomer, only quite recently eclipsed the "original" amateur ethos, even though sports historians have demonstrated that as far back as ancient Greece, sports promoted gambling, cheating, profiteering, privilege, and exclusivity. Neither the ancient Greeks nor their Western European descendants had any conception of "amateur" sports. Professionalism—featuring money prizes, cash payments, and wagers—was the norm for most athletic competitions of public note. Certainly, nobody in colonial or antebellum America ever claimed that sports built character, inculcated the spirit of fair play, or shaped the national identity. Early sports were local, participatory, irregularly scheduled, and loosely organized events; and most events *were* accompanied by fervent gambling and valuable prizes for the winners. The line between amateurism and professionalism was not even drawn in America until the early 1870s, by which time the nation's leading sport, baseball, was firmly within the professional orbit.

Nineteenth-century amateurism was an invented tradition. As the rallying cry of late-nineteenth-century institutionalized sport, amateurism represented an attempt to draw class lines against the masses, and to develop a new bourgeois leisure lifestyle as a badge of middle- and upper-class identity. The amateur ethos was, moreover, an ideological reaction to a well-established professional sporting tradition in the United States. The rising bureaucrats of this movement used the amateur ethos as a mechanism for turning their social prejudices into resilient athletic structures. During the early 1870s, they directed their energies toward the professional, immigrant-working-class sport of track and field, and then, shortly thereafter, toward the more familiar environs of collegiate athletics. By the last decade of the century, the amateurs were enlisted in the emergent Olympic movement. Throughout this process of gaining the hearts and minds of the national sporting audience, the amateurists sought to restore the lost innocence of sport before the advent of wealth and big business. Even though the notion of original purity was largely a myth of their own creation, they sold a vision of an orderly, genteel, harmonious world of sports and healthful recreation, open to all classes, but under the benevolent governance of principled middle- and upper-class men like themselves.[5]

PROFESSIONALISM BEFORE THE BUREAUCRATS' DOMINATION

For most of the nineteenth century, American sports had yet to be monopolized by either corporate wealth or a fledgling amateur system dominated by college presidents, retired military brass, civic leaders, and alumni associations. Until the 1890s, American sports were democratic and pluralistic; as Ted Vincent has written, "a grocer or saloonkeeper had as much chance as a millionaire of producing an event that grabbed headlines in the national sporting magazines."[6] In 1835, an early sports patron, John Stevens Cox, offered a $1,000 prize to any man who could run 10 miles in less than an hour, and $300 more if the goal was reached by only one man. The idea originated in a substantial bet with fellow millionaire, Samuel L. Gouverneur. Henry Stannard, a farmer, beat a butcher, a carpenter, and a house painter, and won a sizable cash prize worth several years' wages.[7]

Commercialized racing (or pedestrianism) was a huge success through the 1850s, particularly in New York, where, for a dime, urban workers, gamblers, prostitutes, and hustlers could see the swiftest runners from Britain and America. Immigrant and working-class athletes, most notably those of the New York Caledonian Society, promoted pedestrianism and awarded substantial cash prizes to the winners. Such track-and-field competitions epitomized the established commercialized sporting tradition that dated back to colonial times.[8]

Early in the nineteenth century, harness racing was the most popular sport for the privileged classes. The most famous race of the century pitted a northern horse, Fashion, against the southern horse Peytona, at the Union Course in Long Island, before nearly 100,000 spectators. By the 1820s, boat races, too, attracted thousands of spectators. Four-to-six-man crews raced for as much as $20,000, and individual bettors occasionally risked tens of thousands of dollars.[9]

Boxing, cockfighting, and billiards were the most popular sports among those of the urban, working-class sporting fraternity, whose members were bachelors or spent most of their time apart from their families. The bachelor sports culture was part of an urban world of saloons, gambling parlors, brothels, firehouses, theaters, and militia-company headquarters, where men drank and caroused in open defiance of Victorian values. Prizefighting, under the bare-knuckle rules, was the favored sport of this underground culture. Boxers were ethnic and neighborhood heroes, leaders of tough street gangs that provided muscle on election days for machine politicians. Boxers competed in a loosely organized, but lucrative, professional circuit. In this same milieu, cockfighting and animal-baiting contests were organized by saloonkeepers, particularly in New York, Philadelphia, Baltimore, and Boston, where workers paid from 25¢ to a dollar to watch such contests.[10]

Organized team sports were the latecomers on the American sporting scene. Professional baseball, the nation's leading team sport, evoked only minimal controversy in its early years.

Even early collegiate athletics (in what would become the sacred realm of amateurism) were remarkably commercialized until the 1870s. In 1852 a railroad entrepreneur, sensing potential profits, transported the Yale and Harvard crew teams to a meet and initiated commercialized collegiate sport and the considerable gambling that accompanied it. Further, within less than a decade, sports historian Ronald Smith writes, "the prestige obtained from winning, the honor brought to the college, and the interest of the public in the physical prowess of the educational elites were all in existence."[11] The pivotal event was an 1869 Harvard-Oxford race on the Thames River. Spirited renditions of "Yankee Doodle" and "God Save the Queen" were sung by a festive, patriotic crowd of nearly one million. The event convinced the *New York Times* editors of the serious effect of the occasion on the development of big-time, commercialized collegiate sport; the paper devoted extensive news coverage and lengthy editorials to the contest, which Oxford won by a mere three lengths.[12]

Lucrative pothunting was important to the development of "amateur" track and field in American colleges. Collegians also received very valuable prizes in crew and track-and-field competitions. Indeed, Harvard crews won expensive black-walnut oars and silver goblets that were worth twice an average laborer's annual income. During the 1860s, Harvard competed for purses as high as $500 in various Boston regattas. Dartmouth College offered opera glasses, silver inkstands, silverware, and special editions of the works of Thomas Macaulay, John Milton, and William Shakespeare as prizes in their early-1870s track meets. This was quite in keeping with the amateur rules that prevailed well into the twentieth century; the value of the award did not matter—what counted was that it could be inscribed or engraved. James Gordon Bennett, Jr., a first-generation Scottish-American, and owner of the *New York Herald*, offered a $500 first-prize trophy for a two-mile run in 1873; the only requirement for entering the race was that one needed to be an enrolled student. Duncan Bowie, of McGill University, who had won $90 at the sixteenth annual New York Caledonian Club meet a year earlier, won the competition. The following year, at Princeton's Caledonian Games, first-place winners received $15 gold-medal prizes; $10 medals went to second-place finishers in each of the 15 events; and the meet's outstanding athlete was given a $50 medal.[13]

As early as 1866, the Harvard University nine, one of the strongest teams in the country, played the leading New York professional baseball teams. The faculty neither frowned on the game nor objected to the team's contests against professionals. By 1869, Harvard played a full spring schedule, beating the Athletics at Philadelphia 35 to 21 and besting the Nationals at Albany 58 to 17. Harvard finished the season by losing, 30 to 11, to the nation's leading professional team, the Cincinnati Red Stockings. Between 1868 and 1874, Yale played 60 percent of its games against professionals. And in 1870, Harvard won 34 games and lost only 9—8 against professional teams.[14]

THE EMERGENCE OF THE AMATEUR ETHOS

Across the Atlantic Ocean, however, a new elitist sports movement was brewing simultaneously with the growth of American collegiate athletics. Invented by Oxford and Cambridge students and institutionalized by the London-based Amateur Athletic Club, which defined *amateur* synonymously with *gentleman*, upper-class British sportsmen alleged that their "social inferiors" could not comprehend the ethos of amateurism and fair play. They proclaimed that exclusion was "the only way to keep . . . sport pure from the elements of corruption; . . . [specifically], the average workman has no idea of sport for its own sake."[15] The English apostles of amateurism created a myth and sanctioned their new practice by a reference to timeless tradition—they connected their new ideas to the ancient Greeks, even though the latter neither distinguished between amateurs and professionals, nor entertained such novel Victorian goals as fair play. Philosopher Paul Weiss discerns that the line between a nineteenth-century amateur and a professional was "mainly a line between the unpaid members of a privileged class and the paid members of an underprivileged class."[16]

As was true in nineteenth-century England, most American colleges scorned sports but tolerated them since they were run by students and were only unofficially connected to the institutions. For example, William and Mary College students pursued hunting, horse racing, and gambling. Between the 1840s and 1860s, Eastern private colleges made rowing the most popular sport. The first collegiate baseball game was played in 1859, as Amherst trounced Williams, 73 to 32. Students developed their own extracurricular programs, usually in open defiance of the regulations of their school's administration. As Ronald Smith notes, young college men, "using what they believed was an inalienable right, structured an intellectual, social, aesthetic, and physical world of their own." By the middle of the nineteenth century, the extracurricular program of fraternal rituals, student government, newspapers, and football rushes was transformed into the lifeblood of student social and physical life.[17]

In the early 1870s, amateurism quickly spread to elite American colleges. Influential spokemen for the view that American intercollegiate sports should remain strictly amateur events solidified this doctrine for the public through their writings and speeches. Even though Yale, the nation's leading athletic power, had integrated many professional features, Walter Camp, Yale's unofficial football coach, and the father of the American game, promoted the English-gentleman model as the preferred exemplar for American collegiate sports. "A gentleman does not make his living from his athletic prowess," Camp proselytized.[18] "He does not earn anything from his victories except glory and satisfaction. . . . A gentleman never competes for money, directly or indirectly."[19]

The collegiate athletic scene was only one, and perhaps not even the most important, arena within which the merits of amateurism were debated in late-nineteenth-century America. Devoted apostles of amateurism outside academe upheld pure English amateurism and lambasted American collegiate abuses of that noble dream. The first cogent argument for strict amateurism was presented in 1872 in a pamphlet written by William B. Curtis. As cofounder of the New York Athletic Club and editor of *Spirit of the Times*, a leading sports journal that championed the amateur cause, Curtis modeled a sports mentality on the English elite. Prior to Curtis's editorship, the *Spirit* had covered professional pedestrianism for several decades—a policy that Curtis summarily ended. Curtis and his compatriot, John Watson, also a journalist, and a member of the Schuylkill Navy Athletic Club of Philadelphia, defined *amateur* as "any person who has never competed in an open competition, for a stake, or for public money, or for admission money, or with professionals, . . . nor has even, at any period of his life, taught or assisted in the pursuit of athletic exercises as a means of livelihood."[20] Certainly, such standards were at odds with the acquisitive, individualistic, materialistic sensibilities of the Gilded Age.

Curtis and his colleagues quickly institutionalized their ideas and stole the spotlight from the once well-established professional pedestrians. Amateur track and field soon became part of the Olympics, and had competitions arranged by colleges and by the new Amateur Athletic Union (AAU), which monopolized quality coaching, facilities, and public legitimacy. A rising first generation of gentlemen who became amateur bureaucrats recast the popular working-class spectacles for future upper-class sports enthusiasts. Lingering puritanical suspicions that athletics were nothing more than a conspicuous waste of time mandated that the rising amateur bureaucrats cleanse and repackage sports with appeals to higher moral purposes. In so doing, the new generation of sports promoters closed class ranks so as not to appear as "inferior tradesmen, apprentices, and other dissolute persons neglecting their trades and employments."[21] Athletic elitism blurred the fact, according to Vincent, that the amateurs were decidedly inferior to the professionals and were barely equal to the quasi-amateur athletes who performed at the massive picnics of ethnic and working-class clubs. In place of local heroism and money prizes, the sanctified amateurs were given prestige, as Vincent cleverly observes, in much the same way that the Wizard of Oz solved the problem of the cowardly lion by bestowing a medal. By the 1920s, track and field ceased to be something working-class people dabbled in on holidays and weekends.[22]

The dialogue that arose within the New York private-athletic-club community had given rise to the AAU—which represented the greatest and most enduring legacy of the early amateur movement. Before the founding of the AAU, several ill-fated, New York-based amateur regulatory bodies were formed during the 1870s. First, in 1879, the National Association of Amateur Athletes of America was founded; but with the establishment of the powerful New York Athletic Club (NYAC), the fledgling organization folded in 1887. Then, on January 21, 1888, the NYAC, along with the Amateur Club of the Schuylkill Navy and 15 other clubs, established the AAU, and by the summer of 1889, they gained control of the amateur movement. The following year, Colonel Abraham G. Mills, AAU legal specialist, proposed a reorganization plan that would change the AAU from a union of individual clubs to a union of regional associations, with the United States being sectioned into five geographical areas. Mills's proposal was ratified, and shortly thereafter, the AAU assumed principal control over track, lacrosse, and basketball, but ceded jurisdiction of collegiate football, soccer, baseball, and rowing. In fact, all college runners, jumpers and throwers were now obligated to register with the AAU. In less than a decade, the AAU moved rapidly to consolidate its power, despite the fact that, before World War I, its influence was wildly uneven, with the exception of Chicago, Milwaukee, Los Angeles, San Francisco, Baltimore, and New Orleans. In so doing, as John Lucas has written, it "created an atmosphere of both fierce loyalties and persistent opposition."[23]

The amateurists' early negative attacks on professionalism were, in fact, quite limited. Most critics willingly accepted professionals so long as did not intermingle with the amateurs. Thus, between the 1870s and the early 1890s, amateurists honed their message about the meanings of amateurism in the media, collegiate circles, and public debates, and developed organizations like the AAU to legitimize their message within collegiate circles and the wider society. Early antiprofessional sentiments and class bias, however tentative, restricted the full emergence of the professional athlete until early in the twentieth century—when the amateur code was firmly established in the emergent Olympic movement. Prior to the 1896 Olympiad, though, amateurists struggled to invent and define their own identity.

THE AMATEURISM-PROFESSIONALISM DEBATE

Despite such ambitious organizational endeavors and the myriad of published statements of support, it was clear to many people that amateur sports bore most of the characteristics of the professional model. Yale's athletic budget clearly reflected this trend: The receipts and expenses were managed by the Yale Financial Union under the partisan treasurership of Walter Camp and the student managers of football, baseball, track, and rowing. The Union usually ran an annual surplus (totaling $96,323 by 1905), which Camp deposited into a secret reserve fund, consisting of four accounts at New Haven and New York banks; the Union pooled funds flowing to and from these major sports. Camp tapped the fund to pay athletic trainer Michael Murphy a salary, and an annual salary of $5,000 to himself (a full professor at Yale earned about $3,500 a year). Yale's athletic budget doubled between 1893 and 1903, equaling the combined salaries of 30 professors, and nearly equaling the incomes of the law, divinity, and medical schools combined.[24] "Somehow, without exercising any great amount of political talent or pull," Camp explained to a Stanford administrator (who had wondered how Yale did it), "I have in the vernacular 'corralled' all the offices in sight. . . . Between you and me it has proven wonderfully successful both from an economical standpoint and a standpoint when measured by athletic victories." Thus, the amateur-professional "dilemma" developed. If a college acknowledged outright the presence of professional sports, Ronald Smith observes, it lost respectability as a middle- or upper-class institution. In other words, be amateurs, and lose, athletically, to those who were perhaps less skillful amateurs; or be outright professionals, and lose social esteem. The solution, according to Smith, was to claim amateurism to the world while, in fact, accepting professionalism.[25] Clearly, amateurism was harder to define in America, where class lines were less distinct and more fluid than in the mother country.

Another case in point was the contradictory nature of summer baseball. The summer resorts in the White Mountains of New Hampshire initiated what for two decades was considered an innocent pastime for college athletes, and not incompatible with proper amateur standards. In reality, summer baseball was semiprofessional entertainment for the uppermost middle class and wealthy Americans, whose children attended the eastern colleges that promoted the amateur ethos. "In those earlier days," a New Hampshire newspaper editorialized, "college ballplayers did not think it at all beneath their dignity to spend the summer at a swell hotel, in exchange for which pleasure they gladly gave their services on the diamond and cared not who knew it."[26] At the conclusion of the summer baseball season, the players were paid by generous donations of the resort patrons, and did not fear that the practice compromised their collegiate eligibility.[27] By the turn of the twentieth century, summer ball for pay was one of the most charged issues in intercollegiate sports, second only to the debate about football's brutality.

The belated question of whether it was acceptable, among the educated and socially elite Americans, to earn a living by playing summer baseball was addressed during the last years of the nineteenth century. In 1879, Lee Richmond, a Brown University undergraduate, became the first college student to play professional baseball. The debate escalated during the 1880s and culminated in a 1898 conference held at Brown. A group of delegates drafted rules and guidelines that explicitly discouraged summer ball but were never ratified by individual schools and, therefore, not collectively institutionalized. The galvanizing case involved Harvard's Walter Clarkson, a young man from a wealthy Cambridge, Massachusetts, baseball-playing family (two older brothers played in the major leagues; one, John Clarkson, became a Hall of Famer). After Yale had consecutive losses to its chief rival, Harvard, a Yale athletic adviser investigated Clarkson's summer exploits, but ultimately could not secure affidavits saying that he had been paid to pitch in a New England summer league. Clarkson had indeed been solicited by the Camden team of the Knox County (Maine) summer league, had been given strict promises of anonymous cash payments, with all expenses paid, and been hosted by "the best [of local] society."[28]

The Clarkson case illustrated the difficulty of obtaining any facts, other than circumstantial evidence, that would disqualify a college athlete on the grounds of professionalism. Moreover, the ambiguous situation encouraged creative efforts to defy poorly enforced eligibility rules. The most prevalent tactics included playing under assumed names, or receiving weekly compensation for a phantom job like waiter or casino attendant. *McClure's Magazine* writer Henry Beach Needham concluded that in summer ball there was "more lying and subterfuge than in any other evil connected with intercollegiate athletics."[29]

During the same year, another journalist launched even more penetrating criticisms about the volatile state of American collegiate amateurism. The "high finance" of eastern collegiate athletics, Clarence Deming believed, created "an atmosphere of wealth" that represented an apt microcosm of the larger society.[30] The student "must not enter a contest for the smallest money prize," he acknowledged, but the athlete could accept endorsement money from tobacco companies, or a college subsidy for scorecard privileges, which enabled athletes to keep the entire proceeds from the sale of programs at games.[31] "He will be told . . . that all this is but a reflection on the academic life of the mania of materialism in the outside world," Deming wrote; but he shrewdly recognized that "not so often [is the athlete] told that, even if such is the fact, it rests upon the culture, the refinement, the scholarship, and the ideals of the universities to set the pace toward the opposite pole."[32]

The summer-baseball question was debated into the twentieth century but never resolved—summer baseball for pay persisted. During his senior year, Walter Clarkson signed a contract with the New York Yankees. The Harvard dilemma illuminated the perplexing relationship of amateurism versus professionalism in American sports.[33] In the English society that gave birth to the amateur ethos, it would have been inconceivable that a college athlete would have turned professional. However, even in elite American circles, a man like Clarkson could, and did, sell his baseball skills in the sports marketplace.

How can the failure of pure amateurism in nineteenth-century American collegiate circles be explained? Smith, the recognized authority on American collegiate sport, attributes this development to deep ideological differences between Britain and the United States. Just as many Americans opposed the English aristocracy, with its House of Lords, landed nobility, privileges, and pensions, they also ultimately refused to accept the tenets of amateurism, since "achieved status in colleges and in athletics became the American way, rather than the ascribed status" of England's elite universitites and their athletic programs.[34] In particular, Smith writes:

> The English amateur system, based upon participation of the social and economic elite and rejection of those beneath them from participating, would never gain a foothold in American college athletics. There was too much competition, too strong a belief in merit over heredity, too abundant an ideology of freedom of opportunity for the amateur ideal to succeed. It may be that amateurism can never succeed in a society which has egalitarian beliefs. It may be that amateur athletics at a high level of expertise can only exist in a society dominated by upper-class elitists.[35]

Thus, the amateurism-professionalism dilemma existed from the very beginning in American intercollegiate athletics. Americans practiced a form of professionalism, while simultaneously cloaking their actions in the ideology of amateurism, which resolved the status problems endemic to late nineteenth-century society.

This argument has its merits. Certainly, critical cleavages existed between American and British society. Contemporary commentators advanced arguments for American athletic exceptionalism; for example, Ralph Paine proclaimed that "the whole difference [between English public- and American private-school athletics] lies in the fact that in England athletics are ruled by the spirit of sport; in the United States, by the spirit of competition."[36] But even though Britain was officially ruled by a monarchy, elitist attitudes were passionately challenged and negotiated with a strong, egalitarian working-class movement that elected labor-party politicians.

More important, the English amateur-sports establishment itself harbored deep, internal ambiguities. The Oxbridge amateur ethos was the exception, rather than the rule, of the nineteenth-century British sporting scene. Originally developed as an amateur sport, and a character-building one, by the public schools, football was rapidly proletarianized during the early 1880s and acquired all the institutional and ritual characteristics with which we are still familiar: professionalism, the League, the Cup, and so forth. Hobsbawm identifies the 1883 defeat of the Old Etonians, by Bolton Olympic, as the symbolic turning point that was widely recognized by contemporaries as a class confrontation. Similarly, British historian Richard Holt finds that the key shift in the amateur question occurred during this same period, with the formation of the Football League in 1885; and with the split in 1894, between the Rugby Football Union and Northern Union, so that working-class players could now have the leisure time to compete with wealthy young men. With the development of overt professionalization, Hobsbawm writes, "most of the philanthropic and moralizing figures from the national elite withdrew, leaving the management of the clubs in the hands of local businessmen and other notables" much less sympathetic to the amateur ethos. In short, professional football dealt a crippling blow to English amateurism when the sport was taken over by the working class and its business patrons. In the process, sport sociologist John Hargreaves writes, workers transformed these sports into "a means of expression for values opposed to the bourgeois athleticist tradition"[37] [of amateurism]. A disdain for constituted authority and official rules; a preference for monetary rewards; and a hedonistic, festive element—these were all brought to British mass sports by working-class athletes in open defiance of the Oxbridge amateurism that Smith claims was so hegemonic.[38]

Americans were no less amateuristic in their orientation than the British. Smith's argument for American exceptionalism, however intriguing, fails to recognize that amateurism was (and is) more an ideological construct than an actual set of practices and agreed-on rules. Amateurism, like the other invented traditions of the period, legitimized certain beliefs, values, institutions, and social relationships.

The invention of amateurism, then, must be understood within the larger context of how a national middle-class elite was formed late in the nineteenth century. Hobsbawm notes astutely that as class borders became more fluid and increasing numbers of people in both Britain and the United States identified themselves as "middle class," the issue of defining a national elite of the upper middle classes became highly problematical. "Since the middle classes were par excellence the locus of social mobility and individual self-improvement," he notes, "entry to them could hardly be closed."[39] The problem entailed establishing an identity and a class presence for the relatively large mass of those who belonged neither to the elite nor to the masses. Amateurism thus provided a needed class presence and ideology for a rising generation of middle-class sports leaders. It was no coincidence, then, that the institutions (academe and private athletic clubs), the individuals (educated, socially mobile white males), and the messages (meritocracy, fair play, respectability) of the amateur movement reflected similar vestiges of middle-class identification in America's Gilded Age and progressive eras.[40]

AMATEURISM TRIUMPHANT

Just two decades after its introduction, amateurism seemed doomed by the early 1890s. The AAU's control of such sports as track and field, and basketball meant little to the larger sporting public, whose principal loyalties went to professional baseball and big-time (professionalized) college football. Basketball, invented in 1891, was in its infancy, and track still retained its old-world, immigrant associations. Mere organizational legitimacy was insufficient for an overwhelmingly professionally oriented sporting culture. Moreover, by the late 1890s, there was scarcely a college which preserved pure amateurism in men's sports. Competition for money and status; contests against professionals; collection of gate receipts; support for training tables; provision for academic tutors; recruitment and payment of athletes; and the hiring of professional coaches—all these pervaded the intercollegiate athletic scene.

During the 1890s, the public debate about amateur sport focused almost singularly on the brutality of collegiate football. Scores of injuries, and several well-publicized deaths on the gridiron led many concerned, influential members of the middle class to call for the game's abolition. Yet, at its bleakest moment, two apologists for the amateur ethos, Caspar Whitney and James Sullivan, emerged and effectively saved the movement from its own contradictions and abuses.

Caspar Whitney was the most influential sportswriter at the turn of the century, and America's most dedicated apostle of amateurism. Born into a middle-class Boston family in 1861, he became a versatile athlete at St. Matthew's College in California, where he captained the football, baseball, and lacrosse teams. He also boxed, fenced, and wrestled. After graduation in 1879, Whitney spent five years traveling, exploring, and writing in the West. In 1888 he became the regular sports columnist for *Harper's Weekly*, a post he occupied until 1899. Less than two weeks after his death in 1929, *The Nation* wrote, in a reverential obituary, that Whitney was "almost the first writer of culture and ability to deal with sports, then not considered worthy of serious treatment in the chief dailies of the country."[41] His opinions received "the widest circulation," particularly his advocacy of fair play and sport for the joy of the game, for which "a whole generation of Eastern college men grew up in lasting indebtedness to him."[42]

Whitney was zealously dedicated to elitist English amateur sports. His most influential writing for *Harper's* grew out of an 1894 trip to England. His explorations of British sports were presented in a multipart series titled "A Sporting Pilgrimage," and were published in book form in 1895. According to Whitney, English college sports were untainted by commercialism, the winning-at-all-costs mentality, and the attendant eligibility scandals that characterized American collegiate sports. "It is simply a tradition that the colleges and universities shall be represented by athletes from the student body," he wrote, and "no one thinks of asking why, or attempts to evade the prerogatives of custom."[43] As was the case in most of his essays, Whitney could not resist drawing a moral: Americans do great harm to college sport by making it merely another business venture—"money, money seems to be the cry, and it will be the curse, if indeed not the downfall of honest university sport."[44]

Whitney's amateurist advocacy revealed his strident anti-working-class sensibilities. He was openly contemptuous of working-class athletes, whom he described as "vermin" and the "great unwashed" who lacked "the true amateur instinct of sport for sport's sake."[45] He pleaded for a return to the "halcyon days" of the 1870s, when "amateur" was still defined in strict class terms, and "amateur contests" were restricted to "the better element"; it was evil, he argued, to "bring together in sport the two divergent elements of society that can never by any chance meet elsewhere on even terms."[46]

Clearly, Whitney's sentiments belie Ronald Smith's explanation of the "failure" of American amateurism. Even though Americans tended to practice professionalism while cloaking their actions in amateur garb, there were the true believers, like Whitney, whose polemics contradicted any uniquely American ideological claims of indifference to the elitist English model. To be sure, Whitney did not represent some fringe, idiosyncratic element in American journalism. Prior to purchasing the nation's most influential sporting magazine, *Outing*, in 1900, he was a correspondent for *Harper's* during the Spanish-American War, and would later fulfill a similar assignment as a World War I correspondent for the *New York Tribune*. Moreover, his nine books and editorship of *Collier's* "Outdoor America" and the American Sportsman's Library conferred on Whitney an international reputation.

While writing his "A Sporting Pilgrimage" series in 1894, Whitney did not yet know that he would soon discover his sporting utopia—the modern international Olympic Games, launched by Baron Pierre de Coubertin—a magnificent athletic festival intended for "the more refined elements," as Whitney described it, and which ultimately legitimized the amateur ethos. Whitney was to become the second American ever appointed to the International Olympic Committee (IOC), and, from 1906 to 1910, was president of the United States Olympic Committee.[47]

James Sullivan, from 1900 until his death in 1914, was the most important American amateur-sports bureaucrat. As indicated in the *Dictionary of American Biography* profile of him, he was America's "first sports czar." Born in New York, in 1860, to Irish-immigrant working-class parents, Sullivan embarked on a journalism career in 1878, with a job at Frank Leslie's publishing house. In 1880, Sullivan founded the first track-and-field publication, *Athletic News*; and between 1889 and 1891, became both business manager and editor of the *New York Sporting News*. Sullivan reached the pinnacle of his editorial career when he became president of the American Sports Publishing Company in 1892, a post he held until 1914—in this capacity, he edited the highly influential Spalding Athletic Library series.[48]

Unlike Whitney, however, Sullivan's influence transcended the print media. Sullivan became the chief power broker for American amateurism, through a distinguished career within the fledgling sports bureaucracy. As an ambitious 25-year-old, he was elected president of the Pastime Athletic Club (of New York) and was the club's delegate to the nation's ruling amateur athletic body. As the first secretary of the AAU in 1888, Sullivan quickly established a reputation as a fierce and resolute defender of the pure amateur code. Between 1906 and 1914, he served as president and secretary-treasurer of the organization. Sullivan also helped form the Public Schools Athletic League in New York, and headed the athletic competitions at the 1893 Chicago World's Fair, and at the 1904 St. Louis Exposition (which hosted the third Olympiad). As sports historian Stephen Hardy notes, Sullivan used the amateur athletic movement as a status vehicle for rubbing elbows with select elites; he stressed the importance of "gentlemen, leading citizens and business men" to the organization and success of the amateur movement.[49] But, Hardy points out, unlike Whitney, Sullivan's mission was not a class-specific one, since he argued that the AAU should be broadened; and that "athletics should be for the masses and not [just] for the classes," provided that the masses were organized under the AAU structure of bourgeois respectability.[50] Hence, Sullivan worked feverishly to solidify the AAU's authority by designing the athletic-sanction notion, which gave the Union monopoly powers.

Sport historians have been seduced by Sullivan's impressive accomplishments but have failed to critically examine the deeper connections and inconsistencies that illuminate a very different picture of American amateur sports around the turn of the century. We should consider an important article written in 1910 by America's first Olympic gold medalist, James B. Connolly. He shrewdly recognized that behind the facade of an orderly, efficient, moralistic banner of amateurism was a handful of self-interested, power-hungry men, like Sullivan, who were elected to the local and national AAU boards, but who pursued policies to suit themselves. Connolly demonstrated that most New England clubs were "fake" ones controlled by half a dozen men and their "safe" friends; the pursuit of lucrative gate receipts lured not the enemies of amateurism, but "its very priests," (e.g., AAU officials) who provided the best athletes with "under-the-table payments" and valuable gifts.[51] For instance, those who ran the New England AAU boxing and wrestling meets often awarded gold watches—known among athletes as "stock" watches—since the following day the prizes went back to a jeweler's stock, once the athletes returned them for cash. According to Connolly, AAU officials handled the watches and "knew both their origin and destination."[52]

Sullivan was intimately connected to this "scandal." As a full-time employee, he was well placed to do great service for the "House of Spalding"—the powerful firm that was intent on becoming the leading athletic-goods trust in America. Although the ostensible project of the AAU was to promote the amateur athletic spirit, Sullivan's position as handler of the Spalding firm's advertising predisposed him, according to Connolly, to promote "that grand American idea, the [Spalding] Trust."[53] With the Spalding Athletic Library which carried instructions for various sports, Sullivan oversaw the publication of "voluminous Spalding advertising wherein Spalding educated the public that everything good in athletics had some connection with his house."[54] Sullivan's colleagues went along as well. Luther Gulick, national chairman of the AAU basketball committee, stipulated that only Spalding balls and baskets were to be used in championship games; otherwise, the referee was to declare a game void.[55]

In short, Whitney and Sullivan played the roles of popular intellectuals and social leaders for amateur sports, who, in the words of cultural historian Andrew Ross, patrolled "the ever-shifting border of popular and legitimate taste," supervised the participants' passports, the temporary visas, the cultural identities, the threatening alien elements, and served the deportation orders; they also occasionally made their own "adventurous forays across the border."[56]

SUMMARY

Despite the long-entrenched legacy of professionalism in American society, American sport by the early years of the twentieth century, embraced the tenets of amateurism. On the surface, amateurism was riddled with contradictions that corresponded neither with the dominant turn-of-the-century American values, nor with the ideological jus-tifications of modern sport which elevated equality, specialization, rationalization, professionalization, commercialization, and quantifica-tion. Melvin Adelman identifies the impetus for the professionalism-amateurism dilemma in terms of the changing nature of the sponsor-ship of sports contests. What distinguishes early professional sports from contemporary forms was a shift from irregular, private sponsorship to regular, full-blown commercial sponsorship. With the notable excep-tion of baseball, the erratic and limited growth of early professional sports' organizational structures—particularly those of track and field—made them vulnerable to a hostile takeover by the rising bureaucracy of amateurists who articulated a class-biased critique of professional-ism, in terms of the ways it corrupted true sport through the exploits of working-class athletes unschooled in the virtues of the amateur ethos. Sport, they argued, should be a form of recreation, not a business. This rising generation of amateur spokesmen effectively turned their biases into resilient athletic structures, and thus defeated a more popular, but unorganized, group of professional-sports promoters.[57]

Despite their considerable initial success, the definition of amateur-ism proved to be a fluid phenomenon. After three years' intensive work on the subject, the Committee on Definition of an Amateur recom-mended, in light of "the rapidly increasing number of men who . . . devote all or part of their time as physical directors, school teachers, playground directors, church and settlement workers, etc.," a revised definition of an amateur; such a person should be defined as "one who has maintained his standing as an amateur in all other respects, except that he has been engaged for pay as an instructor in amateur athletics," since to "classify as professionals those who are doing their utmost to stem the tide of professionalism insofar as it lowers the standards of the true amateur principle" is unjust.[58] In direct contrast to earlier official pronouncements that prohibited any athletic endeavor for pay, a new generation was forced to acknowledge those who were paid to promote amateurism.

Such revisionist efforts were essential to the mainstream of ama-teurist custodians. W. P. Bowen, in his presidential address before the Eighth Annual Meeting of the Athletic Research Society, in 1915, argued against the utility of maintaining a strict, elitist definition of amateur-ism, since it smacked of "the snobbery of the leisure classes of society, and if we want to put amateurism on a basis where it will commend itself to the American public as a whole, we must keep it clear from any possible taint or suspicion of snobbery."[59] Acknowledging not only the popular view that amateurism was a thinly veiled "social distinction," but also the prevailing "wide difference of opinion as to the influence of the professional athlete," Bowen cited a university professor who saw the amateur-professional dichotomy as the source of much dishonesty, and the late bishop of London who considered England's weakness to be "too much amateurism."[60] Clearly, within even the partisan amateurist ranks, dissension and controversy existed.

The revival of the Olympic Games solidified amateurism by linking it to a burgeoning American nationalism. Unquestionably, the Olympic Games have been the grandest effort to promote this ideology of amateurism, and sport for sport's sake. Prior to 1896, amateurists had indeed promoted a negative case against commercialized sports. Western elites then resuscitated the ancient Games in 1896 as a form of invented tradition—a strategy that, according to Hobsbawm, established the legitimacy of national cultures by helping citizens understand the relationships between the state and the people.[61] As such, Olympic spectacles provided the much-needed grist for cultural commentators and sports journalists, like Whitney and Sullivan, to invent a virile national sporting identity that, they believed, reflected America's institutions, social structure, work ethic, and national superiority. After international sports gained legitimacy after 1896, amateurists shifted their rhetoric to a more positive tone and attacked professionalism much less than they had during the 1870s and 1880s.

INVENTING ATHLETIC PROWESS AND BENEVOLENCE

THREE

OLYMPIC SPECTACLES AND THE REDEMPTION OF THE AMATEUR ETHOS

THE INVENTION OF AN IDEAL

The revival of the Olympic Games by a French aristocrat, the Baron Pierre de Coubertin, proved to be the pivotal episode in the making of an American athletic identity. Convinced that the disciplined austerity and sportsmanship required of the English rugby players had produced empire builders and men of character, Coubertin conceived a modern athletic festival that would promote cooperative internationalism throughout Western society. Coubertin's philosophy of "olympism" (the philosophy and world-view of the Olympic movement) embraced the best of ancient Greece; the proven power of English muscular Christianity; rhythm; art; beauty; and a balancing of body, mind, and soul. Such a synthesis might lead a man, the Baron thought (as did Socrates), to "knowledge of himself and of the right way to live."[1] Like other bourgeois liberals, Coubertin was torn between beliefs in both the individualistic ethos and nationalism. These ideological tensions led to an institutional action in 1894 when the International Olympic Committee ruled that individuals could compete only as representatives of their country's national Olympic committees. The contradiction between the internationalist Olympic vision and nationalistic rivalry reflected the world-unifying and world-fragmenting tendencies of advanced capitalism itself.[2]

Coubertin conveniently neglected to put his 1894 initiative (introduced at a glitzy Paris conference) into an accurate nineteenth-century historical context. There is evidence of earlier attempts at revival: An annual festival of "Olympick Games" took place in the seventeenth century when a Catholic landowner organized events on Whitsun, as a way of dramatizing the dissent from dominant Puritan codes of conduct, which interpreted play as sinful. These games, Alan Tomlinson has noted, had an obvious religious or political meaning, "reminding us that play-activities do not belong to some independent realm of the pleasurable."[3]

37

More significant, the revived Olympic Games actually dated back to Athens, where, in 1859, a rich grain dealer named Evangelical Zappas organized a festival. The Greek king gave athletes olive wreaths, money, and other valuable prizes for their victories; an enthusiastic but disorderly crowd had to be vigorously controlled by police and soldiers. The same was true of the 1870 Games, which were a huge success (by today's standards). Widely praised and witnessed by 30,000 spectators, winners received cash prizes in the most sophisticated program the world had ever seen. Ambitious, but much less successful, Olympic contests were also staged in 1875 and 1889. Coubertin's revived Games had more in common with these nineteenth-century Greek Olympics than they did with those held at Olympia 2,000 years earlier. Contemporaneous with these nineteenth-century Greek festivals, historians cited an emergent myth about the ancient-Greek sports culture. British scholar John Mahaffy elevated both the superiority of English sports and an alleged established tradition of ancient Greek amateurism. But it was historian Percy Gardner who created the first idealized picture of the ancient-Greek amateur sporting world, as he read ancient-Greek culture through a distinctly Victorian English lens. Through their imaginative intellectul labor, Mahaffy and Gardner turned the professional ancient Greek athletes into wholesome, middle-class amateurs.[4]

The year 1896 marked the inception of the *modern* Olympics, for it was then that athletic contests took place in Athens between teams representing different nations. It is usual to attribute the revival of the Games to one man, Coubertin, but as Tomlinson reminds us vis-à-vis Marx's oft-quoted thesis, "men make their own history, but they do not make it under circumstances chosen by themselves, but under circumstances directly encountered, given and transmitted from the past."[5] Coubertin's case for a modern Olympics derived from his own historically specific experience as a displaced French aristocrat, who, in Tomlinson's words, "looked towards both the model of athleticism pioneered by the contemporary British upper classes and a world of mind-body harmony in ancient Greece, in order to breed a new generation of men to rule the modern world." In this endeavor, Coubertin confirmed another of Marx's theses: that in periods of revolutionary crisis, people "anxiously conjure up the roots of the past," borrowing "names, battle cries, and costumes" from the past, "in order to present the new scene of world history in time-honored disguise and borrowed language."[6] Coubertin united the world of the Oxford don, Gardner, with American amateurist Caspar Whitney. The idealistic Frenchman had the money, ability, obsession, and clout to achieve what others had only dreamed of. According to modern-day classicist David Young, Coubertin's devotion to Greece was perhaps more theatrical than real—since after the 1896 Athens setting, the Games were whisked off to Paris, St. Louis, and then London. "In the mists of the ages," Coubertin wrote in 1896, amateurism (then only 28 years old) had "come of age."[7] Though amateurism lacked a legitimate historical legacy in ancient Greece, myth became reality.[8]

This newly invented tradition was quickly popularized in early magazine and newspaper articles, which situated the 1896 Games within the timeless orbit of ancient "amateurism." Classicist Paul Shorey wondered in 1895:

> [Can] we recover or in any way reproduce the harmonious beauty of the [Greek] ensemble, the banishment of the professional and commercial spirit, the idealizing influence of genuine religious and patriotic feeling, the untroubled unanimous acceptance not merely of the multitude, but, by great poets, orators, and thinkers, of the perfection of bodily grace and strength as the choicest gift of heaven?[9]

But most other commentators concurred that the modern revival *would* do its originators proud. In a sophisticated essay about the history of Greek athletics and their attendant mind-body philosophy, G. T. Ferris told adolescent readers of *St. Nicholas* that the Olympics would revive "the memory and spirit of an institution which shed a particular slant on the history of ancient Greece"—one which "entered into the life of the ancient Greek to an extent which we to-day can scarcely realize. . . . It was associated with his religion, his civic pride, his ideals of art, and his highest patriotism."[10] Rufus Richardson denied that "a modern contest will ever match the splendor of ancient Olympia," but remained optimistic, nevertheless; Olympia "could never be re-created," [but] "only in thought . . . [since] the athletic instinct never dies."[11] The IOC shamelessly appealed to this instinct: "It was a happy thought of the Committee to bring the first contest to Greece, the mother of athletics," Richardson noted. The modern athletes were "forced into contact with history, and their visit to Greece was an education."[12] The "thorough and unquestioned amateur spirit" of the 1896 contest was a cause for prominent commentators like Richardson to celebrate how athletics have "moved on a high plane and were carried on with a dignity that ought not soon be forgotten"—a dignity reflected in the distribution of wild olive branches from Olympia, as an indication of ancient tradition and the Games' lack of conspicuous materialism.[13]

In truth, amateurism was a mid-nineteenth-century creation of the Victorian middle class, which emphasized the moral primacy of fair play over the pursuit of victory; the preference of versatility over specialization; and personal restraint, modesty, and selflessness over individualism and excesses of emotion. The amateur code led to an almost puritanical conception of sport which went beyond mere games to encompass a whole way of life; this became the dominant view in the late nineteenth century, as sport sociologists Richard Gruneau and Hart Cantelon have recognized. It was furthered by the men of the university world, the upwardly mobile businessmen, and others who became the prominent figures in the formation of sports organizations, by virtue of their influence and authority in the society at large. Amateur sport was established as a prominent feature of Victorian culture only after they transformed apparently useless games and contests into morally useful ones. As Gruneau and Cantelon argue, "those uses had to be limited to moral and personal development, not economic gain, since accepting money for victory assumed that social rewards should be based solely on merit and not upon one's social origin or position in society—a radical, disturbing concept."[14] In stark contrast to the spectacle related to universal participation, and the money-mediated outcomes of athletic contests of professionalism, amateurism was portrayed as the most refined, civilized form of sporting practice.

The amateur ethos was inextricably linked to the burgeoning nationalism in Western society. The struggle between individuals and social groups for cultural power in the modern nation-state transformed culturally-specific ideas and meanings into universal metaphors and common sense. In the American sports world, this effort was led by an emergent group of amateurists, who, having achieved some tactical victories over the residual professional sports promoters during the 1870s and 1880s, were ready to challenge the world by the 1890s.[15] Americans' experience in international sports contests, however, had been limited to occasional Anglo-Saxon competitions in crew, football, lacrosse, and track and field. Baseball was, of course, not widely played by the British, let alone by Europeans. Collegiate football was under the control of individual schools, not the Amateur Athletic Union, and, by the 1890s, it had been transformed, beyond all recognition, from its original rugby and soccer forms. Basketball, invented by James Naismith in 1891, did not attract significant European interest until American soldiers showcased the game behind World War I battle lines. Track and field was the only prominent sport under unchallenged AAU auspices, and thus became the dominant athletic event in early international competitions. Due largely to AAU Secretary Sullivan's efforts, Americans emerged as the world's leaders in the sport early in the twentieth century.[16]

AMERICAN-STYLE OLYMPISM

The Olympics provided an arena in which certain Americans could invent and popularize symbols of their political and sporting culture by linking athletic prowess to national mythology. As such, the Olympics became a self-perpetuating forum for discussions of athletic superiority as a national characteristic. Commentators extolled the virtues of masculine competition, the benefits of the melting pot, and sport for

sport's sake by fusing nationalism and amateurism. The dominant notions regarding American athletic prowess were defined from the beginning in national terms. This was not entirely new, but the regularity
of Olympic contests gave the amateurists their opening for a positive
public-relations campaign (as opposed to the negative campaign against
corruption during the 1870s and 1880s).

Consequently, the most significant point that emerged from the
early commentary about U.S. involvement is the notion of a national
team. Despite the fact that it was only in 1908 that the American Olympic Committee (AOC) made preparations on a national scale, with the
use of regional tryouts, rather than selection by past performances, the
early teams were described as representative of America. In truth, American involvement before 1908 was principally an eastern-college and club
affair. Nevertheless, beginning with the 1896 Athens Games, observers
summarily equated the athletes as representatives of their nations and
races. British participant and sports enthusiast G. S. Robertson admired
the effort the American team made to participate in the Athens Games,
which he attributed to "the natural enterprise of the American people
and to the peculiarly perfect method in which athletics are organized
in the United States."[17] Lauding the American Olympic victors for their
"mastery of modern athletics," influential sports commentator Caspar
Whitney asserted that "even with men of lesser prowess" than the elite
sportsmen who comprised the Olympic contingent, "America must still
have proved an overwhelming victor, for the superiority of the style and
form of our representatives was entirely convincing of American pre-
eminence."[18] Such "mastery" demonstrated to other observers that the
United States was the most energetic and modern nation on earth, as
Whitney and like-minded athleticists linked modern sporting practices
to the cultivation and control of human energies, and to the production achievements of progressive modern civilization.[19]

American Olympic athletes were not instantaneous demigods in the
public mind—they had to be created. In spite of the haphazard organization of the American entry and the average quality of the team's
athletic skills, the American press transformed the athletes into exemplars of the national spirit—middle-class icons who showed the decadent Old World the strength of an emerging world power. Explaining
American dominance in track-and-field events through a selective reading of the results, the *Atlanta Constitution* boasted that "though America
has none of the traditions and but little of the training possessed by these
nations of the Old World, she has evinced her superiority over them in
the games of their own choice, and from the heights of Mount Olympus
she has transferred the laurel branch to her own distant borders."[20]

In the 1896 Games, the American team performed well enough to
encourage sports fans to read about American amateur athletic superiority in the expanding sports pages. The American athletes then made

good on the nationalistic rhetoric by performing even better at the 1900 Paris Games, thanks in part to a clever point-scoring system, devised by journalists, that favored track-and-field events. The labeling of track-and-field events as "American" was not exactly accidental, for, with the creation of the AAU, all college runners, jumpers, and throwers interested in national and international competitions were now obligated to register with the AAU and were rigidly controlled by AAU administrators and the university-appointed coaches and trainers. On the eve of the Paris Olympics, the AAU leadership merely changed its name, for the moment, to the AOC. This established the trend for the first two decades of the century, in which this AOC, composed almost entirely of AAU men, met shortly before the Games to raise money and select the Olympic team; it had no other function. As a harbinger of things to come, the *New York Times* described the 1900 Games as the "world amateur championships" and declared that the United States had, in fact, won them. American explanations of their Paris victories testified to the widening recognition of the power of sports in the national sporting culture, and to the identification of athletic teams in strictly nationalistic terms.[21]

The decision to hold the 1904 Games as part of the St. Louis Exposition allowed sports leaders to define their own version of American-style Olympism. And indeed, American nationalism and cultural jingoism triumphed. James Sullivan (who also organized the A. G. Spalding and Brothers exhibit) was courted by the Expo's officials to situate the Games within a Western ritual that dramatized national power relations and America's turn-of-the-century worldview. A writer for *Outlook* characterized the World's Fair as "an educative force," arguing that its distinct purpose was to "make people see things."[22] The class bias of the Exposition was clearly recognized by F. J. Skiff, director of exhibits, who admitted that the event was designed to teach all, but "primarily and distinctly [the] working citizenry of the country and the world." President Theodore Roosevelt exploited the occasion to pay homage to the virtues of the frontier, westward expansion, and America's policy of manifest destiny. In a world alive with social Darwinism, displays of material and natural abundance became an outward sign of inner strength and a high level of culture.[23]

Indicative of the ideologically charged milieu, the most popular exhibit of the 1904 expo (according to interviews conducted by the Missouri Historical Society) was the Philippines Reservation. Organized by the U.S. government and sanctioned by prominent anthropologists, the scantily clad Filipinos, located adjacent to the American Indian reservation at the center of the fairgrounds, signaled the arrival of the United States as an imperial power. The Filipino and Native American villages were part of the "Congress of Races," whose aim, according to the exhibit's coordinator, W. J. McGee (a leading anthropologist of the day), was to "represent human progress from the dark prime to the highest enlightenment."[24] By objectifying the Filipinos, historian Robert Rydell contends, the exhibit also "confirmed for white Americans a sense of their own racial and cultural superiority," and as such, "transmitted scientific racism from intellectual elites to millions of ordinary Americans."[25] As Rydell documents, the best evidence of the fair's influence on American culture is the fact that one did not have to actually attend the fair to feel the effects of it. Through newspaper stories and magazine articles, together with merchandise advertising (postcards, souvenirs, etc.) the gospel of imperial supremacy was carried to a national audience. In short, the directors of the St. Louis Exposition turned a portrait of the world into what Rydell characterized as an "anthropologically validated racial landscape" that made the acquisition of the Philippines and other expansionist adventures appear to be as much a part of the nation's manifest-destiny policy as the Louisiana Purchase was 100 years earlier. This was achieved, in part, through the "Congress of Races" exhibit.

Within this nationalistic context, McGee welcomed Sullivan's suggestion that "Anthropology Days" contests be arranged to promote the Olympic Games. On August 12 and 13, Africans, Asians, Filipinos, and American Indians competed in both Olympic events and contests representative of their native cultures. The Pygmies, for example, took the laurels in the mud fight; a Filipino Igorot won the pole-climb; and a Sioux Indian took first place in the 100–yard dash. The "Anthropology Days" competitors wore their native costumes—a visible sign of their racial differences—rather than athletic garb. The nativistic spectacle enabled Western spectators to feel morally justified about bringing modern sports and civilization to the emerging Third World. Albert W. Jenks of the U.S. War Department awarded American flags to the winners of various events. A St. Louis newspaper summarized the results by commenting that "the meeting was a grand success from every point of view, and served as a good example of what the brown men are capable of doing with training."[26] The bureaucrats of amateurism were impressed by the tribal athletes' performances and granted small cash prizes to the winners. Future amateur eligibility was not a problem for the Third-World Olympians since they had "proved themselves decidedly inferior athletes," and would not have understood the amateur ethos, anyway.[27]

Just as the "Anthropology Days" spectacle was taken as an authentic ethnographic reflection, so, too, was American "mastery" of advanced sport taken as proof of the nation's power and vitality. However, the time, expense, and travel logistics involved prevented most Europeans from participating. Only fifty-one made the trip. A total of 617 athletes represented 12 nations, but 525 of them were Americans and another 41 were Canadians.[28] American athletes dominated most events. In fact,

Americans scored 22 firsts in the 23 track-and-field events. For the first and last time in Olympic history, American gymnasts, in their 12 events, won all but 5 of the 36 medals. Moreover, Americans swept the rowing, boxing, cycling, and wrestling competitions. Given the marginal international field, Sullivan stretched the definition of Olympic Games to include a host of scholastic, collegiate, and even several professional contests.[29]

Nevertheless, chauvinistic American journalists and sports leaders claimed an international victory as proof of the nation's values, assimilative capacities, and growing athletic prowess. Sullivan shamelessly declared that the 1904 Games "were without question the greatest athletic games ever held in the world."[30] Sullivan, the dominant figure in American amateur sports for the following decade, also publicly endorsed Spalding goods as "the world's finest." Due largely to his efforts (Sullivan was a Spalding employee), Spalding's sporting goods became the official brand and benchmark for all subsequent amateur athletic competitions, and the only equipment recognized by the AAU—an organization Sullivan dominated until his death in 1914.

Coubertin was less sanguine. Not only did the founder of the modern Olympics fail to attend the third revival, but he referred to the chauvinistic St. Louis festival as one that could take place only in America, since "to Americans everything is permissible, their youthful exuberance calling certainly for the indulgence of the ancient Greek ancestors, if, by chance, they found themselves at that time among the bemused spectators."[31] The intellectual Henry Adams's assessments were even more damning since they came from an American observer. Commenting on the 1904 spectacle, Adams saw "a third-rate town of half-a-million people without history, education, unity, or art, and with little capital, ... doing what London, Paris, or New York would have shrunk from attempting."[32] Describing St. Louis as "a new social conglomerate," Adams speculated that one "enjoyed" the Exposition "with iniquitous rapture, not because of exhibits but rather because of their want," since the "pageant [was] as ephemeral as a stage flat."[33] Such old-world assessments were not widely entertained in the United States. Promoted by a legion of intellectuals, politicians, and sports bureaucrats, the 1904 Games, nevertheless ignited an explosion of American athletic nationalism and, according to Dyreson, "convinced the public that sport served the interests of progress and national revitalization."[34]

Interim Games were held in 1906 in Athens (the last Games on Greek soil) as a political compromise designed to allay the Greeks' frustration for the IOC's refusal to make Greece the permanent site of the Olympics. The Greek embassy solicited President Roosevelt to be honorary director of the American committee, which was headed by Whitney. At a White House luncheon on March 6, Roosevelt selected Sullivan to be the official American representative, considering him, according to the

New York Times, the one "embodying in the minds of all present every desiderata of the position." Not only had Sullivan been "in close touch with every phase of the preparatory work undertaken to insure its success," but he raised funds to defray the team's travel expenses; and most important, according to the *Times*, Sullivan had "prevented the attendance of some who, while they might have been athletically capable, bore reputations none too savory for pure amateurism. [A] place on this team," the *Times* concluded, "is in itself a certificate of bona fide amateurism that all can accept without question."[35] In truth, the AOC only accepted athletes deemed worthy by the AAU. Whereas previously, Sullivan had appointed AOC officers at his own discretion (since the organization lacked a constitution and by-laws), after the 1906 contests, the responsibility to plan and coordinate American participation, through the AOC, fell on the AAU. Sullivan assumed unrivaled leadership of the AAU the following year.[36]

The 1906 Games were a success. Twenty nations sent 887 athletes to Athens (30 American representatives went)—nearly twice the number that participated at St. Louis. The Americans staged the most successful collective effort, even though the 1906 results have not been included in the official Olympic records.[37] Even though Coubertin and other international representatives remained vigilant in relation to the amateur sporting utopia, the concept and practice continued to exclude members of the working classes, and, thus, were in direct contradiction to the internationalist, moralistic tenets of sport, which called for equal opportunity for people to compete on a level playing field. Nevertheless, Sullivan was awarded the Greek Golden Cross for his efforts and was showered with praise and honor by journalists, who celebrated his honesty, organizational genius, and amateurist integrity.[38] Even the staid, albeit liberal, journal, *The Nation*, which had traditionally viewed spectator sports with suspicion, had nothing but praise for the 1906 Athens Games and the classical traditions they recalled. "With the institution of quadrennial Olympic Games on Greek soil," *The Nation* editorialized, "let us hope that the ancient Greek traditions and ideals infuse themselves into the world's athletic life and raise its moral tone and standards, so as to make a great and noble power for what is good and beautiful."[39]

THE 1908 LONDON GAMES: A NATIONALISTIC SHOWDOWN

When the celebratory dust settled, it was clear that Greece would not be the eternal host of the Olympics. During deliberations for the selection of the site for the 1908 Games, Coubertin favored Rome, saying this would pay "international homage to Roman antiquity"; he wanted Olympism, "after its return from the excursion to utilitarian America, to don once again the sumptuous toga, woven of art and philosophy, in which I had always wanted to clothe her."[40] But even Coubertin's influence could not prevent England—the home of the Rugby School, muscular Christianity, and the amateur ethos—from receiving its due, as London was selected as the site.

The 1908 London Games proved to be a very different kind of Olympic spectacle. Having proven to the American people, on their own soil, that their race was a "superior" one, the American bureaucrats of amateurism took the ideology a step further. At a time when the United States challenged Britain for the political, economic, and athletic leadership of the world, the 1908 Games simplified the larger struggle in terms easily understood by a receptive American public. The headlines of the *New York Times* prior to the Games reflected the intense desire of the Americans to beat the Britons: "American Athletes Sure of Success"; "Britishers Fear Yankee Athletes"; "We Will Knock the Spots Off the Britishers." Such audacious declarations signaled what became a nationalistically charged showdown between the most powerful industrial and imperial power of the world and the emergent one. Sullivan asked Roosevelt to be honorary chair of the 1908 team and requested $100,000 from him for the undertaking. The first request was accepted; the second one was denied, despite Sullivan's reminder that "national pride and not individual honor was at stake."[41] In all, the 1908 Olympic executive committee featured three Spalding employees (out of eight members). Bartow S. Weeks, AAU counsel, threatened the *New York Telegraph* with a libel suit if the paper printed a story that would have charged Sullivan with graft and unscrupulous motives.[42]

The primacy of this rivalry was also extremely important to the hosts of the 1908 Games. Members of the British middle and upper classes were concerned that the empire's prestige was perceived to be steadily declining. A consequent search for new devices to ensure social cohesion and national identity materialized into a veritable heyday of "invented tradition," characterized by historian David Cannadine as "a time when old ceremonials were staged with an expertise and appeal which had been lacking before, and when new rituals were self-consciously invented to accentuate this development."[43] The opening ceremony of the 1908 London Games represented such an example of a more general proliferation of political ceremonials designed to promulgate respect for the British aristocracy. Indeed, the social and political changes that had altered Edwardian society allowed the ceremonial presentation to be made by what Cannadine describes as an "impotent but venerated monarch as a unifying symbol of permanence and national community."[44] The *London Times*'s assertion that "there is no one living more fitted to open and in one sense preside over the fourth Olympiad than King Edward the Peacemaker," reflected the extent to which such an invented tradition became commonsensical in British public discourse.[45]

The exaggerated idealogical rifts that involved American and British nationalism were dramatized in the opening ceremony when the American flag, despite British disclaimers, was conspicuously not on display in the stadium. The episode roused indignation among American athletes—most notably, shot-putter and standard-bearer Ralph Rose, who refused to dip the flag, in what was a customary courtesy, while passing the royal box during the opening ceremony. One of the American athletes reputedly quipped: "This flag dips to no earthly king"—this initiated a contentious wave of American protestations throughout the London Games.[46]

From the American perspective, the most controversial event was the 400-meter race. American runner J. C. Carpenter was disqualified by British officials for obstructing England's ahtletic idol, Lieutenant Wyndham Halswelle, whose performance had promised to bring the greatest glory to the motherland. The acrimonious situation was fueled by the different track-and-field rules for the countries, a difficulty which was resolved only years later by the formation of the International Amateur Athletic Federation. Despite an unsuccessful appeal to the Olympic jury, chauvinistic American journalists and spokesmen portrayed Carpenter as the winner. "Carpenter of Cornell Easily Beats English Crack, but Is Disqualified for Foul," announced a headline in the *New York Times*; "Officials Claim Bump-Race to be Re-Run, English Crowds Boo American Performers for No Reason Whatsoever." Nationalistic recriminations flew back and forth across the Atlantic during the ensuing days.[47] Whitney offered a conciliatory note by assuring British sports fans that "the hearts of our athletes are of prime quality even though their manners may not be an invariably correct index."[48]

Whitney attributed the American involvement in the controversy to a "mistaking of violent glorification for patriotism by the younger element," and to an "absence of tradition"; he explained the American sporting personality in terms of a "general disposition to 'kick' at decisions" and their "training to beat the rules."[49] Americans reputedly understood that "kicking" and attempting to outsmart the officials did not reflect dishonesty, but, rather, "an expression of [a] frenzy to win [that is] so characteristic of us, . . . that has made us what we are."[50] Whitney continued: "We do things in Wall Street that would put a man behind the bars if he was not ranked as being smart," America's chief guardian of amateurism admitted that "the slickness which enters into high finance has a tendency to creep into our athletics," signifying that Americans' passion for moneymaking as "the highest expression of one's endeavors, one's brain, one's skill, is reflected in athletics by the passion for victory which ignores sport for sport's sake."[51] Thus, in few strokes of the pen, Whitney aptly equated the American athletes' behavior with a distinct *national* character, which dangerously challenged (if not outright violated) the fraternal, amateur restrictions on international athletic competition. Such explanations, articulated by a nationally known spokesman, quickly became part of the popular discourse of the day and thereby soothed dominant concerns about the vitality of the amateurist-nationalist ideology.[52]

By 1908, the nationalist Olympic discourse had become standard fare—ideologically consistent and predictable. In just 14 years, the Games had gained unchallenged media support. Despite the fact that Britain handily surpassed the United States in total medals, the American media, again, claimed victory on the basis of the track-and-field results.[53] Arthur Ruhl, the distinguished associate editor of *Collier's*, described the track-and-field results as consummate "American achievements." Ruhl attributed the American "dominance" to a "particular make-up" that consisted of a "large amount of immediately available nervous energy and the alert power of concentration," which, he suggested, were "characteristically American."[54] The *New York Times* personified the mighty, energetic American sporting nation through caricatures of a robust Roosevelt, who was shown facing a skinny, effete Englishman donning a top hat and monocle. If a broader ideological media perspective was needed, the *New York Evening Call*, the daily Socialist newspaper, added further fuel to the "bourgeois" nationalistic flame by chastising the "snobbish" English sporting officials for having provided only "comfort for the classes rather than the masses."[55]

One late August afternoon in 1908, the dominant version of American athleticism was dramatized on New York City streets. Amid the profusion of bunting and the sound of patriotic hymns, 250,000 people participated in what the *New York Times* categorized as "the greatest ovation in the history of athletics," celebrating those "brawny representatives of young America [who] faced the multitudes in the London Stadium perfectly unconcerned and won the most glorious victory in the annals of athletics."[56]

The *New York Evening Call* exposed the fund-raising efforts for the grand New York parade. Unlike other leftist newspapers that ignored sports, the *Call* had an informative daily sports page that featured regular contributors, including W. O. McGeehan (regarded by contemporary journalist Paul Gallico as "the greatest sportswriter that ever lived"). When it was reported in the *New York Times* that $10,000 had been promised by the AOC for the parade and banquet, the *Call* predicted that the public would be coerced into making "voluntary" contributions. Tammany Hall's pressure on local employers, the *Call* maintained, would simply result in "a sudden interest in the underpaid and hard working employees denying their families the pleasure of a Sunday at the shore in order to give 'voluntarily'" the money necessary to entertain the Olympic athletes and their bourgeois patrons.[57] The *Call* condemned the effort as a ploy by "a bunch of ward heelers, political grafters, and artistic plunderers" who aimed to "steal the city's scant supply of real money to eat up and drink up in a political exploitation of a pseudo-reception to the Irish-American Olympic team." In other words, as the *Call* explained, the "spontaneous" enthusiasm of America's athletic exploits abroad was not equally visible to all social classes.[58]

A casual observer might have mistaken the Olympic parade for a military exhibition. The parade's grand marshal, General George Wingate, accompanied by 16 high-ranking officers, led four groups representing the United States Army, Navy, and Marines, and the National Guard; they numbered some 15,000 troops in all. Behind the militia marched the athletes and the city's elite, followed by athletic clubs of all stripes and throngs of excited schoolchildren. The orgy of nationalistic fervor culminated in a rousing speech delivered by New York's Mayor McGowan, who congratulated "those of our countrymen who have won victories in athletic sports against the world," and praised the "uplifting role of amateur athletics" in producing a "strong and manly race" of coura-geous, patriotic men.[59] Aside from the regeneration of the body, the mayor insisted that sports served to elevate the national reputation. Like most traditional street theater, Olympic celebrations not only refracted cultural meanings, but were also used by people for building, maintaining, and confronting social relationships. Through the Olympics, accord-ing to anthropologist John MacAloon, we seize the occasions of "rela-tively purer sociability, consensually framed as play, and attempt to solve . . . our terrible confusion" about the relationship between the "objec-tive" world of political and social constraints and a more "subjective" one of personal enjoyment and autonomy.[60]

1912 "MELTING POT" VICTORIES AND JIM THORPE'S FALL FROM GLORY

On the eve of the 1912 Stockholm Games, journalist Edward Bayard Moss related the newly invented metaphors of American Olympic prow-ess to a timeless tradition. Just as in ancient Greek mythology the Argo-nauts sailed to recover the golden fleece of the winged ram Chrysomallus, nailed to an oak tree in the garden of Ares, so too, according to Moss, did the United States Olympic team sail for Stockholm in its quest for sacred, modern-day athletic honors. As the United States developed an empire and a major role in world affairs, many people, like Moss, dis-covered a symbolic relationship between athletic success, national vi-tality, and the creation of an American race. In an article written several weeks later, Moss transformed "America's Argonauts" into "America's athletic missionaries," and, through his commentary, honed the already-effective "melting pot" explanation of American athletic prowess.[61] Not only did America successfully assimilate the various ethnic groups into a national team, but class lines, he claimed, were blurred in the process—the team comprised a "heterogeneous gathering of lawyers, physicians, policemen, Indians, negroes, Hawaiians, college men, school boys, clerks, mechanics, and entrants from every walk of life."[62]

An editor for *The Independent*, conveniently ignoring how the amateur code discriminated against many of the best working-class and African-American athletes (many of whom sold themselves as professionals), affirmed Moss's conviction that "American success" was due largely to the "wide range of selection without regard to class, wealth, race, color or previous condition of servitude."[63] Whereas only 20 years earlier, the leading apostles of amateurism, like Whitney, had characterized athletes from less socially privileged backgrounds as "vermin" who could not understand the elevated ideals of true sport, Colonel Robert Thompson, the AOC's president, speculated that the team's melting-pot character provided a "fair criterion in speculation as to what sort of a race we now are building in America"—a view widely popularized by extensive newspaper and magazine comments.[64]

America's 1912 melting-pot victories bolstered nationalist appraisals that the United States was surpassing its old-world rivals. Jim Thorpe's brilliant performance at Stockholm, in particular, appeared to legitimize America's melting-pot ideology. A Sac and Fox Indian from Oklahoma, Thorpe had previously been selected by Walter Camp as an all-American halfback, and was hailed by Sweden's King Gustav V as "the greatest athlete in the world," for winning the pentathlon and decathlon at the 1912 Games. The British complained vociferously about the "negroes and Indians" who disproportionately won medals for the American team. Irish-American journalist-humorist Finley Peter Dunne had an ethnically aware and class-conscious answer, during the London Games, that resonated clearly four years later: "These boys that you see hoppin' around th' thrack," a fictional Mr. Dooley said to his friend Hennessy, "ar-re the rile represinitive Americans. They are the ambassadurs, not the lords ye see makin' a ginuflixion befure th' king."[65] Another American journalist attributed the fact that the United States scored as many points as the rest of the competing countries combined to the nation's assimilation "of all races."[66] Without succumbing to social Darwinian chauvinism like many of his contemporaries, the writer concluded that such "melting-pot" victories proved "how artificial, accidental and unessential are the distinctions which we draw and go to such great trouble to maintain between nation or between race and race."[67] As nativist fears of "race suicide" incited federal policy toward adopting stringent immigration restrictions, American Olympic spectacles convinced many pessimists that the country should not obstruct the successful assimilation process. Charles E. Woodruff, a distinguished ethnologist and United States Army medical-corps doctor, recommended that "if America is to be at the front of civilization, . . . its blood must be constantly recruited from Northern Europe."[68]

On August 12, 1912, New Yorkers again lined the streets from Fifth Avenue and Forty-first Street to City Hall to honor the returning American Olympic athletes. The celebratory parade was itself an American microcosm. Local and national elites escorted by an artillery corps led the march, and were followed by war veterans, Boy Scouts, and citizens' committees. The bulk of the paraders were representatives of athletic clubs, religious athletic organizations, ethnic turnvereins, and gymnastic clubs, and African-American athletic clubs. According to the *New York Times*, the cheering was led by "the youngest of young Americans," public-school children who demonstrated their "real American pride" by competitively chanting "U.S.A. A-M-E-R-I-C-A!"[69] At the parade's conclusion, New York's Mayor Gaynor praised the "victorious athletes'" prowess as "the medium of comment for the people of the world." "You have shown," he said "that you possessed American stomachs, hearts, muscles and heads."[70] Despite such self-congratulatory exhibitions, deeper issues about America's commitment to the amateur ethos remained unresolved.

Six months after Thorpe's stellar performance, America's Olympic aristocrats—Gustavus Kirby (president of the AAU and vice president of the AOC); Bartow S. Weeks (chair of the AAU's legislative committee and an AOC committee member); and Sullivan—exposed Thorpe's earlier brief stint in semiprofessional baseball. The bureaucrats of amateurism in the AAU and on the American Olympic Committee closed ranks and made an example out of Thorpe, suggesting that "Mr. Thorpe is deserving of the severest condemnation for concealing the fact that he had professionalized himself"; and thereby forcing him to return his medals and valuable prizes, which included a sculptured Viking ship given to him by the Czar of Russia, and a handsome bronze bust of the king of Sweden.[71] As historian William Baker surmised, "the muses turned the brightest gold of Stockholm into dross."[72] The custodians of amateurism indeed exploited the situation to demonstrate the inexorability of the eligibility standards—a mighty public-relations effort, for which Sullivan, Kirby, and others received widespread praise.

Ignoring earlier statements about the melting-pot nature of the 1912 American squad, athletic organizations and their media supporters scrambled to explain Thorpe's "mistake" in terms of *his* race, which had been proudly characterized as American just months earlier. The IOC's resolution noted that Thorpe was "an Indian of limited experience and education in the ways of other than his own people."[73] Thorpe's plea that he was "not wise in the ways of the world," and was "simply an Indian school-boy," only confirmed the sentiment expressed by the *Columbia* (S.C.) *State*: that "an Indian may hardly be held with strict justice to so high a degree of moral accountability as his white competitors."[74]

The actual situation beneath the moralistic posturing was more complex. Thorpe was implicated in the summer baseball controversy that bedeviled American amateur sport. As a student at the Carlisle (Pa.) Indian School, Thorpe, like scores of other college students, received money during the summers of 1909 and 1910 for playing semiprofessional baseball in North Carolina. Even though many colleges publicly condemned semiprofessional baseball, athletes (as I noted in the previous chapter) were not disqualified from collegiate eligibility. Thorpe, in fact, competed in AAU-sanctioned track meets during the following years. Nor did the AAU condemn professionalized college athletes who were given scholarships, room-and-board expenses, and under-the-table favors. "If their move against Thorpe was not animated by sinister and personal motives," noted the *Philadelphia Times* in an editorial, the AAU "will have a busy time cleaning up the ranks of collegiate athletics in order to make all amateurs as thoroughly amateurish as the AAU insists Thorpe should have been in order to keep the honors he so clearly won."[75]

The contradictory nature of amateur athletic governance inspired several other commentators to openly support Thorpe. The *Buffalo Express*, for instance, exposed the amateur ethos as it was indiscriminately applied to Thorpe. In a true amateur spirit, Thorpe played summer baseball not for a salary, but for his own professed "love of the game." As a young man of independent financial means, he was not on the diamond, the *Express* reported, "to earn a living or his way through college, as many college men are, and there was no profit in the playing for him except that which was derived from the pure pleasure of having an opportunity to gratify his athletic longings."[76] Moreover, given his accomplishments at Stockholm, the *Express* noted, "he could as well never have seen a ball game, much less played one."[77] Arguing against the accusations that Thorpe's Olympic exploits derived from his baseball professionalism, the *Washington Herald* declared that not only had he not "become a great runner, jumper, and weight thrower through participation in professional baseball," but that his "professionalism endowed him with no advantage over the college amateurs against whom he won his place on the American Olympic team."[78]

How then could Thorpe's unequivocal disqualification be explained? The *Washington Herald* recognized the Olympics' international character as the probable explanation: "The most serious feature of Thorpe's conduct is that he violated not only the rules of amateur sport, but that he sacrificed the reputation of American athletics."[79] The *New York Times* concurred, and articulated what became the most popular view: that Thorpe's disgrace was "a trivial matter in comparison with the humiliation which he has brought upon his country—with the derision and denunciation which all Americans will long have to hear from the foreign critics: . . . that we lack the instinct of fair play."[80] Clearly, the opinion shapers and sports bureaucrats were most concerned with how the Thorpe incident would be interpreted by America's chief Anglo-Saxon rival—the mother of modern athletics—Britain. Saving national face was indeed the operative issue. Concerned that the British would conclude that Americans were driven principally to win at any cost, and that the genteel idea of amateurism was beyond the comprehension of the American athletic establishment, the Thorpe controversy became a nationalistic battleground. The *New York Times*'s London correspondent speculated that "what occurred at Stockholm [including charges of American sprinters obstructing their opponents and attempting to anticipate the pistol] involves no indictment of the sporting spirit of the people of the United States as a whole," but, rather, a "wholehearted dislike of the particular crowd . . . which controls Olympic matters in America and of what are commonly called the political and Tammany methods which that crowd represents."[81] More common, however, was the cascade of British complaints, like those of London's *The Spectator*, which condemned American specialization and professionalism as having simply gone too far.[82]

Most American commentators assured their readers that such elitist diatribes were merely a smoke screen. With the advent of the Olympics, *The Nation* noted, in an editorial, that "the rivalry between nations assumed a new phase, [and that] the Englishman has been forced to reconsider his position."[83] Although traditionally scorned by the mother of modern athletics, American training and preparation had at last compelled the Briton to "face the alternative of adopting the methods about which he feels a little uncomfortable as being tinged with 'professionalism,' or of resigning any hope of regaining his old prestige in the world of sport."[84] With his characteristic bluntness, the fictional Dooley interpreted British charges of American athletic professionalism as merely convenient explanations for their lack of success at Stockholm. "While our athletes were livin' their ordhinry amachoor lives an' takin' no exercise beyant fightin' with th' wasps f'r possession iv th' breakfast marmylade," Dooley said in a parody of a fictional London editorial, "their opponents were practicin' runnin', jumpin', and puttin' th' shot to have an onfair advantage whin they entered th' races." Dooley's parody of an imaginary British editorial continued:

> Our idee iv these spoorts is that they ought to be threated as a pleasant way iv passin' th' afthernoon. Th' thrue amachoor wud disdain missin' a meal in ordher to run a little faster thin his fellow man. He ates a hearty lunch iv veal an' ham pie, with a chunk iv cheese an' pasthry, dhrinks a basin iv tea, goes at wanst to th' game, takes off his coat, hands his pipe to th' starter, an' runs till a light perspiration breaks out on th' forehead or a sinkin' feelin' in th' neighborhood iv th' stomach warns him he has gone

far enough. Anywan who adhopts other methods is a profissyonal an' ought to be barred.[85]

The poignant juxtaposition of Dooley's parody with Thorpe's disqualification illuminates the American ambivalence regarding the amateur code. Although most Americans probably believed in the tenets of amateurism, many could not refuse the opportunity that the ideologically charged 1912 Games provided for mocking the original British conception of amateurism, which was less than a generation old.

Just 16 years after the Olympic revival, the rule regarding amateurs had proved to be especially difficult to enforce, let alone define. There was no single definition of *amateur*. Each national federation defined the term as it wished, and with the gradual increase in permissible ways for amateurs to receive monetary compensation, the term became almost meaningless. After the Thorpe incident, the single thread held the fragile international athletic system together was a rule that an amateur in one sport had to be an amateur in all sports if he or she was to compete in the Olympic Games.[86]

THE POST–WORLD WAR I RESUMPTION

The sixth modern Olympiad, envisaged by Coubertin as an event that boded "gladness and concord,"[87] had been scheduled for Berlin in the summer of 1916. But this spectacle could not be held as the guns of August 1914 had reduced everything to shambles. More than 10 million had died in combat, and another 10 million were wounded and maimed. Athletic games, as William Baker notes, "gave way to a far more grim contest of strength and will. Fields of play became ugly zones of devastation marked by shell craters, barbed wire, and filthy trenches."[88] The vindictive distrust that characterized the Versailles treaty was subsumed under the IOC banner. The brotherly, internationalist auspices of Olympism only applied to the Allied nations; Germany and the Soviet Union were excluded.

Post–World War I political developments brought about new challenges for the IOC's politicized athletic leadership. Indeed, an international socialist movement posed a threat to Western bourgeois nationalism, both before and after the war. Challenging the contradictions between the benevolent internationalist rhetoric of the Games and their explicitly nationalist reality, European Socialists organized their own sports federations to promote the cause of working-class solidarity. In 1920, representatives founded an international sports organization, which, five years later, celebrated the First Workers Olympics at Frankfurt—a four-day event featuring elaborate pageantry, speeches, and Socialist demonstrations; the event involved over 1,000 worker-athletes who sought to achieve a Socialist version of Coubertin's dream.

Western Olympic federations relied increasingly on official govenmental financial support. In the United States, post–World War I federal patronage did much to bring about American sports' golden age of the 1920s by legitimizing international athletic spectacles in the public's eye. AOC Chair Kirby predicted that congressional support would ensure that the trip to Antwerp (the site of the 1920 Games) would be "a truly American invasion in every way"; sailing under the Stars and Stripes, Kirby believed, would signal to the world that the American team "enjoy[ed] the official support of the Government in their effort."[89] Further, private-sector initiatives complemented the official federal support of the U.S. Olympic team. Posters that said, "Help America Win the Olympic Games" appeared in schoolhouses, police stations, firehouses, municipal buildings, social centers, and athletic clubs throughout New York City, during the summer of 1920; and thereafter, the poster campaign spread throughout the nation. A local spokesman explained, "It is the desire of the American Olympic Committee that the support and financing of the American teams this year shall be national in character."[90] The consumer culture had not weakened the nation's vitality; it only strengthened America's resolve to defeat its international rivals on the Olympic battlefield. Indeed, a poignant metaphor in the immediate aftermath of the war was reflected in the official poster of the Antwerp Games, which portrayed an athlete hurling the discus, and which conjured memories of bomb throwers and artillerymen; but also, according to journalist Arthur Drew, it symbolized "the return of peace to an anguished world, and the triumph of fair play over foul."[91]

Reflecting the stateliness of modern athletics, the AOC avidly solicited cooperation and support from the Army and Navy by inviting Secretaries Newton Baker and Josephus Daniels to serve as honorary vice presidents on the committee. Military participation, according to the AOC, "placed behind civilian activity the bulwark of the great branches of government service," which greatly enhanced "the prestige of the United States among other nations competing at Antwerp, and broadened the field from which to glean our champions and in which to sow the Olympic idea."[92] The military quickly warmed to the mission by staging, in efficient fashion, sectional tryouts for soldier-athletes in Philadelphia, Chicago, and Pasadena.

The military's most important contribution, however, was transporting the American athletes to Belgium—an undertaking riddled with legal and logistical difficulties. It was illegal for civilians to travel aboard Army and Navy ships. Military and Olympic officials instigated congressional hearings between March and June, which culminated in joint House and Senate bills enabling the secretary of war to use Army transports for the athletes, coaches, and other personnel. Gustavus Kirby solicited the testimonies of Secretary of War Baker, who was chair of the Senate and House Committees of Military Affairs; the Honorable James Wadsworth and the Honorable Julius Kahn (respectively); and New York Supreme Court Justice Bartow Weeks. The distinguished witnesses consistently emphasized the patriotic nature of American sports. Weeks, who, as a past secretary of the AOC, was hardly a disinterested witness, testified that "our fine young men and women are going to carry our flag to victory over there on battlefields of peace just as they carried our flag to victory on battlefields of war."[93] Weeks concluded his testimony by invoking a trinity of references—to flag, country, and patriotism—plus the words "nation defense," as splendid justification for the official transport of the athletes. Following coaxing by witnesses who assured a wary Congress that such efforts were pragmatic and would not establish a precedent, the bills were signed into law by President Woodrow Wilson on June 2.

American interpretations of the 1920 Games both embraced and departed from Coubertin's idealism. American explanations about Olympic results had always teetered on the cusp between myth and reality. By all systems of athletic scoring used in 1920, the United States emerged as the dominant nation, with the small nation of Finland a close second. There were murmurings, however, among various AOC members, and especially among journalists, that the country had not done as well as the great 1912 American team had done, and that poor AAU and AOC management was the reason. Although the media reverentially paid homage to American athletic prowess, such accolades were overshadowed by the controversies surrounding the team's shoddy management.

For the first time in its young history, the American bureaucrats of amateurism were publicly shamed and challenged. The controversy centered on the government-subsidized travel-and-accommodations efforts. The American athletes vociferously protested the unsatisfactory quarters aboard the *Matokia*, on the trip from New York, as "absolutely unbelievable for finely trained men," and blamed the AOC (specifically naming Weeks, Kirby, Everett Brown, and Frederick Rubien) for poor judgment in making the traveling arrangements. The resolution was endorsed by nearly 200 athletes and required that copies be sent to the secretary of war, the press, and the AOC.[94] The Antwerp accommodations were no better and incited further complaints. As one athlete described the quarters:

> The building was divided by an ill-smelling unsanitary court. The athletes were herded into confused quarters, they slept on straw with lumps in it which put ridges in your body, and sanitation was conspicuously absent. The drinking water was terrible and conditions all round were objectionable.[95]

Protest verged on rebellion when Dean Ahearn, world record holder for the hop, step, and jump, was dismissed from the team on charges of insubordination, which stemmed from his violation of the AOC's curfew restrictions. In the face of threats that some of the athletes would not compete unless Ahearn was reinstated, the committee replied that it would stand by its decision even if 90 percent of the athletes refused to compete. Following a boisterous mass meeting of athletes and Olympic officials, during which Kirby and Weeks were greeted with catcalls and heckling, Ahearn was reinstated after he appeared before the AOC and apologized. The returning athletes kept the controversy alive. Public discontent and suspicion affected the results of the voting at the annual AAU convention, in which Rubien barely managed reelection, and Weeks was defeated for reelection as a delegate, finishing eighth in the balloting. So damaging had been the charges brought against the AOC that at the committee's December 4 meeting, a plan calling for a complete reorganization was introduced.[96]

The subsequent reorganization of the AOC became a source of conflict between the AAU and the burgeoning NCAA during the 1920s. A scathing letter from the NCAA head, General Palmer Pierce, notifying Kirby that the NCAA would withdraw from the AOC, appeared in the *New York Times*. Pierce, who had exposed the undemocratic nature of the AOC's organization in the pages of *The Outlook*, thought it better for the NCAA to remain independent (a decision that was also supported by the Navy and War departments, and by the YMCA), since it had marginal power in the selection of Olympic contestants, managers, trainers, and the conduct of the contests.[97]

All hell broke loose after Sullivan's death in 1914. Without a czarlike bureaucrat, the American Olympic bureaucracy fell into disarray. Newton Fuessle identified the fact that in "back of every contest between amateur athletes in the United States, a curious war is raging" between those who believe in "building stars" and those who believe in "building men."[98] In a polemic against the AOC, the "self-appointed and self-perpetuating hierarchy of bosses" who controlled America's Olympic representation, Fuessle called it "a clannish organization" comprised of officials who refused to cooperate with the colleges and universities, the War Department, the YMCA, the Boy Scouts, or the many playground associations; he promoted a version of American amateurism conspicuously excluded from most congratulatory Olympic commentaries.[99] Fuessle raised the specter of corruption, within the AOC, initiated by the bosses of the AAU over the appropriate selection of American athletes. Fuessle was not alone in this critique. Educators felt the whole tendency of the AAU (which controlled America's participation in the Olympics) was founded upon "undemocratic and unrepresentative principles," and that its influence was "detrimental to the broad spirit of play and physical development that alone can justify the heavy expense of organized athletics."[100] In short, the Olympic movement (i.e., the AOC and its media spokesmen) had won the battle for the hearts and minds of the American public, but had yet to win the war with the larger amateur athletic community over the unresolved dilemma of the amateurism issue.

SUMMARY

"Do not imagine that a democracy can live healthily if its citizens have nothing to hold them together but legal texts and electoral summonses," Pierre de Courbertin wrote in a December 1918 letter. Recalling the clerical and monarchical bonds of old, the founder of the modern Olympics passionately believed that modern society needed "popular spectacles" to dramatize "simple, clear and tangible ideas [and] draw together not only people of all ages and all professions, but of all opinions and all situations." Reiterating the theme of a lifetime's social commentary, Coubertin proclaimed the one "cult" capable of promoting civic unity— "the cult which will develop around youthful exercise, symbol of the endurance of the race and the hopes of the nation."[101] The modern Olympic Games, in particular, provided a forum for cultural performance at both the national and international levels.

By 1920, Americans had read about the meaning of the Games for a quarter of a century. Although it is possible to exaggerate the influence of the Olympic opinion makers on the rest of society, since they spoke primarily to educated, middle-class Americans, they ultimately did exercise crucial cultural power. They not only established the official common sense of ruling groups throughout the nation, but they also articulated moral and psychic dilemmas that later became common in the wider society—which ultimately revitalized and transformed their class's cultural influence. The nexus of nationalism and amateurism was the thread that ran throughout their struggle to establish cultural power within the Olympic forum. Their interpretations not only lavished praise on American muscles and minds, but also legitimized amateurism as the preferred vision of the national sporting culture.

FOUR

THE NATIONAL PASTIME

Baseball, Professionalism, and Nostalgia

Unlike all other major American team sports, professional major-league baseball gained cultural primacy in the United States long before the amateur and semiprofessional games. Although amateur and semiprofessional play sustained the game as the national pastime for more than a century, professional baseball fundamentally shaped the way that most Americans have played and thought about the sport. The creation of the National League in 1876 spawned the key elements—league structure; territorial franchise monopolies; annual championship tournaments; the "reserve clause"; assignment of game officials; and revenue sharing—that dominated commercialized American sports for more than a century. Given the fact that basketball was not invented until 1891 and that professional football only materialized in institutional form in the 1920s, baseball was the only leading American professional sport until after World War I. Despite the ascendancy of amateurism during the late nineteenth century, professional baseball, although an anomaly for its time, provided a model for Americans in understanding big-time commercialized sports.[1]

Baseball's profound influence on the development of an American professional sporting tradition must be analyzed, as Warren Goldstein argues, on two distinct, but related, levels. Professional baseball has both a linear and a cyclical history. The linear record traces the evolution of organizational structures; the cyclical record charts repetitive and generational emotional relationships between fans and the game. Baseball's linear chronicle parallels and reinforces America's business, technological, and labor history; the cyclical level corresponds to cultural and intellectual history. Stephen Fox notes that "baseball remained a way station, content to stay in place, traditional and respectful toward the past, a matter of connection and continuity"; at its deepest levels, "emotional and cyclical, baseball offered Americans a refuge from real life."[2] Despite more than a century of strikes and lockouts, and the recent sharp escalation of profits for owners, and of salaries for players, fans con-

tinue to interpret the current game through nostalgic lenses. We must
consider how the game of baseball as a commercialized social form traversed both material and intellectual levels.

THE PROFESSIONALIZATION OF BASEBALL

Baseball was an amalgam of various ball, bat, and base games played in
the United States throughout the colonial era and into the early nineteenth century. Children's games such as rounders, town ball, stoolball,
one old cat, and base ball had been played in England and America since
the eighteenth century; and all involved hitting a ball with a bat (indeed, Jane Austen mentions a game of "base ball" in *Northanger Abbey*,
published in 1796). Early contests were informal, unorganized, local
events, and rarely attracted spectators or media attention. Around the
mid-nineteenth century, the "New York game" (with a diamond-shaped
infield and nine players per side) emerged as the dominant form. Baseball, however, did not have an unambiguous founding moment, as most
American fans like to believe. The New York Knickerbockers, led by New
York bank clerk Alexander Cartwright, are generally credited with establishing the modern-style rules and conventions of play. But a recently
discovered newsstory with a box score from the *New York Morning News*
describes "a friendly match of the time-honored game of Base" that was
played on October 21, 1845, at the Elysian Fields, "between eight members of the New York Ball Club and the same number of players from
Brooklyn."[3] The account suggests that something strikingly similar to
modern baseball was played throughout the New York City area in the
1840s, and that several rules innovations usually credited to Cartwright
were already in use in 1845.[4]

By the mid-1850s, dozens of clubs were formed by artisans, clerks,
and small proprietors. Like other such urban organizations—volunteer
fire companies, Masonic orders, and workers' benevolent associations—
baseball clubs enabled men of similar crafts and class backgrounds to
fraternize and play together. Clubs drafted their own independent constitutions and by-laws, held regular meetings, and elected officers. Early
baseball, as played by gentlemanly skilled workers, was, as Goldstein
writes, "an alternative to the seamier amusements of early urban America; and it was used as an exemplary activity by an emergent group of
respected middle-class advocates who were beginning to articulate a
defense of sport and recreation in the name of Victorian ideals."[5]

In the late 1850s, baseball eclipsed the English game of cricket as
the principal American ballgame. Henry Chadwick, baseball's chief
nineteenth-century publicist, was the first to see that the game was better suited to the pace of American life than cricket. "Americans do not
care to dawdle over a sleep-inspiring game all through the heat of a June

or July day," the English immigrant wrote. "What they do, they want to do in a hurry. In baseball, all is lightening; every action is swift as a seabird's flight."[6] Chadwick initiated a debate, which persisted into the early part of the twentieth century, about how baseball reflected a national identity. His early writings, however, were premature for a country that lacked a resilient national identity. Cricket's failure in pre–Civil War America had more to do with other historically specific factors. Sport historian Melvin Adelman explains cricket's failure to gain widespread popularity in terms of the respective ball-playing traditions in England and America. Whereas young men and adults in England played ball games during the early years of the nineteenth century, such endeavors were basically children's amusements in the United States. Cricket failed, Adelman contends, because "it was too advanced and too institutionalized for a society that lacked a manly ball-playing tradition." Moreover, "the fate of cricket was not influenced by the fact that it was an English game but that the sport was run for and by Englishmen."[7]

Compared to cricket, baseball arrived in America at a much earlier stage in its development.[8] There was, therefore, according to Adelman, "nothing sacrosanct in its rules, norms, and sanctions, and the structures of the sport that was [not] easily changed by trial and error."[9] The game began in the United States as a club-based fraternal sport that thrived in northeastern industrial cities; indeed, skilled workers dominated the early game. Baseball quickly spread to a range of social groups, who played a variety of styles, from the gentlemanly to the rowdy. Yet, historians differ as to how the rise and popularity of early baseball were related to the cultural matrix of industrial capitalist society. Steven Gelber persuasively argues that through their common work experiences players shared a set of values that could be expressed through baseball. Moreover, the attraction of the game emanated from "the many ways it replicated and legitimized the social and intellectual environment of the urban workplace"—particularly the broadening acceptance of the corporate ideal.[10] Gelber argues that baseball became the national pastime because it *reinforced* the shift to rationalized industrial life and the values that underlay it; Adelman counters by suggesting that Gelber's thesis fails to explain the game's attraction in the 1850s, when scientific management and industrial rationalization were spotty and inconsistent. Perhaps the safer argument is that baseball had paradoxical appeals, and that therein lay its popularity.[11]

The pivotal moment in the game's early organizational development occurred in 1858, with the formation of the National Association of Base Ball Players (NABBP). Despite the fact that all but 1 of the 26 teams hailed from the New York City area, the NABBP pioneered a forum for settling disputes and governing the sport. Curiously, the newly formed national association formally banned professional players on the grounds that sports should be played for pleasure, not profit. The *New York Clipper* summarily charged that such a stance had "something of an aristocratic odor," and that it exhibited a "rather uncharitable disposition towards poor players." Clubs paid lip service to the idealistic interests of amateurism, but, nonetheless, often made secret cash payments to players. By the late 1860s, knowledgeable observers recognized that baseball had become a business, and many recommended the NABBP publicly endorse professionalism. It soon did, and in so doing, provided the pay-for-play movement with a structure and thus endowed professional baseball with a greater sense of stability.[12]

During the 1860s, organized baseball spread rapidly from its northern hub. In 1860, there were 54 clubs represented in the NABBP. Five years later, the membership had grown to 91—48 from New York, 14 from Pennsylvania, 13 from New Jersey, and others from Maine, Kansas, Missouri, Kentucky, and California. The Civil War stimulated player migration and club expansion, thereby weakening the established club networks in the Northeast. By 1867, there were 237 teams represented in the burgeoning national association, but by then, New York State ranked behind Illinois, Ohio, Pennsylvania, and Wisconsin in the number of enrolled clubs. Southern baseball came to the fore when the Southern League, including teams from Georgia, Alabama, and Tennessee, was organized in 1885; the Texas League was organized in 1888.[13] As a result of the game's steady diffusion, national consciousness increasingly replaced local and regional consciousness.[14] Baseball's rapid geographical expansion and popularity between the 1860s and the turn of the century proved to many advocates that the sport usefully linked Americans to a national community, irrespective of local, regional, class, gender, and ethnic differences.

Before the early 1870s, a preferred image of organized baseball had yet to be popularized. A wide range of perspectives of the new sport jostled and often conflicted with each other. Although the professional model was rapidly gaining legitimacy among journalists and commentators, residual fears about commercialized sports continued to exist. In 1875 a sportswriter declared that, "as a general thing, any professional baseball club will 'throw' a game if there is money in it. A horse race is a pretty safe thing to speculate on in comparison with an average baseball match."[15] To counter such criticisms, the first generation of baseball writers emphasized how the game was an effective character builder and a worthy exercise for an increasingly heterogeneous urban population. The moral-uplift component of baseball journalism quelled opposition to the "unsavory" professional practices of paying players and charging admission to games.[16]

In the sports press, stories on the outcome of games, rule changes, gossip, and other areas of baseball interest were vital in the formation of ideas about baseball and the "national character." Early claims of baseball as America's game were shaped by the development of professional-baseball journalism—most notably, Henry Chadwick's efforts. Not only did he introduce the newspaper box score—which became an effective tool for measuring performance—but he also edited and published baseball guides and yearbooks, and chaired the Rules Committee of the NABBP. As early as 1856, William Trotter Porter, editor of the New York-based *Spirit of the Times* (a sports weekly that published the first box scores), was probably the first to call baseball "our national game." In 1866, Charles A. Peverelly, an early authority on recreation, claimed that "the game of Base Ball has now become beyond question the leading feature of the out-door sports of the United States," mainly because of its "low expense, its excitement, and the small amount of time required"[17] (particularly in comparison to the English sport of cricket). Another advocate marveled at how baseball "is a pastime that best suits the temperament of our people. . . . It has become the rage with all classes and conditions."[18] Such statements, penned in the immediate aftermath of the Civil War, advocated baseball as a sporting institution that could help restore fellowship and unity to a divided nation.[19] Chadwick, Porter, and their colleagues gave baseball an emergent (though not yet mythical) national identity that popularized the game and its players in the public mind. In truth, the early sports press prematurely labeled baseball the "national pastime"—based on the erroneous popular belief that the game was indigenous to America, even though Chadwick, as early as 1860, noted baseball's British origins.

These pioneering forays prepared the way for the flowering of Chicago's baseball journalism in the 1880s, which represented a distinctly new style of sports reporting that wove wit, satire, slang, and metaphors into stories and editorial pieces. By way of Cincinnati, St. Louis, Louisville, and Pittsburgh, the Chicago style reached Boston, New York, Philadelphia, and Baltimore, where it became amalgamated with other journalistic innovations. Most notably, Joseph Pulitzer's *New York World* produced the first major daily sports page in the 1880s; and Pulitzer's fierce competitor, William Randolph Hearst, introduced the first modern sports section in the 1890s. Baseball writing was thus the focal point for the organization of ideas about the game.[20]

Just as journalists were pioneering the notion of baseball as a national sport, the game was itself in the process of profound transformation. The NABBP, in the process of refining the management strategies that ultimately segregated players from those who employed them and regulated their work lives, failed to create a structure that would protect players' ability to act as free agents in the sports marketplace. What began as a kind of fraternal world of ballplayers engaged in a new pastime, according to Goldstein, "became part of managers', directors', and owners' ideological arsenal as they battled players over the structure of the baseball business in the late nineteenth century."[21] Given their lack of formally organized collective power, players quickly lost control over their game. Moreover, the very size of player payrolls brought relatively wealthy businessmen into the game—men, Goldstein writes, "whose resources and experience made them formidable adversaries."[22] The petit-bourgeois owners of early baseball teams had close ties with their communities of fans and players, but were squeezed out by a new generation of owners whose resources enabled them to deal with the higher capital requirements, larger salaries, and more permanent facilities that the maturing game demanded.[23]

With the advent of open professionalism in the 1870s, the game became an entertainment business run by owners, boards of directors, and nonplaying managers, with its exhibitions being performed by player-employees. By the mid-1870s, urban growth and the development of an extensive railway system signaled the possibility of a commercially viable national baseball league. What was required for such a scheme to become reality from a capitalist's perspective, according to historian Robert Burk, was "some individual or group with the financial ruthlessness to enforce interclub arrangements restricting competition and protecting markets and with a similar willingness to bring player-employees to heel."[24] Enter William Hulbert, baseball's first, and most important, empire-builder, who, Burk notes, "combined the drive for business dominance of the era's nouveau riche with a traditional Yankee craving for the respectability of [a] well-established position."[25] Determined to ensure that his Chicago White Stockings would become the dominant team in a new, more lucrative baseball empire, Hulbert led a coup with the help of other businessmen from the largest northeastern and midwestern markets. Collectively, in February 1876, they launched the National League of Professional Base Ball Clubs. The name signaled not only their national pretensions, but also the fact that the premier game form would shift from player-controlled teams to clubs under the control of wealthy owners. Journalist Leonard Koppett explains that "it [the league] was the last word that changed everything."[26] In the NABBP, the clubs had been sovereign groups whose policies were determined by the players (read *citizens*), while in the emergent National League, the clubs, ruled by a central government, were much less sovereign; and players became employees, rather than citizens.[27]

The original National League clubs were located in the nation's largest cities—Boston, Chicago, St. Louis, Louisville, Hartford, Cincinnati, Philadelphia, and New York. The geographical structure of the league fluctuated greatly during the early years as Milwaukee, Indianapolis, and Providence clubs entered the circuit. When the Indianapolis and Milwaukee teams dropped out in 1879, they were replaced by clubs in Troy (N.Y.), Buffalo, Syracuse, and Cleveland. The Troy, Buffalo, Syracuse, and Providence clubs failed in the 1880s, and were replaced by clubs in Detroit, Washington, and Kansas City; and by second clubs in New York and Philadelphia. Baltimore and Brooklyn added franchises in the 1890s.

The National and American leagues were firmly established by 1903, with 16 teams located in 10 cities—a structure that remained unchanged for 50 years. Despite westward demographic and economic trends, major-league baseball was confined to the industrial Midwest and Northeast. Nevertheless, baseball played a critical role in the development of an American sports system by creating urban rivalries and, consequently, a sport-place bond based on the geographical structure of competition.[28]

Hulbert's draconian scheme proved remarkably effective. The National League survived intermittent challenges and is now more than 120 years old. It became the prototype for all other professional-sports leagues in the United States throughout the twentieth century. Its early success derived from Hulbert's plan to restrict new memberships; enforce territorial monopolies; codify a regular league schedule; bind players to their teams; and discourage Sunday games and liquor sales at ballparks (for public-relations reasons). The old NABBP died, and its most solvent teams went to the new league. Albert Spalding, Hulbert's partner, a star pitcher, and later a sporting-goods magnate, later explained that the idea for the league "was as old as the hills. . . . It was, in fact, the irrepressible conflict between Labor and Capital asserting itself under a new guise. . . . Like every other form of business enterprise, Base Ball depends for results on two interdependent divisions, the one to have absolute control and direction of the system, and the other to engage— always under the executive branch—the actual work of production."[29]

The emergent National League cartel had the good fortune of being organized before the passage of the Sherman Anti-Trust Act of 1890, which banned monopolies. Prior to the congressional legislation, the National League owners introduced the reserve clause, which effectively bound a player forever to the team which signed him, or until the club decided to release him. Moreover, the owners protected themselves by establishing the idea of exclusive territorial franchise rights. Throughout the ensuing years, the league's cartel arrangement enabled the owners to impose a system of labor control unequaled in American industry. Not only did they dictate the players' place of employment, salaries, working conditions, off-field conduct, and freedom of occupational movement, but they exercised unilateral control over the game's rules. In 1922, the United States Supreme Court reaffirmed baseball management's autocratic structure by ruling that baseball was not subject to antitrust laws because it did not constitute "interstate commerce" in the sense of the contemporary interpretation of the Sherman Act—a conclusion that has been upheld to this day.[30]

Resisting the reserve clause in players' contracts (which, as noted above, bound players to one team for their entire playing careers), the upstart rival Brotherhood of Professional Base Ball Players, in 1890, convinced most of its members to break their contracts with National League clubs and join the new Players' League. John Montgomery Ward, the leader of the Players' League, wrote an article that compared the reserve clause to antebellum slave laws: Embracing the vision of the Knights of Labor and the Farmers' Alliance, Ward characterized ballplayers as members of a producing class pitted against the parasitic, nonproducing, capitalist league moguls. Let the players reclaim their rights as proud workers, he argued, and their just rewards would come to those who were honest laborers.[31] Ward's populist rhetoric notwithstanding, major-league players earned two, and sometimes three, times more than the typical American worker. While average U.S. wages, calculated in current dollars, held conspicuously constant at about $500 through 1915, players' salaries averaged roughly $1,400 during the 1880s and increased sharply to $3,500 with the advent of the rebellion involving the Players' League. After the Players' League was crushed, salaries, not surprisingly, dipped back to 1880s levels, and remained consistently around $2,500 between 1900 and 1910.[32]

In fact, a three-way battle had erupted between the Players' League, the National League, and the American Association. Although the Players' League fought the good fight (and even won the legal battles), it failed to win the war. In short, it was no match for the National League owners, who ultimately bought out the Players' League's financial backers, and thereby buried the most radical experiment in professional-sports history.[33] As a result, public interest in the national game dwindled as fans became disgusted with baseball's chaotic state; they grew increasingly tired of reading about the political and economic problems of the game. Although professional players saw themselves as the employees they were (and attempted several times to gain collective-bargaining rights with their employers), most of their working-class fans did not see them as workers. As Goldstein writes, both owners and fans have had longer relationships with given clubs than the great majority of players; such relationships have strengthened their commitment to the long-term fortunes of the club—an attitude that makes any one player expendable.[34] While the national game remained overwhelmingly popular, baseball's business side—which featured battles between labor and management; labor discipline and blacklists and Pinkerton agents; franchise shifts; booms and busts; cartel agreements that were made and broken—was rocked with the instability of the gilded-age corporate culture. At the conclusion of the 1890 season, all three major leagues were drained by the losses incurred by cutthroat competition. Spalding, baseball's leading power broker, reported, "Not in the twenty years history of professional club organization was there recorded such an exceptional season of financial disaster and general demoralization as characterized the professional season of 1890."[35]

Baseball owners employed the language of capitalistic paternalism to solidify their position, and posed as saviors of the national pastime. During the labor disputes, Spalding characterized himself as General Grant, who was battling the rebellious players in the name of peaceful

union and, of course, efficient capitalism. Like other influential owners, Spalding believed that the game's success depended on rationality,
bureaucracy, and a strict division of labor. Spalding's partisan account
of this history appeared in 1911, the same year as Frederick W. Taylor
published *Principles of Scientific Management*, in which he posited that
baseball was an example of how training, efficiency, and spirit created
an ideal workforce. Responding to contemporary discussions about
industrial efficiency and scientific management, journalist M. Cready
Sykes speculated in 1911 that professional major-league baseball was
the most efficient endeavor "in getting the utmost product from every
tiny contribution of energy."[36] The "science" of the modern professional
game was based on "a system of swift and accurate efficiency that makes
every step, every shift of position do its instant effective work."[37] Baseball was, without doubt, "the most perfect thing in America to-day,"
and according to Sykes, it was only fitting that the game was developed
by "a people of high nervous organization and of a temperament quick
and eager."[38]

Clearly, baseball had undergone a managerial revolution in just one
generation. Baseball magnates insisted on the separation of management
from players, and introduced contractual relationships. Through the
channels of popular opinion, the depiction of selfless, civic-minded baseball owners, who were pursuing business practices out of a concern for
the greater public welfare, became part of the common sense of professional sports. Baseball owners, officials, and propagandists benefited
enormously by insisting that players were boys in a man's world of salaries, contracts, lawyers, and big business, while at the same time prefer-
ring to see themselves as benevolent fathers rather than magnates. Consequently, rather than appealing to capitalistic ideology, owners appealed
to familial language, acting as though their paternal care had been
scorned when players attempted to organize, and to negotiate with them
as equals.[39] The National League's three-man "war committee" of Spalding, John Day, and John Rogers portayed the league as the true, traditional defender of baseball integrity and its player opponents as having
"no moral foundation."[40] Promanagement sportswriters depicted the
Players' League's leaders as spoiled and greedy boys who wore fur-lined
overcoats, silk hats, patent-leather shoes; and who sported gold-headed
walking canes and smoked expensive cigars. Chadwick, editor of the
National League's *Spalding Guide*, labeled the brotherhood's manifesto
against the league a "revolutionary pronunciamento" of a minority third
that had used "terrorism" to drag along the rest of its members; Chadwick dubbed Ward the "mastermind" of "secessionists," while a Cincinnati paper called him John "Much-Advertised" Ward, capable of
overblown "oratorical flights."[41]

Not all journalists championed the owners' case; the players did have
their defenders. In fact, the *Sporting News* needled Spalding and (A. G.)
"Awful Gall" Mills, and blamed the showdown on the National League's

own "mean, niggardly, close-fisted acts" and "high handed manner."[42] *Sporting Life's* Francis Richter expressed similar opinions. Other opponents of the reserve clause saw in it an intolerable restraint on individual freedom, the right to work where one chooses, and the ability to attract the highest compensation for one's labor—all of which were notions deeply embedded in the dominant American values: social mobility and meritocracy. Opponents characterized the clause as "tyrannical," "barbaric," "un-American," and the "creator of a special class of slaves." Yet such critiques were consistently marginalized. As a contemporary newspaper columnist expressed it, baseball "is run as a dictatorship, . . . tied neither to John Paul Jones nor Betsy Ross; and George Washington never played it, but you would think that the Declaration of Independence carried a complete set of baseball rules as a postscript."[43] And, according to renowned baseball writer Hugh Fullerton, who was critical of the game's oligopolistic structure, baseball was "the strangest, and most contradictory business in the world."[44]

The capitalistic separation between management and labor portended more than just workers' alienation. The very structure of the emergent sport, involving sporting-goods firms and consumers, shaped not only the demand for the game, but the very character of it. As Stephen Hardy persuasively argues, sporting-goods firms (Spalding and Brothers, in particular), through their involvement with governing bodies, helped change informal activities into commercialized spectacles and, therefore, established the foundation for an even larger sports industry—an interlocking network of rules committees, trade associations, manufacturers, and professional groups. Although the sports marketplace has remained formally free, the nature of the product has since late in the nineteenth century been determined by a narrow range of firms.[45]

The preceding passage is only a cursory sketch of the development of major-league baseball's professional structure. This late-nineteenth-century history is well documented, and readers should examine the abundant literature for details and a closer explanation. For the purposes of this discussion, it is worth noting that major-league baseball introduced the franchise concept to the lexicon of American professional sports. A franchise is quite simply similar to a private government. In the context of American professional-team sports, the governing body for independent team franchises is the commissioner system. This structure was introduced in 1903, when the adoption of a national agreement formalized the control of major-league baseball under two league presidents and another person, whose responsibility was to regulate the sport. In 1921 (amid accusations that Chicago White Sox players were complicit in throwing the 1919 World Series), baseball owners endowed a single commissioner with broad powers over the operation of the game. Political economist John Wilson shrewdly ascertains the larger significance of the commissioner system in relation to the further evolution of professional sports. Through the commissioner system, he writes, "baseball could become a thoroughly capitalized industry and yet appear to have no capitalists and no proletarians."[46] It could also "cleverly produce and package a product and yet, with the Supreme Court's 1922 imprimatur not appear to be commerce at all. In short, it could retain much of the 'civility' of the amateur tradition while at the same time becoming thoroughly professionalized."[47] The restructuring of self-regulatory control solidified the baseball-cartel arrangement by making the sport appear to be a "natural monopoly" in which complicit action was necessary for the health of the game. The scheme worked so well in baseball that it was adopted by other professional sports throughout the 20th century.

FROM STRUCTURE TO IDEOLOGY

Still absent, however, was a baseball ideology appropriate for a modern capitalistic nation. Baseball had been repeatedly cast, as early as the 1850s, as the national pastime and the exemplar of American values, and was commonplace by the 1890s. However, there were widespread disputes about the game's true origins. The fact that baseball could be traced back to rounders threatened to tie the sport too closely to the British culture from which late-nineteenth-century Americans attempted to distance themselves. In short, baseball lacked a creation myth that could effectively link the country's most popular team sport to American tradition. Within this context, the mythification of the origins of American baseball arose from the related exigencies of nationalism and big business, and was, Cyrus Patell speculates, perhaps the first time but "not the last time that cultural mythology would either be created or invoked to mask the [base] economic realities of baseball."[48]

The promotion of baseball as a distinctly American tradition was based on the game's indigenous origins: Tradition inventors shrewdly decided that only if the game originated within the United States could they lay claim to its connection with the national psyche. The myth about baseball's U.S. birth began to materialize in 1889 at New York's Delmonico's Restaurant, where a celebrity crowd gathered to honor a group of baseball players who had just returned from a well-publicized world tour under Spalding's entrepreneurial leadership. During the banquet, one of the featured speakers, Abraham G. Mills (fourth president of the National League, and former leader of the Amateur Athletic Union) said he wanted it distinctly understood that "patriotism and research" had established that the game was American in origin. Contemporary wisdom had generally recognized British rounders as baseball's proper ancestor. Chadwick, a pioneer sports journalist who was acknowledged in his time as the "father of baseball," claimed that, as a boy in England, he played a game similar to early American baseball.[49] Nevertheless, the audience enthusiastically greeted Mills's audacious pronouncement with cries of "No rounders." According to the *New York Clipper*, this assertion "forever squelched" the British claim that baseball was a descendant of rounders.[50]

The official story about the beginning of baseball is, thus, an invented tradition. Spalding, the game's first star pitcher, later founded the sporting-goods company that still bears his name, and became one of the great commercial moguls of America's gilded age. Peter Levine, Spalding's biographer, has argued splendidly that Spalding was very much a part of a middle class that was trying to find ways to reorder a world seething with rapid growth and change; strange new faces and languages; violent confrontations over work and life conditions; and underlying fears that an old American breed had lost its vigor.[51] Moreover, as publisher of the influential *Spalding's Official Base Ball Guide*, he shaped public and institutional opinion about baseball and its historical legacy. In 1907, Spalding established a blue-ribbon commission to investigate and resolve baseball's origins. The commission, under Mills's leadership, included Arthur P. Gorman (former U.S. senator from Maryland); Morgan G. Bulkeley (ex-governor and ex-senator from Connecticut, and the first president of the National League); James E. Sullivan (president of the Amateur Athletic Union); Alfred J. Reach (former professional baseball player and sporting-goods entrepreneur); N. E. Young (veteran ballplayer, and the fourth president of the National League); and George Wright (famous ex-player and a prominent Boston businessman).

The commission conducted no first-hand research, but, rather, sent letters of inquiry to old-timers who had been associated with organized teams in the antebellum era. Late in its investigation, the commission received a letter from Abner Graves, a Denver mining engineer, who confidently reported that in 1839, Abner Doubleday interrupted a marbles game that was being played behind a Cooperstown, New York, tailor's shop. Doubleday allegedly drew a diagram of a diamond; explained the rules of the game played on the diamond; and authoritatively designated the activity by its modern name of base ball (then spelled as two words). With only this circumstantial evidence from the elderly Graves's testimony, reported by Spalding, the Mills Commission drafted a letter dated December 30, 1907, testifying that baseball originated in the United States, and was first played by Abner Doubleday at Cooperstown in 1839. This conclusion, Spalding emphatically proclaimed, helped free baseball "from the trammels of English traditions, customs, conventionalities."[52] Just as no self-respecting American would jeopardize his work ethic by waiting up to three days for the conclusion of a cricket match, according to Spalding, no Briton "who had not breathed the air of this free land as a naturalized citizen" could be expected to appreciate America's game.[53] Thus, the invented tradition of baseball as a distinctly American game was inspired in large measure by transatlantic rivalry, and by a more general effort to differentiate American culture from anything that hinted at the old-world motherland.

While true, the idea that baseball had evolved from a wide variety of British stick-and-ball games, did not suit the mythology of a phenomenon that had become so quintessentially American. "We may accept the psychic need for an indigenous creation myth"; but why, asks Stephen J. Gould (scientist and baseball aficionado), was Abner Doubleday—a man who had no recorded ties to the game, and who, in the words of writer Donald Honig, probably "didn't know a baseball from a kumquat"—considered the creator?[54] Interestingly, Doubleday was the captain of the Union artillery who sighted the situation and gave orders for firing the first volley in response to the Confederate attack on Fort Sumter. Doubleday later commanded divisions at Antietam and Fredericksburg, became a minor hero at Gettysburg, and retired as a major general. Needless to say, Doubleday's heroic role in a pivotal event in American history was not lost on the inventors of the myth. As Spalding wrote to the Mills Commission, when submitting Graves's dubious testimony, "it certainly appeals to an American pride to have had the great national game of base ball created and named by a Major General in the United States Army."[55]

But Gould delves deeper into the episode for clues as to why the myth received nearly universal (and immediate) acceptance in American society. As the nation's leading authority on evolutionary theory, Gould concludes that Americans are particularly uncomfortable with evolutionary modes of explanation, and prefer, instead, creation myths that identify heroes and sacred places. Evolutionary explanations provide no particularly palpable symbols of reverence, worship, or patriotism.[56] The Doubleday/Cooperstown myth gave baseball a quasi-religious status. Indeed, each year, thousands of Americans make the pilgrimage to Cooperstown, the site of the National Baseball Hall of Fame and Museum. There they can see statues, photos, and miscellaneous relics of their heroes; they can visit the "hallowed ground" of Doubleday Field, where the young Doubleday "immaculately conceived" the game. And each year, sportswriters dutifully select great players of the past for "enshrinement," after which they become baseball "immortals."[57] Reflective of the American culture's attraction to neat creation myths, the major leagues in 1939 celebrated baseball's centennial, culminating in a dedication ceremony for the Hall of Fame. The U.S. government abetted the hyped festivities by issuing a commemorative stamp, marking 1839 as the birthdate of the "National Game."[58]

The Doubleday myth created a fertile framework within which the game could be used to extol the virtues of the American character. Baseball's attractiveness as an invented patriotic pastime resonated with an invented national consciousness. The decade following the release of the Mills Commission's findings witnessed a flood of journalistic assessments linking baseball to the American identity. Spalding led the effort. He polemicized: "To enter upon a deliberate argument to prove that baseball is our National Game, that it has all the attributes of American origin, American character, and unbounded favor in America," is to "undertake the elucidation of a patent fact; the sober demonstration of an axiom."[59] If such emphatic statements were not convincing enough, he used alliterative license to connect the game's prestige to the populace. Baseball, like no other sport, he said, is the exponent of "American Courage, Confidence, Combativeness; American Dash, Discipline, Determinism; American Energy, Eagerness, Enthusiasm; American Pluck, Persistency, Performance; American Spirit, Sagacity, Success; American Vim, Vigor, Virility."[60]

Variations of these themes resounded throughout the established popular magazines and scholarly publications of the early years of the twentieth century. For example, Henry S. Curtis (a strict amateurist and an early opponent of professional sports) noted in the *Journal of Education*: "Baseball is not only our national game, but far better than the lean Yankee with the stripped trousers and the many-starred coat," "it represents our national spirit," and gives "the clearest picture of those qualities which distinguish us from others and which have made us what we are."[61] Baseball, according to another patriotic editor, is "not so much an institution," but "an expression"—[an] "index of our national genius; . . . baseball presents the American spirit bared of furbelows."[62]

Clearly, baseball was connected to preferred bourgeois nationalist, capitalist visions. The game's newfound ideology asserted that baseball was an indigenous, American rural game, which reflected all that was best in the country: Crowds at the games included people from all classes;[63] baseball owners were benevolent citizens who operated the franchises in the "public interest"; the game was open to anyone with talent; and most players came from humble origins. All these cultural meanings became conventional wisdom and acted as a bulwark against threatening social developments, proving the legitimacy of elite values that prevailed on the national and global levels. Indeed, middle-class Americans saw that their values were still relevant; and working-class and immigrant men found that social solidarity and respectability could be achieved in the realm of popular culture.[64]

The invented mythology of baseball was ultimately convincing because it was tied to nationalism. Nationalism encouraged the integration of the working class into the capitalist system; among workers, the historical competition for jobs gave rise to a sense of identification with the "better" classes in American society. And the price for a share of the pie was assimilation or class conciliation. Moreover, the progressive social and political reforms gained prior to World War I ultimately reduced the worker's impulse toward revolutionary change, and prompted most workers to turn to the state for protection against the worst abuses of the capitalist robber barons. During the first two decades of the century, workers had a stake in the nation-state and embraced new, non-class-defined symbols of community—like baseball. It is the symbolic values of the nation that explain its powerful hold over people's imagination.[65]

The immigrants' relationship to American baseball confirms this thesis. Baseball provided second-generation immigrants acceptance and identity as Americans. In 1919, Hugh Fullerton, a leading sportswriter, wrote in the *Atlanta Constitution* that baseball "is the greatest single force working for Americanization. No other game appeals so much to the foreign born youngsters and nothing, not even the schools, teaches the American spirit so quickly, or inculcates the idea of sportsmanship or fair play so thoroughly."[66] Historian Peter Levine has recently explained that baseball, by its very status as America's national game, "symbolically permitted an immediate sense of belonging to a larger American community in ways that few other sportive experiences provided."[67] However, this cultural phenomenon was not limited to baseball, since many immigrants also played basketball and football as well. These overlapping leisure experiences reinforced immigrants' acceptance of American ways and values.[68]

The American national sporting tradition was tied to the early-twentieth-century search for foreign markets and coincided with calls for international expansion. Sports and imperialism came to be seen as natural ways to deal with both surplus energy and industrial goods. As part of the official rhetoric of American diplomacy, baseball as a form of cultural imperialism was portrayed only in a positive, benevolent light.[69] In this sense, advocates unabashedly claimed that baseball's geographic diffusion brooked no national boundaries. According to Spalding, baseball won its right to be called the American national game because of the way it always "followed the flag"—to Alaska, Hawaii, the Philippines, Puerto Rico, and Cuba; and "wherever a ship floating the Stars and Stripes finds anchorage to-day, somewhere on nearby shore the American National Game is in progress."[70] The game trope in American imperialist rhetoric helped to popularize the "body politic" metaphor. In capitalist society, as cultural studies scholar Bill Brown explains, activities are real to the extent that they can be represented as "games." Spalding and his cohorts did present baseball as a game, a tradition, to non-Americans or new Americans.[71]

The most widely publicized effort to export the American sporting tradition was the 1888 world tour led by Spalding, and the 1914 sequel sponsored by Charles Comiskey. Both tours featured two all-star-caliber teams that displayed the national pastime to audiences on every continent. The world tours demonstrated to the game's proponents that it could be reproduced anywhere and under any circumstances, so that the sport, as Brown recognizes, "represented a medium for eliminating differences of time and space, for making the world seem familiar, for reducing it to an American globalized village." Indeed, baseball "as [a form of] cultural imperialism operated not at the level of force, but through its benign, but powerful, civilizing influences." For Spalding's 1888 tour, this meant not only promoting the game itself, but also advertising the mass-produced athletic commodities of his fledgling sporting-goods corporate empire.[72]

The Americanist ideology and cultural imperialism fused in dramatic fashion during the 1914 worldwide baseball tour. On a balmy December day in 1913, a contingent of major league baseball stars aboard the *Lusitania* was enthusiastically greeted at Manila Harbor by American citizens. With a Filipino band playing "The Star-Spangled Banner," the atmosphere, according to New York Giants manager John J. McGraw, was "American, and Americanism stuck out all over the place."[73] The nationalistic fervor was sustained throughout the ballplayers' stay in the Philippines. Prior to a game, the baseball missionaries escorted the commander of U.S. forces, Major General J. Franklin Bell, to the pitcher's mound, and he addressed the crowd. Decked out in a crisp, white military uniform, the "gray old fighter" affirmed his lifelong admiration for the game, and suggested that the tour would "not only stir patriotism wherever Americans are encountered," but should "impress foreign nations of the cleanness and manhood of Americans."[74] Prior to throwing out the first ball to catcher Jack Bliss, the general insisted that baseball "fostered clean living, skill, and fair play, makes men, and is therefore a big factor in the upbuilding of a nation."[75]

The results of the tour were best captured in the following doggerel:

> We've hiked around this mundane sphere
>   Like sprinting round th' bases,
> We've roused th' rooters' ringing cheer
>   In strange and alien places;
> We've boosted Uncle Sammy's fame
>   And caused some world sensations,
> And made th' grand old baseball game
>   The talk of all th' nations.[76]

The press portrayed the tour as a grand success—baseball brought the world into America's expanding, benevolent orbit.

The connection between baseball and the national-character tradition was further popularized by the way in which it created tangible political resources for the state. Gradually the U.S. government saw sports, like baseball, as important instruments for enhancing political legitimacy. Although Abraham Lincoln was the first president to demonstrate an interest in the game, it took nearly a half century for the introduction of the idea of inviting the chief executive to throw out the first ball. In 1910, Washington club owner Clark Griffith pioneered this promotional scheme by inviting President William Howard Taft to throw out the first ball at the Senators' opening-day game. The robust Taft thus became the first presidential fan. Then, after the election of Woodrow Wilson, a knowledgeable baseball enthusiast, in 1912, he became the first president to attend a World Series game, when he traveled to Philadelphia for a game between the Red Sox and Phillies.[77]

The heightened sensitivity to baseball as the exemplar of Americanism prompted major league owners to stage on-field patriotic displays, which signaled the game's resolve to promote World War I preparedness. The *Spalding Guide* claimed that major-league-sponsored military drills, for instance, "anticipated" and "nullified" the possibility of any public charges of "slackerism." Teams urged star players to serve as Liberty Loan spokesmen. National League President John Tener, proclaiming baseball's role in sustaining American democracy, said that "there is no sport or business or anything under heaven which exerts the leveling influence that baseball does."[78]

Warren Harding pioneered the use of baseball as an electioneering tool. During the 1920 presidential campaign, Harding's handlers worried about his being too closely associated with the "aristocratic" sport of golf. Advertising executive Alfred Lasker suggested Harding stage a big-league contest in his hometown of Marion, Ohio—which he did. The game enabled Harding to connect with the American masses. Exploiting the occasion to employ baseball jargon in a criticism of Wilsonian liberalism, Harding declared himself a "team player," opposed to the "one-man play" that Wilson had supposedly exhibited in his campaign for the League of Nations. "It is my observation that the National team, now playing for the United States," Harding said, "played loosely and muffed disappointingly in our domestic affairs, and then struck out at Paris." Packaging himself as a true populist, Harding hailed team play in America: "Hail to a hundred million of American rooters, the citizenship of the republic; expect Uncle Sam to put them over or bat them out as the situation requires, and count upon team play in government, team play in citizenship and everybody in America first."[79]

By 1922, Harding was referred to as the "president of the fans." He was reportedly a "regular rooter" who always kept a complete scorecard and knew the "inside stuff" of the game. Although political historians emphasize the Harding administration's high degree of corruption and Harding's ineffectiveness as a leader, his close association with baseball evoked widespread admiration. For example, sports editor Francis Richter noted that Harding belonged to the baseball fans of America, the plain people from whom he had come, and from whom he inherited his love of the game. He was free of snobbery and "truly loved the National Game of the American people, just as he loved and revered all things American."[80] When Harding died in office in 1923, many people thought that not only did the nation lose its chief executive, but that baseball lost its most prominent fan. In unprecedented fashion, the entire sports world observed a day of mourning, and canceled all events that were scheduled on the day of Harding's funeral.

The following year, the World Series came to the nation's capital as the Washington Senators dueled the New York Giants for the supremacy of baseball. Harding would have been thrilled, as his successor, Calvin Coolidge, addressed a large enthusiastic crowd who greeted the Senators. Coolidge, while not remembered by baseball men as an avid fan, actually attended more games in a single term than any other president, according to George Rable. Coolidge once claimed that the integrity of the game and its players should inspire all citizens, and that "while baseball remains our national game, our national tastes will be on a higher level and our national ideas on a firmer foundation." Just prior to the 1924 series, the *New York Times* (on October 2) noted, in an editorial, that "baseball news is the most eagerly sought" among its readers. "A Presidential campaign, the war in China, the meeting of the League of Nations in Geneva, even mysterious murders and social scandals have to take second place to the reports of the desperate encounters on the diamond," the *Times* noted.[81] On October 10, after star pitcher Walter Johnson won the seventh and final game of the series, Washingtonians went into a frenzy. "Thousands are tramping the streets in the wildest celebration ever seen in baseball," one newspaper reported: "From the White House to the Capitol, the clamor rises. The streets are full of jostling, joy-crazed citizens, blowing horns, manipulating rattlers, firing pistols and making a din that can be heard for miles."[82] Western Union sent a record 2.2 million words over the wires; and news of the game was relayed by WEAF to other stations from coast to coast, reaching a record 500,000 radios.[83]

Two years later, high-ranking government officials attended a gala Golden Jubilee Dinner honoring the National League's fiftieth anniversary. Cabinet members, governors, and senators joined prominent business leaders in a "democratic gathering of more than 1,000" at New York's Astor Hotel.[84] Unable to attend, President Coolidge extended his greetings and best wishes through a telegram to league President John Heydler, wherein he acknowledged the league as "one of the leading exponents of the national game. Anything which tends to interest the youth of the country in participation in a wholesome athletic sport is to be encouraged."[85] As master of ceremonies, Heydler used a portion of star player Cap Anson's bat (preserved by A. G. Spalding and Bros.) as the toastmaster's gavel. Pennsylvania Senator George Wharton Pepper closed the speaking program by praising baseball, its officials, and its fans for making the sport such a central component of American life. Pepper commended the National League magnates for their efforts that preserved the stability of the national pastime: "Suppose there were no National League," he speculated; "the country would be full of independent professional ball clubs raiding one another for players. There would be no central authority to unify rules and provide umpires." And even more debilitating for the nation's fans, "there would be nothing to read about [in the morning papers] except miscellaneous news, foreign affairs and the concerns of government. The *Congressional Record* would be a poor substitute for the thrills of a big-league game."[86] Pepper concluded his partisan homily by praising the 1922 Supreme Court ruling that gave the game and its cartel arrangement a sanctioned exemption from American antitrust laws.

Governmental patronage was not the only vehicle through which baseball came to be closely connected with the state. National loyalty and patriotism were also promoted through sports rituals and pageantry that linked baseball and nationalism. For example, on May 15, 1862, at the Union and Capitoline Grounds in Brooklyn, patriotic fans decked out the park in national bunting, and hired a band to play "The Star-Spangled Banner," for the first time at a professional sporting event.[87] Although not institutionalized until the second decade of the twentieth century, flag salutes, pledges of allegiance, the singing of the national anthem, and the omnipresent emblems, flags, and insignias all evoked feelings of national unity, consensus, and the legitimacy of the nation-state. Moreover, the national spirit was reflected in the names of various major leagues: National Association of Professional Base Ball Players; National League; American Association; Union Association; American League; and Federal League.

By the second decade of the twentieth century, claims about baseball's nationally unifying characteristics were ubiquitous in American social commentary. "A great many people have been searching during ever so many years for the religion of democracy. I believe I have found it," proclaimed New York journalist and Marxian socialist Simeon Strunsky. "What I have in mind is a great democratic rite, a ceremonial," he noted, "an ideal faith," one that is "solemnized on six days in the week during six months in the year by large masses of men with such unfailing regularity and such unquestioning good faith that I cannot help thinking of it as essentially a religious performance"—Strunsky was referring to the seventh-inning stretch.[88] Philosopher Morris Cohen was even more inclusive. "By all the canons of our modern books on comparative religion," he wrote in 1919, "baseball is a religion, and the only one that is not sectarian but national."[89]

The invention of the American baseball tradition, like most other invented traditions during this period, was principally a middle- and upper-class endeavor. The personalities, meanings, associations, and control of the pastime were firmly situated in the circles of economic, political, and cultural elites in the United States. Recognizing these connections, however, does not imply that only middle-class and elite Americans made these values hegemonic. Workers, immigrants, and African-Americans also accepted, and affirmed, much of this invented ideological structure. Lest this process be interpreted as another instance of top-down social control, we need to pay attention to the reasons why workers and immigrants also bought this tradition and cultural paradigm. Seen in this light, the history of baseball involves what cultural historian Raymond Williams referred to as the "social relations of cultural production"—social processes actively shaped by human actors, and shaped by, but not fully determined by, the capitalist mode of production.[90] If baseball as a cultural spectacle failed to fully eradicate class conflict, as bourgeois advocates had hoped it would, it did become one of the unifying enthusiasms that bridged class divisions and encouraged national solidarity.[91]

INTELLECTUALS AND THE SEARCH FOR AMERICAN INNOCENCE

Given major league baseball's checkered early history, how can we explain its uncanny hold over the national imagination for more than a century? Sportswriters and scholars alike have theorized about baseball's place in American culture since 1858—thus, there is certainly no shortage of explanations. Baseball historian David Voigt suggests that the game has compelled every generation "to get right with baseball" as a distinctly American rite of passage.[92] Historian Edward Pessen acknowledges this quandary in which sports-minded intellectuals find themselves in explaining the nature of baseball's attraction. What is it about baseball, he asks, that induces so many of us to love it so, or at least say we love it so? "The romance between intellectuals and the game of baseball," baseball writer Roger Kahn wrote in 1957, is "one-sided to the point of absurdity."[93] We obviously love something and simplistically call it "the game." But in fact, Pessen recognizes, "it's a complex of memories, associations, longings, focusing on things clean and aesthetically pure, things infinitely more pure, things infinitely more fun to think about, than the mournful political, economic, social realities, tensions, and discords afflicting the real world out there."[94]

Such observations point to the high-profile status of nostalgia among intellectuals and baseball people. Typical of this tradition, A. Bartlett Giamatti, the Yale Renaissance scholar who served as president of the National League and commissioner of major league baseball, believed that baseball is "so much a part of our history as a people" that it represents "America's plot, America's mysterious, underlying design," the "tale America tells the world—indeed the story we tell ourselves."[95]

Baseball played an important role in nuturing feelings of community
for a culture in flux during the twentieth century:

> For those native to America, particularly in cities, the game, whether
> watched or played, recalled the earlier, rural America, a more youthful,
> less bitterly knowing country; for the immigrant, the game was another
> fraternal organization, a common language in a strange land. For so much
> of expanding and expansive America, the game was a free institution with
> something for everyone.[96]

Most of Giamatti's writings on baseball were attempts to account for
what he called "this love affair between America and baseball that has
matured and changed but never died."[97]

Michael Novak claims that baseball is "American" because it em-
bodies the Protestant, individualistic, rural values that defined early
American society.[98] In other words, nineteenth-century America was ripe
for the emergence of baseball because it reflected those social forms of
life which lay at the heart of the young society. The most influential
scholarly interpretation, however, is Allen Guttmann's liberal-modernist
thesis: that baseball helped Americans make the transition from a rural,
preindustrial society to an urban, industrial one. Guttmann theorized
that it was natural for baseball to become the national pastime because
the United States was a quintessential modern nation. It was only fitting that the game's fast pace, complex set of rules, methodical organization, and materialistic approach to professionalism should take hold.
Baseball's special attraction among team sports lies in its combination
of primitive-pastoral characteristics and its extraordinary modernity—
representing, according to Guttmann, a "ludic symbol of our ambivalence about our abandoned past and about the unknown future that
we are all, willy-nilly bound for."[99] Both Novak and Guttmann bolster
their interpretations with claims that the game reflected the national
appetite for democracy, pastoral settings, and rugged individualism, and
a desire to "return home."[100]

What I have argued, however, is quite different: that baseball's
popularity as a distinctly American tradition neither reflected an innate
national character nor merely evolved from the modernization process.
Rather, this selective tradition was constructed by certain groups of
people to legitimize particular values and activities, and to discount
competing alternative ones, during a tumultuous period when Americans attempted to reconcile a dynamic society with the existing liberal
state that had been designed generations earlier for a corporatist,
agrarian-commercial society.[101]

Middle-class reformers, capitalists, journalists, ministers, gamblers,
workers, athletes, and spectators shaped the meanings of baseball to
coincide with their own worldviews. As sport historian Steven Riess
wrote in 1977, baseball mythology gave middle-class native whites "con-

fidence that their society was democratic, that the traditional American values developed in an earlier pristine period were still applicable in their modern world, and that the various divisions in American society could be alleviated by such mechanisms as the edifying and integrating latent functions of baseball."[102] To them, baseball constituted a powerful paradigm for promoting an idealized version of an American identity, which appeared to be threatened by endemic class warfare arising from the disruptive transition from industrial to monopolistic capitalism. Spokesmen who utilized the baseball-as-an-American-tradition paradigm pointed to the ways the sport inspired teamwork, greater awareness of the rules of the game, and sportsmanship—notions resounding with strategies of class conciliation. Through their administrative clout in national sports organizations, their prominence in major magazines and newspapers, and their social networks established with capitalists and political elites, bourgeois baseball advocates used the game to popularize the virtues of discipline, hierarchy, individualism, and nationalism. This ideology went virtually unchallenged, Riess explains, because "there was abundant evidence in the media or to casual observers at the ballpark that [it] was the reality"; and because the game was a "prescriptive construct of a burgeoning baseball business," he maintains, "contemporary sportswriters had been co-opted by club owners."[103]

To this day, baseball's preferred ideology runs untrammeled throughout the nation's cultural landscape. Journalists, popular intellectuals, and filmmakers continue to stoke the flames of baseball's "innocent," mythical past. Americans have eagerly imbibed the nostalgic references of Hollywood films like *Field of Dreams, The Babe,* and *A League of Their Own.* Such films reflect the huge rise in the selling of baseball memorabilia since the early 1980s. In fact, baseball-card collecting has become an obsession: A 1909 Honus Wagner card recently sold for nearly half a million dollars; and a 1952 Mickey Mantle card goes for over $30,000. Baseball-card conventions now feature stars from an earlier era, like Ted Williams and Joe DiMaggio, who offer autographs for $100. The baseball that Babe Ruth supposedly swatted for his sixtieth home run in 1927 was sold for $200,000 in San Francisco, and a 1919 Joe Jackson autograph currently commands in excess of $25,000. There is now a Nellie Fox Society in Chicago, a Burleigh Grimes Museum in Wisconsin, and a Dizzy Dean Museum in Mississippi—these celebrate the memories of players from bygone eras. Major league owners and their profiteers have astutely recognized the profit potential of America's appetite for baseball nostalgia. Several professional teams don vintage uniforms. Old-timers' games continue to grow in popularity. And, Baltimore's new $105 million Camden Yards ballpark recalls the classic 1920s stadiums, with old-time Coca-Cola ads, ushers wearing bow ties and suspenders, and baseball nostalgia piped into both men's and women's restrooms. "The beatification of baseball's past and the consequent miasma of woolly commentary, mawkish sentiment, and cardboard portraits," are, writer Nicholas Dawidoff recognizes, more than a cultural "fad"; these "social balms" are responses to an increasingly fractured society that is so swamped in baseball nostalgia, he writes, "that the game threatens to be obscured by a cloud of kitsch."[104]

Contemporary intellectuals benefit from such "mass cultural false consciousness"—while nineteenth-century intellectuals strictly avoided any taint of popular culture, many now appropriate it.[105] Ken Burns, a widely respected observer of the contemporary American scene, created an 18-hour documentary of the game for public television. Buoyed by the enormous commercial success of his earlier Civil War epic (which reportedly sold $60 million worth of videotapes and accompanying coffee-table books), Burns's "Baseball" was given an even more lavish media launch with spin-offs that included uniform jerseys, coffee mugs, and a $60 coffee-table book. Like the Civil War series, Burns's "Baseball" has been offered by most public libraries and private video stores.

Billing his work as an objective archival reconstruction of the national pastime's glorious history, Burns produced not exactly a photo-documentary of the game, but, as one baseball historian characterizes it, "an illustrated history of baseball geared to the sensory imperatives of television entertainment."[106] While visually satisfying for most viewers, it was riddled with factual errors (Larry Gerlach has spotted more than 100), chock full of clichés and facile metaphors about how baseball has represented "all that is good in America"; for music, it used the familiar "Take Me Out to the Ballgame" and "The Star-Spangled Banner." The chorus of "experts" featured in the series paid homage to the well-established homilies developed a century earlier: How baseball is the only game without a clock, and is played on grass, where the object is to get to home plate safely. What is so striking about Burns and his middle-aged male backup singers, critic James Wolcott noted in *The New Yorker*, is how "homogeneous their tone is," as if "they had become part of the fraternal order of 'Field of Dreams.' The entire series sags beneath this mopey air of male menopause." At its conclusion, the themes and lore of the series are recapitulated so as to evoke the audience's greatest nostalgic sensibilities. As Wolcott writes, with verve and precision:

> As a lone piano nudges the National Anthem to life, we see ballpark lights at red sunset, a string of Kodak moments showing Little Leaguers missing fly balls and children running to home plate, and black-and-white footage of baseball stars seeming to beckon us from the great beyond. On the voice-over track, John Chancellor utters one last ode to baseball, celebrating its "imperishable hope" and its natural rhythms: "It follows the seasons, beginning each year with the fond expectancy of springtime and ending with the hard facts of autumn.[107]

The American public's overwhelmingly positive reception to the documentary is all the more revealing when we consider that it aired during the most controversial labor stoppage in major league history. In response to the owners' demand for salary caps, the players' union struck in early August and came to terms only after their employers (warned by Congress that their antitrust exemption would be annulled) persisted in their solidarity until the early spring of 1995. For the first time since the tumultuous days of 1903, the World Series was canceled. As the vitality of professional baseball began to weaken, Burns's "Baseball" provided a surrogate for a nobler, innocent past that, miraculously, thrives in the literature of mythic heroes and performances; and that flourishes, without rebuffs, in the American nostalgic sports imagination.[108]

Clearly, American baseball fans use nostalgia consciously and unconsciously to avoid contemplating the uncomfortable present state of the game. Even though Americans have traditionally, according to Guttmann, "averted their gaze from the profit margins, personal lives, and political connections of the franchise owners because they preferred, then as now, to follow the action on the field," such conscious neglect has become much more difficult since the players achieved free agency in the mid-1970s. Even though the players have not come any closer to owning "the store" than they did at the advent of professionalism in the 1870s, free agency has made it more difficult for baseball to sustain the illusion of being a pastime, rather than a business, as is often cited as the root of baseball's current malaise. Guttmann summarizes the dilemma: "Many Americans desire nothing better than to dream of a pastoral world where the grass is green, the sun is bright, and the crisp spring air carries the delightful sound of bats and balls."[109]

Today, in an era of declining economic expectations, imperialistic acts of aggression against Third World countries, and unprecedented political apathy and alienation among the populace, dominant groups and individuals scramble for a common language to ameliorate the apparent social and cultural contradictions. It's the business of sustaining the belief that American democracy still works the way Thomas Jefferson said it was supposed to work, according to *Harper's* editor Lewis Lapham, the belief that "the American people still speak a common language and hold to a common definition of the good, the true, and the beautiful."[110] Referring to baseball, he observes that "the 'boys of summer' perform a kind of tribal dance" meant to "restore at least a semblance of meaning to the nation's most cherished hopes." The search for an idealistic, pristine national identity in the lexicon of baseball is a uniquely American tradition. Perhaps it is this feeling of nostalgia for an undetermined, but benign, future that V. S. Pritchett described as the "emotion of being an American."[111]

HOLIDAYS, PATRIOTISM, AND SPORT

FIVE

THANKSGIVING FOOTBALL RITUALS

In 1893 a four-hour Thanksgiving Day parade of horse-drawn coaches traveled up New York's Fifth Avenue and wove through Harlem to the Polo Grounds, where more than 40,000 spectators watched Princeton beat a strongly favored Yale team 6 to 0.

For several days prior to the well-publicized event, "fakirs swarmed uptown like an invading army," noted the renowned writer Richard Harding Davis, "with banners and flags and artificial flowers in the true [school] colors, and with tiny leather footballs and buttons and rosettes and ribbons and tin horns and countless varieties of [school] badges."[1] Manhattan shop windows were adorned with photographs of the collegiate football stars, and the "legitimate gambling on Wall Street was neglected for the greater interest of betting on the game."[2] Many Americans like Davis (who was paid $500 for his featured article in *Harper's Weekly*) recognized the Thanksgiving Day football game as "the greatest sporting event and spectacle combined that this country has to show"; "Thanksgiving Day is no longer a solemn festival to God for mercies given," he wrote, "it is a holiday granted by the State and the nation to see a game of football."[3] The most prominent dialect-speaking fictional character of early-twentieth-century American humor, Mr. Dooley, confidently pierced such intellectual explanations with the homespun wisdom and brogue of a working-class Irish saloonkeeper from Chicago's South Side. "In iv'ry city iv this fair land," Mr. Dooley said, "th' churches is open an' empty, the fleet anise-seed bag is pursooed over th' smilin' potato-patch, an' th' groans iv th' dyin' resound fr'm manny a futboll-field."[4]

This newly invented Thanksgiving sports tradition connected an Americanized game with the sacred ideals and customs of a nation just one century old. Edwin Cady proposes that the Big Game is a "collective representation of the American Dream,"[5] wherein believers and participants expect to be saved not only by their own faith and works, but, equally, by the nation's faith and works. This theme animated the Mayflower Compact and has been celebrated during Thanksgiving holidays ever since. The late-nineteenth-century Thanksgiving Day game merely updated the American Dream text for a modern corporate capitalist society. It dramatized, according to Cady, the concepts of "team against team, individual with team, person against person, team against individual: unity in diversity, diversity in unity, agonism and fraternity, . . . risk and fierce competition and catharsis, yet decorum"—all surrounded and buoyed by the atmosphere and communal joy of the great party.[6]

Behind the colorful, festive spectacle stirred a movement that would have far-reaching effects on the development of the national sporting culture: The emergent bureaucrats of amateurism exploited the holiday venue to disseminate their new version of sport for sport's sake to the wider American community—the amateurists promoted college football as an exemplar of middle-class respectability and rational recreation, and popularized their vision as the legitimate, preferred nature of American sports. Unlike baseball, the nation's leading sport, with its overtly professional elements, football was almost the exclusive property of the colleges. Consequently, this new group of sports advocates was able to articulate a class-biased critique of professionalism in terms of the ways it corrupted true sport. Sport, they argued, should be a recreation, not a business. Moreover, this rising generation of amateur bureaucrats used its social, political, and economic connections to effectively institutionalize its biases as resilient athletic structures.[7] As historian Donald Mrozek recognized, sport's attainment of respectability among the middle and upper classes was critical in shaping the speed in which sport developed and the particular directions it ultimately took. The creation of the Thanksgiving Day game venue was an important moment in the amateurists' struggle for cultural authority.[8]

This subtext of the Thanksgiving football tradition illuminates the importance of social-class formation in the development of a national sporting culture. In the fluid social order of late-nineteenth-century America, a growing number of people, who belonged neither to the elite nor the masses, sought to establish a distinctly middle-class identity through what historian Eric Hobsbawm characterizes as "effective networks of interaction." Higher education was one such network, and a universal criterion for determining social status during the nineteenth century. Schooling provided not only a "convenient means of social comparability between individuals or families lacking initial personal relations," but, on a national level, higher education helped the middle class establish common patterns of behavior and values, in much the same way that institutionalized sports helped do this. The Thanksgiving Day game represented the tendency of middle-class elements to link their own search for identity with national symbols and institutionalized sports—a process (as I noted previously) that Hobsbawm labeled "the invention of tradition."[9]

THE INVENTED THANKSGIVING TRADITION

The American calendar marks an annual cycle of secular and religious celebrations that give the year an American flavor and provide for the annual renewal of national myths and ideals.[10] The giving of thanks for the harvest of the Pilgrims, as canonized in the Thanksgiving story, in particular, provides a structure through which Americans understand their history. Cultural historian James Robertson suggests that national myths, like the Thanksgiving story, provide "a logic for the reconciliation of the contradictions in important aspects of American life and experience."[11] How the stories at the core of such myths are told is not important to the continued functioning of the myths, so long as they are told to, and heard by, Americans.

Thanksgiving is the oldest and most truly American of the national holidays. First celebrated by the Pilgrims, it has changed less in its intention than any other American holiday. Modern celebration of Thanksgiving Day is a ritualistic affirmation of what Americans believe was the Pilgrim experience—confronting, adapting to, and settling, the New World. The holiday reaffirms values and assumptions about cultural unity, about identity and history, about inclusion and exclusion. The importance of assimilation, family, kinship, and freedom is invested in the Thanksgiving holiday with an aura of religion and patriotism. The Thanksgiving story affirms the historical and mythical origins of a new-world Christian civilization, people, and nation.[12]

As a bona-fide national holiday, Thanksgiving dates only to 1863. The traumas of the Civil War inspired President Lincoln to officially proclaim several days of thanksgiving to pay homage to national unity and to appeal to God for divine guidance. Southern states did not immediately accept a holiday that celebrated a revitalized Union, and observed the holiday only after Reconstruction. Succeeding presidents followed Lincoln's act of proclaiming an official day of thanksgiving, anthropologist Janet Siskind observes, thus "appropriating the ritual for the nation over the individual states and laying the groundwork for its further development as a political-religious ritual of nationality."[13] President Grant's 1869 Thanksgiving address formally established the holiday in American cultural life.

Thanksgiving celebrations remained remarkably consistent into the early 1870s. On this exclusively religious, familial occasion, Americans were encouraged to reverentially fill the day with prayer, bible study, religious testimony, and quiet kinship gatherings. This invented tradition was then transformed by the idea for an annual Thanksgiving Day game between the previous year's two leading college football teams— an idea hatched in 1876 by the student-run Intercollegiate Football Association. It thereby reflected a larger, evolving relationship between sports and Protestantism, which was recognized by a YMCA official as early as 1892. The Thanksgiving Day football game, he wrote, "points the way to a Christian solution." "Because the old way of keeping Thanksgiving Day Christian is no longer adequate to hold the young men does not prove that young men are becoming un-Christian"; rather, he concluded "it suggests a new way to make them more Christian than they ever were under the old observances."[14]

Before the middle of the nineteenth century, most Christians opposed sport for its alleged tendency toward idleness, carnal pleasure, gambling, and physical immodesty. A generation later, according to Elliott Gorn, "as people reinterpreted the meaning of faith in an age of industrial capitalism, technological innovation, physical science, and social upheavals, religious thought itself became more flexible, affirming physical health, exercise, and competitive games in ways that would have been abhorrent to earlier puritans and evangelicals."[15] Most important, a chorus of well-respected, mostly Protestant Americans began to articulate a defense of sports and recreation in the name of Victorian and religious ideals. The highest Victorian values—discipline, productivity, order, self-control, and self-reliance—were attached to formally taboo physical activities, which ultimately justified the explosion of organized sports.

THE CRADLE OF AMERICAN FOOTBALL

Football was a well-established ritual that thrived, from the 1850s, in students' hazing and initiation rites, usually in open defiance of the faculty's regulations *in loco parentis*. During the early 1870s, Harvard, Yale, and Princeton played association football, a game that resembled soccer. Harvard broke ranks and played a series of matches with McGill University under the rugby rules. In 1876, Harvard and Yale agreed to concessionary rules—marking the pivotal point in the downfall of soccer and the rise of a rugbylike game in America.[16] These early forays into intercollegiate athletics were grounded in the belief that worthy opponents would be selected on strict social-class criteria. Such individual selection of acceptable social partners reflected the way in which higher education provided a sanctioned rationale for drawing class lines in a theoretically open and expanding social system.[17] The Intercollegiate Football Association was formed in 1876, and it scheduled its championship game on Thanksgiving Day. The event quickly became the most prominent nineteenth-century collegiate athletic contest and did more than anything else to legitimize amateur intercollegiate sports.

Early Thanksgiving Day games attracted only marginal attention outside northeastern collegiate circles and the immediate New York City area, and went unmentioned in most midwestern and southern newspapers. Even in New York, where the Thanksgiving Day championship was held, typical crowds numbered only several hundred. The annual game's popularity blossomed during the late 1880s, as it became an opening occasion on the elite social calendar. Yale and Harvard selected the Polo Grounds as the site for the annual event, and during the ensuing years, Thanksgiving Day football emerged as a spectacle that symbolized collegiate prestige in American culture. In 1885 the *New York Herald* noted, in an editorial, that "even if the turkey should be tough or the pudding not quite to his liking, the average citizen can still maintain his equanimity by journeying uptown and witnessing the pick of teams of muscular collegians strive for the supremacy in football."[18] That year, Yale trounced Wesleyan, 61 to 0. Just two years later, 10,000 spectators enjoyed a much more evenly played contest, as Yale defeated Harvard, 17 to 8, in a game that finally attracted extensive front-page coverage in the New York dailies. The distinguished crowd included not only the New York governor and many other notables, but, according to one newspaper, "nearly every man in New York who had ever been within hailing distance of a college diploma; . . . collegians from every seat of learning along the seaboard were out in force with their peculiar colors and war cries."[19]

Despite frequent diatribes about the corrupting influence of professionalism on amateur collegiate sports, the Thanksgiving Day game became a commercial success by 1890. Increased expenditures for coaches, trainers, uniforms, transportation, and baggage handlers were more than offset by the sizable gate receipts. In 1893, for instance, reserved tickets cost $15; and private boxes ran $150 apiece! Despite such relatively steep ticket prices, temporary grandstands were built to accommodate overflowing crowds. Noticeable increases in the seating capacity for the Thanksgiving Day game incited critics, like *The Nation*'s editor, E. L. Godkin, to conclude that the event was rapidly becoming "a spectacle for the multitude."[20] Harvard was the first institution to build a modern stadium, signifying that the nation's leading university recognized big-time football as a legitimate activity of higher education. During 1904, Harvard's football team was the institution's most profitable undertaking, recording a surplus of more than $50,000; this compared notably with the departments of the faculties of Arts and Sciences, which had a combined deficit of over $30,000.[21]

"Football as an amateur sport in the colleges of the Middle West has almost passed out of existence," wrote a contemporary commentator.[22] A highly rationalized, profit-oriented entertainment business had taken its place. "Victory has come to mean advertising, full treasuries, improved athletic fields, expert coaches," the commentator noted, "and the satisfying howl of approval from an ever-growing bleacher crowd. Faculty control is a myth." Big-time collegiate football increasingly reflected the dominant business ethic as colleges became universities and universities expanded, paralleling the growth of big business. College

governing boards, drawn from the business elite, set policy and con-
doned the commercial and business aspects of athletics. By the early
1920s, leading Ivy League colleges *averaged* nearly 40,000 spectators per
game throughout their football seasons.[23]

The early commercial success of the collegiate football spectacle and
its subsequent widespread popularity were closely related to its prominence in newspaper reporting. Michael Oriard has written that the New
York Thanksgiving game was "the engine that drove football's early
economic development and demonstrated the financial bonanzas that
might be realized on a regular basis by building one's own 50,000 seat
stadium."[24] It was also the engine that drove the expansion of daily
sports coverage. After Joseph Pulitzer's *World* instituted the first separate daily sports section in 1887, other leading New York dailies—the
Times, the *Herald*, the *Journal*—quickly followed suit. Between the 1880s
and mid-1890s, the *World's* sports coverage increased by six times, while
one of its competitors, the *Sun*, expanded its coverage by 15 times. The
New York dailies employed name writers like Stephen Crane, used extensive illustrations, graphics, and cartoons. Nineteenth-century newspapers devoted the most space to the big game. The decision to play
the season's finale in New York on Thanksgiving Day, Oriard writes,
"transformed a sporting contest into a social event whose potential as
[a] spectacle could be exploited by inventive publishers and reporters."[25]
By the 1890s, in fact, the highest advertising rates were on the sports
pages. The high-profile tradition of Thanksgiving Day game coverage
grounded the tradition in a historical narrative that accumulated more
and more power over time.[26]

The game and its deeper cultural meanings were initially directed
at parents, educators, and sportswriters. But middle-class adults were
not the only Americans introduced to the newly invented Thanksgiving Day football tradition. Richard Harding Davis wrote the first published short story about football—it focused on a Princeton football star
who befriended a poor, invalid boy, and it appeared in *St. Nicholas*, a
popular children's magazine.[27] A cadre of early sports fiction writers
followed Davis's lead. Further, as early as 1889, children learned about
the history and significance of the annual Thanksgiving event: Also
writing in the pages of *St. Nicholas*, Walter Camp, dean of American
football (and the unofficial Yale coach) presented a sophisticated four-
part series on college football that covered the game's history; the origins and development of its plays, rules, and positions; the training and
diet required; and the nonphysical qualities (honesty, brains, diligence)
of a good football player. In the series, he told the impressionable readers about the amateur ethos: to "play not for gain but sport."[28] Camp
devoted the entire third essay of the series to detailing the festivities,
excitement, cheering, and pregame preparations of the Thanksgiving
Day contest.

Press coverage of the Thanksgiving Day game spread quickly from its New York hub. Regional papers profited from syndication and wire services, providing their readers with stories about the big eastern games, so that much of the early information about football reflected a homogeneous character. By the early years of the twentieth century, Oriard maintains, newspapers across the country, despite regional differences, presented relatively uniform formulas of reading about football—"the sign of a national sporting culture in regional variants."[29]

The Game's Geographical Diffusion

Before the turn of the twentieth century, collegiate football moved rapidly from its Northeast cradle to the Midwest, the West Coast, and the South. A 1905 study of 555 American cities revealed that 432 of them had football teams. Geographer Carl Abbott suggests that the formation of college conferences reflected unique cultural expressions that contributed to the definition of American regions and to corresponding regional consciousness. One contemporary commentator recognized this sense of regional identification, especially on the development of particular styles of play. "For many years," Herbert Reed wrote in 1916, "the fundamental difference between East and West lay in the fact that Eastern men were prone to develop the defense first, while Western coaches . . . began with the attack."[30] The geographic diffusion of the collegiate game led to the development of regional conferences. The Western Conference (predecessor of the Big Ten) was formed in the 1890s. While western intercollegiate conferences also appeared to have been conceived to attack the growing problem of professionalism, in the East, colleges approached the issue on an individual basis.[31] In fact, the elite northeastern universities were defined as Ivy League schools according to the selection of colleges choosing to play each other in football. In their 1919 Thanksgiving Day football coverage, the *Chicago Daily Tribune* included results and summaries of some 50 games, half of which were played west of Illinois.[32]

The first official southern game, between Washington and Lee and the Virginia Military Institute, was actually played just eight years after the pioneering 1869 Princeton-Rutgers contest. But the growth of southern football was clearly related to the popularity of the Thanksgiving Day tradition. As a common cultural denominator, football compensated for Southerners' initial resistance to such Yankee traditions as a national Thanksgiving celebration. In 1894, for instance, the *Nashville American* awarded five front-page columns to the big game between the southern powers, Virginia and North Carolina. "It was the social event of the year," the *American* proclaimed; "no ball or reception can attract a larger aggregation of society people than did this Thanksgiving football game."[33] As southern historian Andrew Doyle has observed, a generation of progressively minded new southerners of the 1890s adopted football to emulate the preferences of the northeastern bourgeoisie and to gain respectability among the national sporting establishment. The collegiate football spectacle thus informed the southern mind about the new American game, southern modernity, and the cause of a national holiday.[34]

The spread of southern collegiate football changed the style of football play from an exclusively running game to a quicker, pass-oriented one. In 1895, Auburn University coach John Heisman instituted a blocking offensive line for running backs. In 1899, Herman Suter's University of the South (Sewanee, Tenn.) Tigers defeated Texas, Texas A & M, Houston, Tulane, Louisiana State, and Mississippi. Most significant, the leading southern schools perfected the forward pass by 1906, a tactical innovation which eventually transformed the game.[35] By then, southern schools like Vanderbilt, Clemson, and Alabama became national football powers, thanks to the popularity of the holiday game, and to the northern coaches who taught the game's techniques and tactics to southern students. Heisman's Georgia Tech squad won four straight national titles between 1915 and 1918, which reflected, as well as any other factor, the shifting geographical dynamics of the game in just four decades.

By the early part of the twentieth century, football was a major Southern spectacle, and it has since evolved into what two scholars have characterized as a "statewide religion" celebrated with all "the ritual and pageantry and spectacle of a High Church ceremony."[36] Football, according to Novak, reflects the region's dominant evangelical traditions of emotion, inspiration, and charismatic speaking, and surges of personal conversion. The region is marked by patriotism, militarism, prayer, music, conspicuous consumption, politics, sex, white supremacy, and sports. Moroever, in the new South, sports like football were a means of reconciling change with tradition. As Doyle has discovered, Alabamans in the 1920s rallied to the intersectional successes of the Crimson Tide's football team. Rose Bowl glory redeemed southern manhood and honor against the onslaught of northern journalists like H. L. Mencken. More important, football represented a triumphant embrace of the team-oriented, scientific organization of industrial capitalism. Alabama's dominant, middle-class progressives "embraced football as a means of inculcating the competitive self-confidence so vital to capitalism while simultaneously upholding the traditions that bolstered the southern social order."[37]

By the mid-1890s, the commercialized Thanksgiving Day football tradition was also firmly established in the midwestern collegiate scene. Indeed, Notre Dame emerged as a major football power in the 1920s, by blending modern means of material success with age-old religious rituals, myths, and metaphors.[38] Three decades prior to this, however, Michigan and Chicago developed regional dynasties by hiring professional coaches. The University of Chicago, for instance, became a football power *before* it was recognized for academic excellence. Just months after the university's founding, President William Rainey Harper appointed muscular Christian Amos Alonzo Stagg to a tenurable athletic director's position. Stagg, a former all-American football player and Yale Divinity School student, realized that he could "influence others to Christian ideals more effectively on the field than in the pulpit," and accepted Harper's call to "develop teams which we can send around the country and [which can] knock out all the colleges."[39] Harper's marketing skill and Stagg's morality were vindicated in what one historian has called "the first greatest game of the century"—the 1905 Thanksgiving Day classic that attracted 27,000 spectators, and in which Chicago defeated its chief midwestern rival, Michigan.[40]

In 1885, former Harvard footballer Oscar S. Howard began a campaign to convert the San Francisco region from rugby to American football. His efforts bore fruit in 1892 as California and Stanford played their first Thanksgiving Day game. The *San Francisco Examiner* noted that the emergent tradition embodied all the trappings of the New York spectacle. The annual event was regarded as the unofficial West Coast Conference championship until 1905, when both schools dropped football (as did other schools, in a protest against the game's brutality) and went back to rugby for the following 13 years. The *Examiner* dramatized the 1919 resumption of the Thanksgiving football classic between Stanford and California as "the return of the American game"; and noted that "the ancients of rival colleges rejoice that soft and gentle days of rugby have gone their way and Spartan blood flows again."[41] The following year, California went undefeated, won the Rose Bowl, and was declared the national champion. Receipts from Western Conference games during the 1922 season totaled more than $1,500,000. Clearly, by 1920, the balance of power in college football had shifted from the game's northeastern cradle to the South, Midwest, and West Coast. Cornell, in 1922, was the last Ivy League school to win a national championship.[42]

The World War I preparedness campaign bolstered football's geographic expansion. Draped in patriotic garb, the game became a training ground for citizenship and military readiness. Preparedness leaders worked to transform football from a mere specator sport into a basic component of civic education. The politically charged wartime atmosphere prompted sports-minded leaders to link football and the national spirit. In so doing, football advocates broadened their public appeals for the sake of convincing less militant Americans that the sport tempered the fighting instinct and cultivated worthwhile civic values. "Somehow in our schools we must cultivate [a] full form of belonging," wrote Joseph Lee, president of the Playground and Recreation Association of America.[43] Lee pointed to football as being the most suitable preparation for war, due to its cultivation of team loyalty, which could readily be equated with national allegiance.

Wartime discussions were specific as to the desired physical qualities cultivated by football, which prepared young men for war. Amherst College professor Raymond Gettell specified "the elements involved in any struggle for physical supremacy," and identified "strength, speed, skill and cunning" as the most important ones developed by football.[44] Reflecting the editorial sentiments of a 1914 *Puck* magazine, which inverted a well-known adage by implying that war should now become the moral equivalent of football, Gettell maintained that in no other game are the fundamentals of international relations and warfare more closely paralleled than in football. George E. Johnson addressed the staunchest progressive audience, in the pages of *The Survey*, about the role of the "fighting spirit" in American society. "Universal peace will never be realized until both militarist and pacifist find the same outlets for human activity which make alike for peace and progress, " he wrote.[45] When boys engage in fighting games—football, boxing, wrestling—they usefully "preserve and add to the bone and sinew of hardihood and heroism; of strength and sacrifice, of love and ideals."[46] Manly sports like football made strong fighting men for combat, and upright citizens imbued with patriotism, corporate sensibilities, social decency, and endurance for the challenges during peacetime.

The football field became an important substitute battleground and training arena for American fighting prowess. Popular writer H. Addington Bruce, no stranger to sports commentary, believed that football's unrivaled popularity could be accounted for in only two ways: "Either the man of the twentieth century is a brutal, debased creature; or else, to an extraordinary degree, and alike for players and spectators, football meets a real human need."[47] Nothing in organized sports compared to the spectacle presented at college games, he thought. "A visitor from Mars," observing an important college football game, might be led to believe that some "decisive conflict was in process, bearing vitally on the destinies of the nation."[48]

The seriousness of Thanksgiving Day football in World War I-era American culture was dramatized in the military academies' annual confrontation. Prior to World War I, the Army-Navy Thanksgiving Day game commanded increased coverage in the national holiday sports headlines. Not bounded by a particular geographic region, and a showcase for the nation's military establishment, the Army-Navy rivalry was the premier national collegiate sports spectacle. Begun in 1890, the Army-Navy rivalry was transformed from a private military exhibition into a grand public sports showcase by the early twentieth century.[49] The annual game attracted the wealthy and upper classes, politicians, celebrities, and the military brass. Noted sportswriter Arthur Ruhl described the crowd's unique composition by noting the numerous "fine old war-horses with grizzled mustaches," the "awkward enlisted men in shabby khaki," the honorable European "Excellencies"; and "Secretaries of the Army, Navy, Admirals, and Generals, bigwigs galore and their lovely nieces and daughters"—the atmosphere, according to Ruhl, was "very American."[50]

The 1919 Army-Navy game was one of the most widely discussed sporting events in American history: About 45,000 spectators saw the Midshipmen from Annapolis edge the West Point Cadets, 6 to 0, at the Polo Grounds. For weeks prior to the game, the *New York Times* had carried articles about it; and the *Times* devoted several pages solely to the game, on both the day of the game and the day after it. The *Times* proclaimed football's authenticity as an American game and hailed the 1919 season as "the most memorable year in the history of American football."[51] It recognized the tremendous boost given to the game by its widespread popularity among American troops in Europe during the war, and speculated that the 1919 season "will hardly show better played contests than" the Army-Navy game.[52]

Symbolic of the geographic diffusion of football, the Army-Navy Thanksgiving Day contest moved west into the American heartland. It was staged at the dedication of Soldier Field in Chicago, and over half a million people competed, in a national lottery, for about 100,000 tickets. Despite cold temperatures and a steady snowfall, a crowd of 110,000 celebrated Thanksgiving by watching Army and Navy struggle to a 21 to 21 tie. *Chicago Tribune* journalist Robert Kelley recognized the significance of the event when he wrote that "football had its greatest pageant, its high spot of color here this afternoon, and so did sport in the United States."[53] Some 200 newspapermen produced thousands of words for their readers throughout the country. Chicago telegraph officials, in fact, verified that more wires were used to cover the 1926 Thanksgiving Day game than in any other sports event recorded until that time. President Calvin Coolidge was "prevented by government business from being at the game," but he followed the play-by-play on a White House radio.[54] American sailors throughout the world heard the first sporting event ever broadcast outside continental boundaries. Aided by modern mass-communication technologies, the people of the nation joined together in the sporting spectacle—college football and the Thanksgiving holiday fused in dramatic fashion.

The Meanings of the Thanksgiving Day Game Tradition

Most people learned about the new American game of football, and its Thanksgiving Day tradition, on the sports page, not at the ballfield. Football as a "cultural text" was indeed narrated by urban sports journalists who consistently emphasized several, standardized themes: the importance of the social spectacle around the game itself; the amateur ethos of collegiate sport; the cultural significance of holiday sporting events; contradictions on the gridiron between the thrill for the big run or pass and the plodding science of tight ball control, set plays, and coaches' dictatorship; and the meaning of modern masculinity amid brutally violent mayhem. All of these narrative themes emerged before the turn of the century and reflected the principal concerns of the media's football interpreters and promoters.[55]

Oriard's important, provocative thesis about the production of football commentary requires attention to what Goldstein terms the "dual histories" of sports. According to him, the history of sport exists on a linear level—of institutional developments, rule changes, and innovations in game forms; and at a cyclical level—of emotions, feelings, motives, and meanings. The symbolic-laden Thanksgiving Day football narratives engaged both levels. The geographic diffusion of the Thanksgiving tradition resides most visibly at the linear level; yet the deeper, inscribed meanings surrounding this tradition reside at another, more treacherous intersection for historians—between idea and practice.[56]

Thanksgiving Day football was invested with diverse meanings by its participants as well as its interpreters. The event became a grand spectacle for students, who transformed the spirit of campus life by creating their own unique, rich set of symbols and rituals to dramatize their school loyalties. The big holiday game sometimes entailed winning or losing a coveted trophy: Stanford and California struggled for the prized Axe; Minnesota and Michigan vied for the Little Brown Jug; and Purdue and Indiana competed for the Old Oaken Bucket. In fact, school spirit—expressed in terms of loyalty to the football team—was often a precondition for acceptance in college social circles.[57] Yale President Arthur Hadley recognized that the football ritual seized "the emotions of the student body in such a way as to make class distinctions relatively unimportant," and to make students bond in "the old-fashioned democratic way."[58] And parents exploited the big game for their own status aspirations. Nineteenth-century spectacles marked the opening of the leisure class's winter social calendar. For these games, elites displayed their college allegiances in conspicuous fashion by chartering elegantly decorated carriages—pioneering a version of the modern-day "tailgate picnic," replete with sumptuous lunches and champagne. Philosopher and social critic Thorstein Veblen theorized that such rituals represented a "modern survival of prowess," which enabled the wealthy to flaunt their power and prestige.[59] Donald Mrozek reaffirmed Veblen's thesis that elites were obsessed with sports for purposes of consumption, fashion, and display; he identified the wealthy as "pioneers of sports as a leisure activity which required no justification."[60]

Such collective experiences were interpreted most visibly by sports-writers and social commentators. As Oriard argues, the richly detailed record of football journalism provides sports historians with a vast reservoir of the "varied and changing readings," as mediated by the sportswriter, of particular athletic contests and an audience.[61] "Football interpreters' power to determine their readers' understanding," Oriard writes, "resided in the issues they raised and the ways they framed them," and, as such, did not comprise a consensus or single discourse.[62] Oriard's thesis directs our energies away from assigning a specific class imprint to a particular interpretation, and toward a recognition that there was no single voice for each class or group interest in sports commentary (the social elite viewing football this way; the common man, that way). Rather, "football's multiple narratives reveal an interplay of interests, both within and between identifiable groups, that were as often self-contradictory as they were opposed to each other."[63]

Social commentators, for instance, regularly noted the relationship between football and American culture. "Out of the old Rugby game the people of the United States have made a game of unified team play that is distinctive and unique, corresponding to something fundamental in American instincts which it expresses and satisfies," one *Outlook* writer contended.[64] William Lyon Phelps, Yale's renowned professor of English literature, viewed the game as an expression of the aesthetic impulse and a celebration of the human spirit. Amherst College professor Raymond Gettell spoke to the way in which football retained the "vital elements of physical combat" as well as "the skilled interrelation of individual efforts directed to a common purpose."[65] The game, according to Gettell, who obviously entertained versions of the dominant social Darwinist mentality, reproduced that "organized social effort by which man first attained supremacy over the world of nature, and by which the more highly organized and more closely cooperating peoples have conquered and surpassed their less advanced rivals."[66] Like football, the Thanksgiving story affirmed adaptability and physical prowess as defining American characteristics.

Football advocates who opposed such moralistic diatribes downplayed the sport's violence as incidental and necessary for the greater social good. Others upheld American colleges' increasingly secular commitments and demonstrated how football offset a disappearing religious worldview with the new entrepreneurial ethic. As early as 1891, middle-class parents were assured, in the pages of the prestigious *North American Review*, that football was not contrary to education, as was popularly believed. Not only did the game promote and demand order, regularity, and restraint; but it "put an end to all those villainies that have not yet been born, but for whose arrival preparations are being made by their mother, the devil," said Joseph Hamblin Sears.[67] In addition, football play would add 20 pounds and 10 percent to boys' grades, and, most important, increase one's "manly self-respect and ability to reason with common sense" by 50 percent.[68]

Fears of football's excessive brutality did not subside with its fundamental, White House-brokered reform in 1905. Middle-class suspicions persisted throughout the twentieth century, despite the popularity of both the Thanksgiving Day tradition and the geographical diffusion of the American game.[69] During the mid 1920s, a *Literary Digest* writer addressed criticisms of football's brutality and excessiveness, on the eve of the big game, by identifying the ways in which the game "fosters fair play and clean living." "Here is a game which calls for drudgery, discipline, and hard work," values of crucial importance for the American middle class; moreover, football is a game that demands "loyalty, service and team play [hallmarks of the World War I preparedness effort a few years earlier], for clean living, for fine spirit."[70] Noted sportswriter Sol Metzger preached a similar message in the pages of *St. Nicholas*. Presumably writing to young people and the parents who monitored their children's reading materials, Metzger documented football's reform and the corresponding advances in early sports medicine, and reassured many wary middle-class readers that "nothing quite takes the place of football in making you young fellows smile through hard knocks and misfortune, or better trains you to keep on fighting through it all."[71] Clearly, much of the football commentary was directed at the unconverted.

But an equal amount of such commentary was written for those sympathetic middle-class Americans who were enamored with the strenuous-life ideology. Camp, author of nearly 30 books, more than 200 magazine articles, and numerous newspaper commentaries, assured readers of the game's relevance in a rationalized, corporate society, through his use of the metaphor of a hierarchically structured, efficiently operated corporation. Football's evolution from chaos and primitive physicality toward reason and order proved to Camp that the game developed, in young men, the character and experiences for success in modern America. As influential as Camp's football commentary was, Oriard shrewdly cautions us about concluding that Camp's readers always followed his expert advice. In fact, football spectators' influence won out many times, thereby shaping the game as well. As Oriard documents, spectators desired open, brawny play, rather than brains and deliberate strategy (despite Camp's insistence that brains would win over brawn); hero worship prevailed among the greater public, despite Camp's insistence on teamwork; and fans often welcomed extravagance, as evidenced by the popularity of the Thanksgiving spectacle.[72]

In fact, the spectacle of collegiate sports was at odds with much of the middle-class commentary in established journals of opinion. A host of commentators in *Atlantic Monthly* saw "over-specialization," "moral laxity," "vicarious spectatorship," and "exclusivity" in big-time collegiate football.[73] L. B. R. Briggs predicted in 1918 that intercollegiate athletics "like America, will stand or fall according as they choose between luxury and simplicity, trickery, and integrity, the senses and the spirit."[74] In retrospect, such analysts failed either to recognize or acknowledge the postwar middle class's growing enthusiasm for materialism, frivolity, and spectacles, which characterized their experience during the 1920s.

Not all cultural commentary embraced the way in which football prepared young men for an emergent corporate order. For influential sportswriter Caspar Whitney, creeping professionalism and the game's geographic diffusion endangered football's increasingly vulnerable amateur ethos. Whitney was willing to accept the game's abolition, rather than having to witness "the exhibition of our college boys, sons of gentlemen, resorting to the intrigues of unprincipled professionals."[75] Despite the fact that by 1893, collegiate football had already become a highly commercialized spectacle, Whitney remained steadfast in his original intent of favoring the amateur code against the tendency of players and coaches who were "obeying the spirit of the law, [but] spend[ing] their time diligently searching for an evasion of the letter."[76] The game's geographic diffusion portended further disaster. The western and southern hinterlands were a great abyss for amateurism, according to Whitney; the people there displayed "an ignorance of what amateur sport is" and "a general scramble to take part in athletics as one would take part in the manipulations of the Stock Exchange to get all that can be made out of it by fair or foul, honorable or dishonorable means."[77]

Both Camp and Whitney promoted idealistic visions of football that were at once influential in shaping public opinion on sports and sometimes contradictory to the ideas of their own readership. Camp's crusade for rationalized, scientific football conflicted with the game's roots in the collegiate extracurricular program created by students as an antidote to the demands of faculty and the preferred academic curriculum; Whitney's Victorian gentlemanly notion of sport for sport's sake was at odds with universities' emergent vocational orientation; the new corporate sensibilities that privileged teamwork, not for pleasure, but for efficiency; and the growing professionalization of intercollegiate sports. Both the scientifically based and the amateurism narratives, Oriard recognizes, represented aspects of football whose roots lay in different parts of a rapidly changing American society. The Thanksgiving Day football tradition provided a dynamic context for these two seemingly contradictory narratives to be indiscriminately synthesized and linked to the nationalistic meanings of the holiday venue. Whether Americans read the Thanksgiving spectacle through rational, modernist lenses, or through Victorian bourgeois ones, or merely enjoyed the event as a commercial, decadent, secular celebratory alternative, they ultimately embraced the legitimacy of sports as a shaping influence of the national character in one way or another.[78]

SUMMARY

Since the late nineteenth century, many Americans witnessed the decline of traditional Protestant verities and the emergence of nationalism as a replacement. Muscular Christianity synthesized sports and morality in ways acceptable to the late-nineteenth-century American middle class. And the Thanksgiving Day collegiate football spectacle, as a new cultural phenomenon, legitimized the emergent political culture through references to the historicity of Anglo-Saxonism. "Football is the expression of the strength of the Anglo-Saxon," W. Cameron Forbes wrote in the early years of the twentieth century. "It is the dominant spirit of a dominant race, and to this it owes its popularity and its hopes of permanence," he speculated.[79] He was the grandson of Ralph Waldo Emerson, a Harvard graduate and football coach at his alma mater in 1898–99, and later banker and statesman; and his language reflected the key aspirations and worldviews of the *fin-de-siècle* American middle class.

Simultaneously, after the nation's 1876 wave of centennial celebrations, civic, religious, and folk liturgies were intermingled with commercially constructed holiday rituals centered on consumption. The advertising industry popularized turkeys, pumpkins, and cornucopias in the public iconography of the Thanksgiving holiday by equating them with the dominant connotations—bounty, prosperity, and abundance—of the American experience.[80] The stuffed turkey, the sweet potatoes, the pumpkin pie, the Macy's parade, and football are integral components of the modern Thanksgiving experience. The Thanksgiving fare conjures up images of bygone days in a purer, simpler America.[81] Participation in this tradition is part of the feeling that one is a member of the nation, of the imagined community.

SIX

FOURTH-OF-JULY
SPORTING CELEBRATIONS

FROM "SPREAD-EAGLE" PATRIOTISM TO SERIOUS PLAY

Since its inception in 1777, Americans have regarded the Fourth of July as the national Sabbath—a sacramental occasion to affirm popular sovereignty, protest against aristocratic privilege, and celebrate the idea of American unity through impassioned oration, parades, patriotic sermons, and nationalistic bombast (all of which derived from the British).[1] Coming once a year between planting season and harvest, the midsummer Fourth-of-July celebration marked the defining historical moment and confirmed the stability of the republic. Like Thanksgiving, the Fourth presented many pseudoreligious trappings that blurred distinctions between the sacred and secular. Historian John Miller has observed similarities to religion in the Fourth's symbolism; its glorification of the nation's patron saints; its emphasis on the sanctity of the written text; its missionary fervor that focused on the United States as a redeemer nation; and its power to weld people into a community.[2]

The Fourth's significance spread widely after the adoption of the Constitution. By 1800, celebrations were principally staged under Federalist auspices; Republicans, believing their political opponents had misappropriated the American Revolution, staged their own, more democratic celebrations. The annual holiday became more common in the aftermath of the War of 1812. Writing a year after the nation's centennial, a *New York Times* editor described early celebrations as a "mass of Old World fancies ingrafted on the lusty vigor of the young Republic" and dominated by "sometimes bombastic, sometimes turgid" speeches and odes, colored with "freedom and tyranny, science, art, mechanics," and religious allegories.[3] The founding fathers and mothers observed the day whose meaning was "too deep and sacred for our apprehension," in a manner which "would now seem laborious."[4]

In truth, pre-Civil War Fourths were more diversified than the *New York Times* editor acknowledged. Although official celebrations have always downplayed social divisions and had reaffirmed national solidarity, tensions simmered underneath such spectacles. Americans of all classes and races used the day to articulate a wide range of social and political ideas. The day was exploited by abolitionists, temperance advocates, suffragettes, Sunday-school and peace activists so as to promote their special causes, which often deflected attention from the official meanings of the day. Workers dramatized their importance as enlightened, educated citizens by using the Fourth to symbolically affirm their political freedoms, celebrate the country's liberation from colonial rule, and embrace traditional craft ideals. Labor historian Leon Fink revealed that the Knights of Labor often organized the only Independence Day parade in a town, as a means of promoting their political vision of equal rights for all citizens, rather than having the community pursue progress under the leadership of a business class. Immigrants organized parades and picnics as a means of bolstering the status of ethnic and religious subcommunities. Moreover, the Fourth provided an occasion for African-Americans to celebrate their heritage at barbecues and multiplantation gatherings, where slaves heard speeches filled with words and phrases like "freedom," "independence," "revolution," and "death to tyrants." In short, the class, ethnic, and racial dimensions of the Fourth's celebrations reflected the contested nature of "American independence."[5]

After the nation's 1876 centennial, the Fourth's celebrations became increasingly leisure-oriented occasions. American colonists drew from their rich old-world holiday and recreational heritage that sanctioned weeklong wakes, Plough Monday, Shrove Tuesday, and other occasions as times to feast, drink, dance, and play sports like stoolball, skittles, quoits, hurling, and football, and to run footraces.[6] The *New York Times* recognized this general trend and noted that such joyous festivities were the result of the fact that "the war drum beat no longer"—the *Times* said, "The Federal Union is restored and strengthened and . . . out of all the heat and passion of the past has arisen a nobler national life; and a grand addition to the world's work for humanity has been secured."[7] The new focus on sports and commercial amusements, however, was more the result of larger social forces that transformed Independence Day from a civic-religious, republican festival to a holiday marked by sports and leisure than the result of a nominally reunified nation.

As more and more Americans became fond of organized sports and athletic contests, they elevated such activities as surrogates for "Yankee Doodle" and other songs of years past. Major urban newspapers dramatically expanded their Fourth-of-July sports coverage. Across the nation, newspapers devoted increasing coverage to holiday horse racing, regattas, and baseball. Not only did Americans turn to commercial sports attractions on the nation's birthday; but they often journeyed out of town to participate in contests, in which large cash purses were awarded to the winners.[8] Cultural leaders quickly reined in the winds of change to ensure that sports-filled Fourth celebrations bridged the transition from spread-eagle patriotism to subtler messages of class conciliation and ethnic assimilation for an urban, industrial society. Despite the pervasive class, racial, ethnic, and gender exclusivity of organized sports, a new generation of cultural leaders shrewdly catered to the masses' interest in sports and games to reinforce the ideals of patriotism, democracy, and national unity.

BASEBALL AND AMERICA ON THE FOURTH

Baseball became the principal postbellum Fourth-of-July American sport. "It's our game," proclaimed poet Walt Whitman; baseball "has the snap, go, fling of the American atmosphere—belongs as much to our institutions, fits into them as significantly, as our constitutions, laws; is just as important in the sum total of our historic life."[9] During the 1840s and 1850s, the Olympic Ball Club of Philadelphia (the first baseball club with a written constitution and field rules) gathered to read the Declaration of Independence, sing songs, and play a ballgame on the Fourth. Fourth-of-July baseball games since the Civil War both popularized the emergent game and linked it to the modern American character. There was no more appropriate context for dramatizing the connection between the national pastime and American independence and democracy than that of Independence Day.[10]

Fourth-of-July baseball games were popular in large and small cities alike. The history of celebrations of the Fourth in Portland, Maine, illuminates this: Organized baseball made its debut in Portland on July 4, 1864, when a Harvard College nine routed a newly organized Bowdoin College team, 40 to 13. The success of the Bowdoin-Harvard game sparked considerable attention among the city's young men, who organized a team; and among Portland's governing fathers, who included baseball in the city's celebration the following year. By 1880, baseball had become a mainstay in Independence Day festivities throughout Maine, with Bangor, Lewiston, Auburn, Rockland, and Machias all featuring holiday doubleheaders—a trend that intensified further when minor league baseball came to the state in 1885. In fact, the annual Portland-Biddeford game was the most widely discussed state sports tradition, prominently featuring local Irish-American stars like Galligan, Kearns, O'Rourke, Reilly, O'Connell, and Madden in starting line-ups.[11] On July 5, 1885, the new *Portland Sunday Times* featured a story about a doubleheader between Portland and Biddeford—attended by 1,300, on the front page, under the masthead, plus results of earlier baseball games and regattas. No doubt, an important factor in this journalistic recognition were the visits that six major league baseball teams made to the city.[12]

Baseball was warmly embraced by Portland municipal and religious organizations alike. In 1903, Catholics bested Protestants on the diamond, as the Holy Name team narrowly defeated a YMCA squad, 10 to 9. Across town, on the Westbrook Seminary grounds, the All Souls team edged the Woodfords, 25 to 23, prompting a *Portland Sunday Times* writer to exclaim that "the Universalists of Portland never waged a hotter theological discussion than the baseball game they waged Saturday afternoon."[13] Later that day, on an oceanfront field, the local Fort Williams Regulars exploded for a six-run fifth inning to defeat a visiting Coast Artillery team from Fort Slocum, New York.[14]

Fourth-of-July baseball games were staged in remote, regular-Army posts as well. Civilians and military units from neighboring posts often joined forces to celebrate the Fourth. During the Geronimo campaign in 1885, for instance, a company of the Thirteenth Infantry played a cowboy team for two barrels of Milwaukee beer—a rare treat for regulars stationed along the arid Mexican border. The soldiers won, and hospitably shared their beer with both the losers and spectators. Besides baseball, Fourth celebrations at frontier military posts featured a wide variety of races and contests. Individual and team winners at Fort Keough's 1887 program received $5 and $10 prizes.[15]

Beginning in the 1890s, journalists, intellectuals, politicians, and sports enthusiasts utilized an expanding mass media to demonstrate that baseball was a uniquely American tradition. This trend reached its apogee with the invention of the Doubleday myth and was canonized by Albert Spalding's 1911 book, *Baseball: America's National Game*. In a *New York Times* interview prior to the book's release, Spalding hinted at his thesis by describing the psychological impact of the game as corresponding precisely to the national character, and, consequently, as a reciprocal creator of that character.[16]

The game's leading advocates maintained that baseball provided experience involving a wide range of emotions and values, which, collectively, sustained the national identity. H. Addington Bruce argued that Americans displayed physical fitness, honesty, patience, respect for lawful authority, initiative, quickness of judgment, and an appreciation of social solidarity on the diamond. An *Atlantic Monthly* essayist hailed the game as "a great democratic rite," while an *American Magazine* editor believed baseball to be "not so much an institution as an expression" that "presents the American spirit bared of furbelows."[17] Baseball's rapid geographic expansion, and its popularity between the 1870s and 1920s, proved to many people that the pastime usefully linked Americans to a national community, irrespective of regional, class, and ethnic differences.[18]

In 1918, one of the most noteworthy games was played by Army and Navy teams, before more than 40,000 onlookers at London's Chelsea Football Grounds. Except for the numerous members of the English royalty—the king and queen, princesses, dukes, Mrs. David Lloyd George, Mrs. Winston Churchill, and military generals—the sight was, according to George Earle Raiguel, "a familiar one to American eyes: just such a sight as might be seen at a ball game anywhere in the U.S.A. on the Fourth."[19] The Stars and Stripes were omnipresent, signaling "a wholehearted acceptance of America as a comrade in play and a near relation in the great work that lies before the two big English-speaking families," noted the English journal *Living Age*. It continued: "Admirals enjoyed themselves with the light-heartedness of A.B.'s and private soldiers could hardly laugh more delightedly than did generals."[20] After an American attaché informed the king about the ceremonial tradition of presidents throwing out the first ball, the king followed suit and "showed the keenest possible interest in and appreciation of our national sport."[21] After the Navy players defeated their Army comrades in a closely contested game, the excited crowd suddenly became quiet. According to *Living Age*:

> Across that silence drifted the soft, almost pathetic, first chords of "The Star-Spangled Banner," played by the [Royal] band of Welsh Guards. Hats came off. Sailors and soldiers stood to attention, saluting. After all that noise, the quietude, accented by the poignant music, came near being painful. The meaning of this most significant of all ball games was carried along the air. There was more cheering afterwards, but cheering of a radically different kind. The crowd awoke to consciousness that the afternoon had passed into the history of two great nations.[22]

At the anthem's conclusion, the king gave Admiral Sims and General Biddle the American salute. The crowd went wild. According to Raiguel, "the British voted baseball a great game."[23]

PLAYGROUND REFORMERS AND THE SPORTING FOURTH

The newly developed sporting Fourth was not without its opponents and critics. In the mid-1870s, many Americans could not recite the Declaration of Independence, nor did they care for long-winded patriotic orations—a development that evoked great uneasiness among the nation's cultural leaders, who interpreted such trends as signs of impending social malaise. An older generation of social commentators detested the growth of the leisure-filled and commercially oriented Fourth. As early as 1874, the *Worcester* (Mass.) *Daily Press* characterized the Fourth as "the most abused" day of the year; decried the drunken, recreational manner by which workers and immigrants "desecrated" the day as they chased greased pigs, climbed greased poles, and competed in sack and wheelbarrow races.[24] In 1897, A. B. Riker wrote: "To all thoughtful people it must be apparent that the manifestation of patriotism is declining among us. . . . Time was when men sacrificed self for country. Now they sacrifice country for self."[25] Riker regretted that the Fourth had "degenerated into a day of desecration . . . whose significance is by no means duly apprehended by the present generation."[26] In Worcester, drinking was so widespread that the papers claimed the day was devoted only to "liquid patriotism." Such laments and condemnations persisted until World War I. The 1914 Fourth, for instance, was described by one observer as the "denaturing of another picturesque holiday." Just as Thanksgiving and Christmas witnessed "the loss of spiritual significance," and Memorial Day had been "weened away" by regattas and track meets, the Fourth, too, had "joined the tame procession with its pageants and sports" and the "unspecialized relaxation of the many."[27]

Criticisms of the leisure-oriented Fourth traversed class and ideological boundaries. Although workers had traditionally appropriated the Fourth as a day for sport, games, drink, and carousing, labor leaders and socialist intellectuals usually expressed a profound ambivalence toward such activities. From the Knights of Labor in the 1880s to the American Socialist Party of the early twentieth century, leftist leaders increasingly encountered workers hopelessly enamored with commercialized leisure. The left vanguard (many of whom were themselves middle-class) had difficulties making sense of such popular aspects of the working-class culture. When they occasionally bothered to discuss commercialized leisure, they, curiously, suggested bourgeois, Victorian notions of culture and "rational recreation" as "civilizing influences" for the masses. American and British socialist leaders thought workers should devote their increased leisure time to self-improvement and the struggle for socialism, rather than to mass cultural diversions; thus, their opinions were increasingly at odds with the very people they sought to organize and politicize.[28]

Many American workers and immigrants participated in a broad "movement culture" that involved ethnic and neighborhood holiday festivities. In Pittsburgh, historian Francis Couvares has explained, local working-class fire companies organized Fourth celebrations that were short on patriotic homilies and long on leisure activities. Maine socialists held their first annual field day on the Fourth and, simultaneously, adopted a working-class version of the Declaration of Independence.[29] Nevertheless, workers and immigrants were strictly counseled about the assimilationist implications of mainstream holiday celebrations. An 1876 editorial in the *Chicago Vorbote* described the pompous preparations undertaken around the country for celebrating the independence of the "American exploiters" from the "English exploiters"; and painted a dire picture of the sufferings of American workers under the capitalist system, stating that they had no reason to commemorate the centennial of a republic that was the political instrument of the "monied aristocracy."[30] The general denunciatory tone of leftist Fourth-of-July commentary persisted well into the twentieth century. In 1908, the social-ist *New York Evening Call* noted, in an editorial, that "unless we were annually reminded of the fact [that this is a land of liberty], by a read-ing of the Declaration, we might forget that we are free."[31] The larger project behind the festive event, the *Call* speculated, was to keep alive the "spirit of '76": "Remember the Old Revolution, and there will be few thoughts of the New Revolution."[32] Similarly, historian Lynn Abrams tells how the German Socialist party branded "bourgeois" patriotic fes-tivals as propaganda weapons of the dominant classes.[33]

Five years later, the *Call's* condemnations were much more specifi-cally directed toward Fourth-of-July sports and leisure. The *Call*, in a lengthy, detailed editorial, "The Spirit of Play," noted that more than 30,000 people saw prize fights; in one such fight, "for the glory of the American punch and to the credit of Yankee swat," French-Canadian boxer Willie Ritchie and Jewish-American boxer Leach Cross "kept up the reputation of the little, old U.S.A."[34] More than 300,000, mostly males, attended professional or semiprofessional baseball games; and another 100,000 spectators, "in their sane and sober senses," watched "various other athletic contests," the *Call* reported. In addition to the sports spectators, "the sweltering, perspiring, hapless mess of human-ity in search of fresh air"—numbering 300,000, by the *Call's* estimate—"swarmed" to Coney Island, where they were forced to "dig down deep to get the money to pay the traction companies."[35] Moreover, the upper classes hailing from the Wall Street district, with their yachts, house-boats and summer estates, "suck[ed] summer recreation out of those who work"; the result of this leisure-oriented celebration of the Fourth, the *Call* concluded, was that "not a person in Greater New York could, in forty-five minutes, reach the open" air—people were obstructed by the railroad companies and professional baseball promoters.[36] Indeed, the *Call* noted that "Those who go to baseball games, or to the horse races, or similar places have lost all regard for or touch with simple, natural pleasures. They are ridden by the beast of professional sport."[37]

While the old guard of cultural leaders saw frivolous amusements as being the bane of patriotism and national unity, an emergent gen-eration of educated, middle-class individuals saw the opposite—advo-cates of the new strenuous life believed that the popular games and pastimes of mass culture pointed to an athletic route for creating new civic standards. "We get easily differentiated from each other in the struggle for bread and a living," a writer for *The Independent* surmised; "there is no such thing as a commonwealth of intercourse remaining. A good playground seems to be exactly what we all need."[38] Not surpris-ingly, Luther Gulick, president of the Playground Association of America (PAA), agreed: "We are a nation because we have a government, but we are not a people, partly because as yet we possess no adequate social language."[39] "If it is true that we remember those we play with more fully, and feel more at one with them" than in other domains of social experience, Gulick reasoned, "then it seems as if it were also true that there is no way in which a community can be brought together and made to feel and act as a unit so well as by playing together." Fourth-of-July celebrations, he believed, provided a unique opportunity for people to play together and, at the same time, express "social ideals in action."[40]

Such statements did not imply "elite declension," as some historians have argued. The old-stock northeastern WASPs never died out; nor did they lose their hold on wealth, power, and influence to a "new class" of salaried managers and professionals. Rather, they merely revitalized familiar bourgeois values and adapted them to the new corporatist realities. Their move from an "overcivilized" modern existence to more intense forms of physical or spiritual experience—what cultural historian Jackson Lears terms "antimodernism"—was not simply a case of escapism or flutterings of a "dying elite," but a matter of accommodation and protest in the face of the emergent order. As Lears explains, antimodern impulses, which exalted "authentic" experiences as worthy ends in themselves, reinforced the "shift from a Protestant ethos of salvation through self-denial to a therapeutic ideal of self-fulfillment in this world."[41] The older morality embodied an industrial "producer culture," while the new mentality reflected the values of a "consumer culture" in a bureaucratic, corporate state.[42]

Twentieth-century middle-class social reformers acknowledged the importance of sports for promoting Americanism among working-class and immigrant communities, but did so from a particular class perspective. Workers and immigrants had traditionally celebrated holidays with sports, games, and drinking, to express a wide range of values. Workers and immigrants exploited legal holidays to vent their frustration, brought on by industrial work discipline, bosses, and elites whose governing rules encroached on their nonwork activities.[43] While nineteenth-century critics condemned and chastised the working classes for such activities, twentieth-century middle-class reformers channeled traditional pursuits into more socially desirable forms. Thus, fireworks, public drinking, unregulated street play, and "brutal" sports were replaced with "rational," "morally useful" recreations centered on church, school, and civic organizations, which collectively promoted middle-class values and the vitality of the nation.

Formidable middle-class advocacy of rational recreation materialized only when social conditions deteriorated to crisis proportions. Nineteenth-century condemnations, which deplored the "unhealthy constitution, the pulmonary men and women, the childless wives, the dyspeptic men, the puny forms, and the bloodless cheeks" that characterized the American urban population and were destined to become the unsolved riddles of twentieth-century recreation, fell largely on deaf ears.[44] In an 1869 issue of Frank Leslie's *Illustrated Newspaper*, a story titled "Playing Baseball Under Difficulties in the Streets of New York" noted that "there are few places in the city proper of sufficient size to permit ball-playing; but as the young fellows will play, they choose the most convenient streets, and fire away in spite of all travel and obstruction."[45] Such observations were taken more seriously during the 1880s and 1890s, as America's urban population quadrupled and the problems with urban space became much more complicated. Only when the drive for public playgrounds was well under way did, in fact, genteel social reformers infuse the movement with theories about play, child development, and uplifting social behavior, in a direct reaction to the industrial and urban growth in the late-nineteenth-century period.[46]

This transformation in middle-class cultural values and strategies was clearly manifested in the ambitious campaign for a "Safe and Sane Fourth," spearheaded by the PAA. In this campaign, launched in 1906 under the auspices of the Russell Sage Foundation, middle-class holiday reformers expressed deep concern over the fires, vandalism, and the large number of fireworks casualties (first exposed by the *Chicago Tribune* in 1899, and later cited by the American Medical Association in 1903) on the nation's birthday. Ironically, the sanctioned "guns and bonfires" that John Adams recommended in 1776 for the "Great Anniversary Festival" became the focus for reform early in the twentieth century, and the "Safe and Sane" movement became the principal vehicle for national collective action.[47]

The growth of large urban areas, widening class divisions, and the influx of un-Americanized Eastern European immigrants allegedly threatened the nation's foundation. The effort to remake the Fourth on the playgrounds, advocates insisted, provided meaningful lessons in Americanism for workers and immigrants, whose noisy, hedonistic behavior subverted the day's true significance. Thus, urban reformers seized the opportunity for changing the image of the Fourth as a means of reviving civic consciousness, which, many believed, had been eclipsed by larger social and economic transformations. As such, the "Safe and Sane Fourth" movement was primarily an exercise in educating youth and immigrants in the basics of American citizenship; the reformers included metropolitan school superintendents, parks commissioners, heads of athletic organizations, social settlement workers, clergymen, military officers, police commissioners, and an assortment of socially prominent private citizens.[48]

More important than the sheer numbers of supervised playgrounds and holiday participants was a growing ideology of play. As Stephen Hardy has argued, within this philosophy lay "the groundwork for altering the concept of sport so that it would become a tool by which urban youth, the victims of a fragmented community, might fit into the new industrial order."[49] Leaders insisted that Fourth celebrations provided an opportunity for people to play together and, simultaneously, gain instruction about American democracy and their duties as citizens. Joseph Lee, of the PAA, believed that, through supervised play and organized team sports, youth loyalty could be redirected toward the larger community. In Lee's opinion, the playground's greatest function was to transform a "budding loyalty," which was being "perverted by lack of opportunity," into the foundation of the future citizen."[50] Similar progressive sentiments can be found in the writings of Lee F. Hanmer, associate director of child hygiene at the Russell Sage Foundation, who believed that sports and recreation were important antidotes to the "evils" caused by mass immigration and the subsequent decline of patriotic consciousness.[51]

The "Safe and Sane Fourth" movement did more to promote the ideology of holiday sports than any other factor during the early twentieth century. A survey of the *Readers' Guide to Periodical Literature* confirms this: Between 1882 and 1928, of the 173 articles published on the Fourth of July, nearly half scrutinized the "Safe and Sane" movement. Moreover, the successful promotion of a safe-and-sane Fourth spilled over into the organization of other, less-established holidays, like Columbus Day. Prior to World War I, nativist prejudice against Italian Americans underlaid popular resistance to the holiday as a legitimate American tradition. Middle-class reformers like Everett Mero (secretary of the Citizens' Public Celebration Association) saw the opportunity to transform Columbus Day into an occasion for "promoting American nationalism among all the peoples who come hither from every corner of the earth."[52] With the leadership of the Boston Public Recreation League and the financial support of various municipal organizations, an impressive parade, comprised of 30,000 representatives of 26 nationalities, marched through the streets of Boston on October 12, 1912. Floats prominently displayed the city's athletic activities: One float featured 100 men performing calisthenics; another presented a basketball game in progress; and another, gymnastics. Several floats were devoted to children's athletics; and several yacht and canoe clubs marched as well.[53]

In just six years, the sporting Fourth program of the Playground Association was effectively nationalized. In 1913 the *New York Times* reported that safe-and-sane athletic events were held on every available field and park in New York from early morning until sundown. Some 35,000 competitors from the Public Schools Athletic League, various YMCA branches, intersettlement athletic leagues, church athletic leagues, the Military Amateur Athletic League, the Amateur Athletic Union, and parochial schools participated in full-scale track-and-field competitions in 25 parks throughout the city. "Nearly every nationality was seen in action at some point" by 40,000 spectators, the *New York Times* reported.[54] In Chicago the 1913 Fourth occasioned an Olympic-like festival which featured a wide array of amateur ethnic athletic clubs, fraternal societies, church groups, and municipal teams. For example, the Slavonic program was a typical display of ethnic solidarity in its commemoration of the adopted nation's Independence Day; mass Sokol-society calisthenic drills done by hundreds of boys and girls preceded similar exhibitions by the adults, and were interspersed with choruses. At the conclusion, athletes and spectators joined together in singing the national anthems "Where is My Home?" and "Ho, all you Slavs!" Prior to organized municipal recreational activism, such culturally pluralistic sporting spectacles were unprecedented in American urban history. One commentator concluded that American playgrounds for children were "the distinctive contribution of this country to the world's play."[55]

The 1909 Springfield (Mass.) Fourth parade became the preferred model for subsequent patriotic festivals across the nation. Springfield's effort to discourage the use of fireworks was carefully organized to make the day "a true civic festival" and "an object lesson in the value of human liberty and the meaning of American citizenship."[56] Several days before the Fourth, a detailed program was distributed to every home in the city. According to William Orr, a member of the executive committee of the International Athletic Association (representing secondary schools), America's communities did not know how to enjoy themselves in a safe and rational fashion. The masses "have yet to learn how to express adequately, and with good taste, patriotic fervor and enthusiasm for humanity."[57] Orr and other cultural leaders strove to teach "the great deeds of the [founding] fathers and the present duties of the sons," through the use of historical tableaux, pageantry, mass singing, games, and athletic contests.[58] The morning parade in Springfield featured local militia groups; Buffalo Bill Cody and his Wild West Show; a battalion of teenage boys, who were dressed in red, white, and blue, and armed with wooden guns; grammar-school children portraying key moments in colonial and revolutionary history; and ethnic marchers displaying "the characteristic qualities of each people and the contribution each was making to American life."[59] The afternoon was, however, devoted to athletic contests and river sports.

Despite its considerable success and popularity, the "Safe and Sane Fourth" movement was not without its critics and internal contradictions. The socialist press lampooned the manner in which middle-class reformers banned fireworks for the masses but allowed state and federal authorities to showcase "acceptable" cannons, gun salutes, and military drills in the official celebrations throughout the country. According to the *Chicago Daily Socialist*, "the youth of the city were shown how men are fed and clothed and housed and trained to kill men who are also trained and fed and housed to kill other men"; the "sane" celebrants of Chicago's "civilized spectacle" yelled, cheered, ate junk food, and talked about the "thrilling life of the soldier."[60] Having already published several advance articles prior to the Fourth, the *Chicago Daily*

Socialist now prominently featured a front-page cartoon strip, titled "Its Going to Be a 'Sane Fourth,'" depicting three scenarios: the Jack Johnson-Jim Jeffries fight, called "the celebration at Reno"; military manuevers, called "the celebration at Chicago"; and children playing with fireworks—"savage celebrations elsewhere."[61] Chicago's militaristic display was not exceptional. For example, Portland, Maine (population 58,000), featured U.S. Army, Navy, and National Guard displays throughout the city, and hourly cannon and gun salutes by naval reserve ships anchored in the city's harbor.

Dominant Fourth celebrations also exposed the contested, contradictory racial dimensions of American society that were simmering underneath the festive mood. Indeed, conflict materialized along ethnic, class, and racial lines. The most telling Fourth event was the 1910 Independence Day fight between the Irish-American Jeffries and the African-American Johnson—billed as the fight of the century, between the "Hope of the White Race" and the "Negroes' Deliverer." Never before had a sporting event generated greater press coverage and public controversy. The fight polarized the race issue in American society along lines consistent with the dominant national ideology—and appropriately, it was staged on the Fourth. Mediated by visions of racial supremacy, morality, yellow journalism, and commercialization, the bout reflected central concerns in the national psyche. Promoted by the czar of modern American boxing, Tex Rickard (who offered a hefty $100,000 purse), the fight was witnessed by numerous celebrities and women and popularized boxing as a legitimate American sport.[62]

Before and after the fight, renowned writers, collectively, penned nearly 150,000 words per day on the fight. The contest, according to the *New York Times*, was a foremost topic of conversation among all sorts and classes of people. The *Chattanooga Times* hesitantly admitted that "the interest of the majority of the ninety-odd millions of people in these United States is centered on Reno today."[63] Most newspapers caricatured Johnson as a gorilla, or as a dim-witted, watermelon-eating, dialect-speaking brute whose victory would increase the physical contact between "proud" black men and white women. Billed as a contest for racial supremacy, popular commentary treated Johnson's resounding victory as "proof" that the best fighter came from "the lowest and least developed race."[64] A national wave of race riots occurred in the wake of the news of Johnson's victory.

Historian Leonard Sweet has written that Fourth celebrations traditionally provided an opportunity for blacks to reconstruct the genius of ancient Africa, recount the heritage of slavery and suffering, nourish a sense of racial solidarity, and honor African-Americans' contributions to American society. In the words of black clergymen and journalists who chronicled the July 4, 1910, Johnson-Jeffries prizefight, the event in which Americans had chosen to honor the nation's birthday revealed more of "the psychology of the American people in their attitude toward the Negro" than all the tomes ever written on "the negro problem."[65] President Theodore Roosevelt's European tour and his African hunt were relegated to less-eye-catching columns in the *New York Times* than the fight. As Sweet writes, if judged by the numbers of people assembled at Times Square, "the affair eclipsed in importance the 1908 presidential election"; clearly, this was due to the monumental stakes involved in the contest: "the supremacy of the white or black race."[66] The *Chicago Daily Socialist* documented the race riots that occurred (after Johnson's victory) in Washington, D.C., New York, Omaha, Little Rock, Houston, Roanoke, Pittsburgh, Louisville, Philadelphia, Wilmington, New Orleans, St. Louis, Atlanta, Cincinnati, Baltimore, Kansas City, Pueblo, and Shreveport. Moreover, three days after the fight, the *Chicago Daily Socialist* published a front-page article—"Crude, Y' Know, Says England"—about the way that leading London newspapers deplored these race riots. Critiquing the racist Anglo-Saxon tendencies, the *Chicago Daily Socialist* revealed that the British excused the riots when talking to other Europeans, who were less aware of the race situation in the United States, where "Americans are the trustees of the predominance of the whites over the blacks, and we believe that they will be true to the trust."[67] Failing to recognize Britain's own complicity in upholding global white supremacy, the *London Globe* noted, in an editorial: "It is against human nature to expect the whites to accept the negroes' insolent assertion that Johnson's victory established the superiority of the blacks without instant protest."[68]

WARTIME CELEBRATIONS AND THE AMERICAN GOLDEN AGE OF SPORTS

Although the first two decades of the twentieth century exposed deeply entrenched contradictions in American holiday athletics, the World War I context absorbed many of them into a national sporting culture.[69] In 1918, with an Allied victory in sight, many American commentators characterized the Fourth's celebration as the most glorious one since the 1876 centennial. "The democracy of the world has adopted" the American Fourth, said the *Springfield Republican*, a newspaper that predicted that July 4, 1918, would stand in world historical annals as the day that marked the cementing of "a brotherhood among many peoples, as they have joined to insure the world's safety and progress and freedom."[70] *Current Opinion* noted that "our national fete-day became an international fete-day celebrated in many lands—England, Italy, Brazil, Peru, Uruguay, Chile, Argentina, Nicaragua, San Salvador, Algeria, Australia, and New Zealand."[71] New Yorkers watched as 75,000 marchers of 42 different nationalities "snap[ped] their hyphens" and "toss[ed] away the unworthy pieces" in a grand 10-hour "melting pot" parade along Fifth Avenue.[72]

The throngs of ethnic Americans were accompanied by sailors, marines, shipyard and munitions workers, Red Cross nurses, YMCA and Salvation Army employees, and patriotic spokesmen. "Fifth Avenue," as one writer asserted, "never saw so much history concentrated in a single parade. Any humble citizen who learned the lesson of each float and each banner could go home last night and write a complete history of the world, from Alexander the Great down to Woodrow Wilson."[73] In Philadelphia, an equally spectacular parade was accompanied by thousands of immigrants, who signed a pledge of allegiance to their new country; this was appropriately staged at Independence Hall. Simultaneously, President Woodrow Wilson made a well-publicized pilgrimage to Mount Vernon, along with representatives of every group of foreign-born citizens, to present wreaths at George Washington's tomb.[74]

In New York that day, 50,000 boys, girls, amateur athletes, and military personnel participated in a wide array of games and athletic contests in New York's most spectacular safe-and-sane celebration, coordinated by the Mayor's Committee on National Defense. "Athletes of all sizes and abilities," the *New York Times* reported, "gave their efforts for this, the city's great athletic and patriotic fixture."[75] The athletic carnival attracted 250,000 spectators. The most noteworthy performance of the day was Villar Kyronen's record-breaking three-mile run (of 15 minutes, 31 seconds). In Chicago, despite a comparable public athletic program, the war spirit set the tone for the leading athletic contests: An American Soldiers' Athletic Carnival was organized as an honorary departure extravaganza for the Eighty-sixth Division, stationed at Chicago's Camp Grant. The proceeds of the holiday celebration were used to purchase athletic equipment for the soldiers still fighting on the Western Front. Following a four-hour military parade through a Chicago suburb, the games began, featuring some 50,000 officers and enlisted men. In Portland, Maine, Danish residents celebrated the Allied victory, under the direction of the Jacob Riis Patriotic League, with morning and afternoon track-and-field contests at Odd Fellows Park.[76]

Such wartime safe-and-sane Fourth spectacles quelled the criticism of old-guard critics of holiday sports, like Louis Weinberg, who asserted in 1915 that "without a common feeling revealing itself in beautiful forms, all gatherings of people tend to be vulgar, foolish or stupid."[77] Citing the various nationalistic and royalist traditions of pomp and pageantry, he speculated that to "make a community group a social unit inspired, aroused and thrilling to a common emotion requires the presence of a common tradition."[78] Clearly, the unifying traditions in the wartime era were found in sports and athletic contests, even though skepticism persisted.

The search for meaningful, unifying traditions in post–World War I American society bedeviled a *Chicago Tribune* editor, who said that "we are growing impatient with and weary of the flapdoodle and rhetoric and eagle screaming of the Fourth of July, and [want] something tangible." Reminding his readers that the Fourth "is no surface affair," but the "symbol of an ironbound nationalism," the *Tribune* editor quoted from a patriotic homily of former President Roosevelt, who had stated, in no uncertain terms, that America has room for only "one flag, one language, and one loyalty."[79] On the fourth day of official prohibition, amid widespread cries for "100 percent Americanism," and with virtually every law-enforcement agency in the nation readied for rumored anarcho-socialist demonstrations," such editorial sentiments evoked sympathetic attention. Given the troubled state of the postwar union, it is no coincidence that alongside the patriotic editorial was another story—occupying equal space—titled "The Big Fight."[80]

The 1919 heavyweight boxing bout between Jack Dempsey and Jess Willard dominated the nation's sports pages for weeks prior to the showdown.[81] After Willard's defeat of Jack Johnson in 1915, white fighters and promoters had unofficially closed the door on black boxers so as to make the sport more attractive to middle-class male and female spectators. Willard, rich from previous ring earnings and shrewd investments in Oklahoma oilfields, was badly out of shape; his opponent—a scrapping, smallish fighter—hailed from the working-class environs of Manassa, Colorado. On July 4, 1919, in Toledo, Ohio, Dempsey, a half-foot shorter than Willard and 60 pounds lighter, decisively seized the heavyweight crown from Willard, whose puffy white skin stood in sharp contrast to the tanned, hardened body of the younger challenger. During the first round, Dempsey knocked Willard down seven times. At the bell, Willard staggered to his corner, with both eyes nearly closed, his jaw broken, his cheekbone split, and one ear permanently injured. Willard's trainer threw in the towel at the end of the third round. Dempsey then reigned as champion for seven years, taking on every credible challenger in sight, except African-Americans.

Like the Johnson-Jeffries bout nine years earlier, Dempsey's victory in the heavyweight championship bout was front-page news throughout the country and created a bona-fide national sports spectacle.[82] Due, in no small measure, to the success of the 1919 July 4 bout, boxing became the most widely publicized postwar sport. Illegal in many states before the war, boxing became a legitimate American spectator sport after the military demonstrated its value in training soldiers in hand-to-hand combat, and in relieving the monotony of daily drill exercises. American soldiers learned to adapt basic boxing techniques to bayonet fighting and, at the same time, became avid converts to the sport. After the war, the military successfully campaigned against state laws that had prohibited prizefighting. State legislatures began to reverse their prohibitive statutes, and even conservative newspapers like the *New York Times* weighed in on the side of boxing by characterizing the sport's opponents as "a half a century behind the times."[83]

The Dempsey-Willard bout was a precursor for the most widely publicized American sporting event of the 1920s. Prominently staged at Philadelphia's Sesquicentennial Exposition, before 125,000 spectators, the Dempsey–Gene Tunney championship fight was followed by millions of radio listeners. At ringside sat movie stars Charlie Chaplin and Norma Talmadge; baseball superstar Babe Ruth; businessmen Andrew Mellon, Charles Schwab, and Vincent Astor; and governors, mayors, cabinet secretaries, and elegant society women. The *New York Times* published 75 articles pertaining to the fight during August and September alone. The *Times* noted that of the many fine exhibits on the Philadelphia fair grounds, "none will be remembered longer than the [Dempsey-Tunney] gladitorial combat; ... after a century and a half of independence it can be regarded as a crowning glory of our civilization."[84]

The spectacle dramatized social tensions in American culture. Tunney's handsome features, social eloquence, and honorable military service represented middle-class respectability. In stark contrast, Dempsey, barely literate, and with shady underworld associations, emerged from rough-and-tumble, working-class environs in Colorado. As Elliott Gorn writes, Dempsey's early life "evoked the discord of poverty, labor violence, and exploitation"—issues that resonated with many boxing fans.[85] Such social contrasts between the two boxers became part of the national folklore, and were interpreted by men and women alike. For instance, a female journalist had previously heard that prizefighting took place in "brutal halls of bloodlust" connected with "sordid treacheries of dope and fouls and 'framing' in furtive sports clubs"; but on closer observation of the Dempsey-Tunney fight, she thought that a "cloud of governors, a bevy of millionaires, the Pennsylvania Boxing Commission and the Liberty Bell" guaranteed that "the air would blow clean on the fight."[86] In her mind and by her description, boxing had arrived as a legitimate sport and a spectator event. The bout's connection to national commemoration further legitimized boxing in the American psyche. The significance of the fight was not lost in the *New York Times*, which ran a three-tiered front-page headline the following day and devoted seven full pages (of the first section) to the contest![87]

The nation's sesquicentennial was commemorated on the Fourth in grand sporting style. President Calvin Coolidge secured the cooperation of state and municipal officials, along with patriotic, civic, and business societies, to ensure that American Independence Week (June 28–July 5) rededicated the "ideals and principles which brought the Republic into existence." Thousands of Philadelphians watched the Fifty-first Annual National Senior AAU Track and Field Championships, which featured leading American, Canadian, and European athletes. The *New York Times* framed its July 5 edition with a special front-page headline: "July 4 Celebrants Crowd All Beaches in a Record Crush." In fact, nearly 1.5 million beachcombers flocked to Coney Island, Atlantic City, Asbury Park, and Long Island, producing record traffic congestion in the New York metropolitan area. About 25,000 spectators watched as their Giants lost to the Boston Braves in 11 innings at the Polo Grounds. The Giants-Braves game, and the seven other major league contests that day, testified to the growing acceptance of Sunday sports. Elsewhere in New York on the Sabbath, 18,000 saw American bicycle champion Willie Spencer defeat the premier Italian cyclist, Orlando Piani, at the Velodrome, and 2,000 watched the Canadian cricketers play an all-star New York squad. In all, the *New York Times* devoted three full pages to Fourth-of-July sports, covering events in Chicago, Louisville, and throughout New England.[88]

SUMMARY

Celebrations of the Fourth have always been occasions for public discourse and for dramatization of the themes, values, and beliefs of American nationalism. From the earliest days of the nation, Fourth celebrations strengthened the principles of liberty and solidified the bonds between elites and the masses, through noncontroversial, self-evident displays of national unity. The intentionally vague and generic quality of newspaper commentary of eighteenth-century celebrations firmly established the holiday and its patriotic traditions in the national imagination.[89] Since the late nineteenth century, sports provided alternative, but increasingly important, forums for Americans to express a variety of social ideals in action. The appeal of sports and games among the American masses reinforced, in particular, the ideals of patriotism and democratic participation—despite the pervasive, often discriminatory class, race, ethnic, and gender dimensions of organized sports and the hierarchically structured parades that presented selective versions of social relationships. The ritual of playing the game made people feel part of the American community.[90]

While Thanksgiving sports promoted the amateur ethos through myriad collegiate football spectacles, many Fourth sporting contests promoted professionalism. Although playground reformers crusaded for middle-class respectability—sobriety, restraint, sexual propriety, and rational recreation for young people—they often coopted the large-purse, working-class tradition to combat and remove the evils of drink, rowdiness, and gambling associated with sports. In this endeavor, middle-class sports reformers' efforts were supported by the local and national media. Moreover, unlike Thanksgiving, Fourth celebrations became much more explicit Americanization and community-uplift exercises. The difference can be partially explained in terms of the way in which Fourth celebrations were infused with the ethos of civic boosterism. Cultural leaders exuded urban pride at integrating social opposition, by emphasizing cross-class solidarity in the face of economic and political competition from outside their cities. Yet, as Hardy maintains, playgrounds and municipal recreation were different things to different people. Their expansion early in the twentieth century signaled local lobbies' insistence on protecting their environs from the suffocation caused by urban development. "But at their core," Hardy writes, such activities "stood as evidence of an active and conscious attempt to shape and reshape the physical and social dimensions of community" life.[91]

Despite their successes, middle-class reformers only partially transformed Fourth celebrations. Workers and immigrants were not passive bystanders. While many embraced some of the reformers' visions and values, they regularly adapted the official events to suit their own alternative interests. Had working-class and immigrant traditions completely succumbed to preferred bourgeois sensibilities, the Fourth would have ceased to be a day of popular celebration. Rather, by the early part of the twentieth century, the explicit class nature of Fourth celebrations merely reflected the developing national sporting culture. As Lynn Abrams concludes in her study of industrial capitalist German popular culture during the same period, the attempt by employers and cultural authorities to control working-class enjoyment in patriotic festivals was "repeated over and over again across the entire recreational spectrum; the principles underlying the imposition of the national, patriotic festivities had their equivalent in the bourgeois uplifting nature."[92] By the 1920s, American citizenship, as dramatized in Fourth celebrations, had effectively been redefined as a leisure, sporting lifestyle. National icons and myths still captured the public imagination, but were drowning in the pool of consumerism. Automobiles enabled people to take excursions to out-of-town sports events, beaches, and amusement parks; and subsequently, main-street celebrations and patriotic pageantry were canceled or curtailed. No longer did people dabble in separatist recreational events on the nation's birthday, or waver on its preferred, official celebration; they embraced "the promise of American sport."[93]

WAR GAMES AND NATIONAL VITALITY

SEVEN

SPORT, FITNESS, AND NATIONAL PREPAREDNESS

PREWAR PHYSICAL DEGENERATION

Pre–World War I discussions about physical fitness and national preparedness had a profound influence on the American sporting culture. Despite the fact that sports and a vigorous athletic lifestyle pervaded the nation's cultural landscape, distinguished statesmen like Elihu Root believed that the country, on the eve of a world war, had lapsed into a lethargic state of "indifference and sluggish patriotism."[1] Influential cultural, political, military, and educational leaders concurred with Root's diagnosis and recommended that sports be recast so as to rejuvenate national vitality. Patriotic preparedness advocates linked the strenuous life to a larger crusade, which involved combating working-class dissent; schooling unassimilated immigrants in American ways; increasing labor productivity; stoking nationalist sentiments among the native-born, and reviving the dominant WASP cultural authority at a critical historical juncture. Like other progressive contemporaries, they, in the words of Mark Dyreson, "transmuted their particular historical values into what they thought were universal values, and prescribed their brand of athleticism as a tonic for producing a classless, harmonious civilization."[2]

Numerous groups and organizations—including federal, state, and local government bodies—waged a campaign for Americanizing a diverse, multicultural population. Initially, reformers differed sharply over the best means to achieve national unity, with businessmen and ultranationalists stressing the need to acculturate immigrants immediately and completely—and, if necessary, by force. Others, particularly the social-settlement reformers, urged a gradual approach to create an interdependent society based on Anglo-American values that the immigrants themselves would help shape. In time, these two views merged, with the latter position virtually disappearing by late 1917.[3]

The movement was anchored at the national level by the National Americanization Committee (NAC). Frances A. Kellor, the committee's director, personified the dominant middle-class's gravitation to the cause. With a distinguished background in social work, Kellor, by 1915, let her nationalist inclination take charge over her earlier progressive sympathies. Under her leadership, the NAC moved in the direction of forced assimilation; and her book *Straight America* argued that military preparedness, industrial mobilization, universal service, and Americanization were all essential to a more vital American nationalism. Exploiting the language of interdependency to protect their own class interests, Americanization advocates sought to transform mostly rural peasants of dubious national loyalties into contented and reasonably rewarded American workers who would accept the elite leadership of American society.[4]

Organized middle-class women began supporting Americanization efforts in the 1890s, but their numbers increased appreciably after the sinking of the *Lusitania* in May 1915, when the Daughters of the American Revolution and the national General Federation of Women's Clubs joined the campaign. Historian Gayle Gullett has explained that women joined the Americanization movement because the fundamental question of this campaign—defining American citizenship—merged with the basic issue they sought to resolve—namely, how to transform women's citizenship. Women reformers, Gullett writes, rejected women's traditional citizenship status, which relied on the male head of the household to speak for all the female members of the family, and, instead, "called for a full and independent citizenship for women that included the ability of women to speak for themselves, shape state policy, and change American nationalism."[5] Women reformers extended citizenship to their immigrant sisters, but demanded that the newcomers learn, from them, how to become acceptable women citizens by remaking their homes into American homes. Thus, "women progressives placed themselves, white, middle-class, native-born, at the center of their model for the female citizen and made the citizenship of all women distinct from that of men."[6]

As World War I expanded women's role in American society, it also divided them. Some women's organizations, like the women's section of the Navy League, supported American military involvement. Alice Howard, a longtime suffrage leader, organized a women's division within the government's Committee of National Defense, under which women in local chapters provided a range of volunteer services in support of the war effort. Other women had campaigned for American neutrality and sought to counter preparedness sentiment. The Woman's Peace Party, founded in 1915, attracted a large number of suffragettes who insisted that Americans must not enter the war. Even after the United States declared war in 1917, some women, such as Emma Goldman, continued to voice their opposition to the conflict.[7]

Cultivating an American physical culture emerged as a national topic when surveys demonstrated that degenerative diseases increased 85 percent between 1880 and 1910; and that prior to 1915, nearly half of Navy and Marine applicants were rejected due to "physical causes." Another survey, published in the *American Physical Education Review* confirmed that 81.7 percent of the male applicants for the U.S. Army, during the years 1915–16, were rejected![8] A growing cadre of health experts, social commentators, and journalists feared that the impending war would only exacerbate the deleterious urban effects on American youth. One writer for *The Independent* observed the "narrow, sunken chests and projecting shoulder blades" commonplace among city dwellers. "Physical America is beginning to shrink," he wrote, concluding that "the wear and tear of modern life is telling on us."[9] Many people agreed with the dire predictions of Elmer Rittenhouse, president of the Life Extension Institute, who speculated that "unchecked physical decline" portended "a weak, soft-muscled, flimsy-fibered people for the defense of the Republic and the perpetuity of the race."[10] A Cincinnati physician emphasized skill, strength, and endurance as the principal qualities necessary for efficient citizenship, and judged that "happy [is] the nation whose citizens have achieved such a high degree" of these skills during their school life; and who, as a result, "will never falter before the service or sacrifice which their country may demand of them at any time.[11]

Moreover, by the early part of the twentieth century, decades of declining birthrates and poor health among middle- and upper-class white women caused serious alarm among wealthy Americans of Anglo-Saxon Protestant descent. With cries of "race suicide," they predicted that immigrant populations and the "prolific poor" would soon overwhelm white, native-born "racial stock." Fears of population decline among the "better classes" called attention to the low maternity rates of educated women. While many scientists continued to dwell on the dangers that athleticism posed to the female reproductive system, historian Susan Cahn has observed that some eugenicists looked to sport as a way to increase the fertility, and improve the physical vigor, of middle- and upper-class American women. "A reinvigorated motherhood," Cahn writes, "would enable the 'fittest' race to expunge weaker strains and take its natural place atop the social order."[12]

Theodore Roosevelt interpreted these trends in apocalyptic terms. Unsurpassed in his mastery of the sermonette on strenuous sports, Roosevelt proclaimed that "all the great masterful races have been [strenuous] fighting races, and the minute a race loses the hard fighting virtues," it loses its "proud right to stand as the equal of the best."[13] Roosevelt's unwavering belief in militarism, imperialism, and racial destiny was, however, at odds with the spirit of fair play as espoused in the amateur ethos. "Without force," he wrote, "fair dealing usually amounts to nothing."[14] As Michael Oriard recognizes, this tension between force and fair dealing "lay at the heart of the Progressive Era mentality so thoroughly in its representative man."[15] Roosevelt's favorite metaphor, "the game [of life]," reconciled these contradictions by effectively denying them.[16]

Such bellicose statements typified a prominent group of the educated, northern bourgeoisie that avidly embraced the cult of strenuosity, in the belief that, in the words of an *Atlantic Monthly* editor, a "delicate, indoor genteel race" might receive a "saving touch of honest, old-fashioned barbarism."[17] Jackson Lears concludes that, to a bourgeoisie that was feeling enervated and fearful of lower-class unrest, "the worship of force presented paths to class revitalization."[18] Not surprisingly, their support for combative sports like football and boxing, and for outdoor life in general, reflected upper-class tendencies to equate organized athletics with strengthening the "imperiled" national spirit, and with stoking the country's vitality on the eve of World War I.

The militaristic character of American society was perceptively analyzed by philosopher William James. "If war ever stopped, we should have to re-invent it to redeem life from flat degeneration," James thought.[19] Resisting an urge for a pacifist, socialist critique of the "bestial side of the war regime," he nevertheless questioned the "sacramental" belief that militarism was anything but a "transitory phenomenon in social evolution."[20] James argued that societal militarism, while dominant, need not be the only path toward class conciliation. Observing that the "intensely sharp competitive preparation for war by the nations is the real war," he interpreted the contemporary preparedness activities (including sports and athletics) as the "moral equivalent of war."[21] Five years later, after the "guns of August" had been fired, Paul Phillips, an Amherst College professor of medicine, linked James's philosophical insights to the wartime preparedness crisis. Noting how eminent educators and philosophers agreed that the "survival of the fittest" among "the civilized nations" no longer required the "ultimate test of life and death as in lower animals but [could] be nourished on more peaceful competition," Phillips posited football as a worthy surrogate through which "the barbaric man rises."[22] If during such moments of controlled barbarism, educators and sports officials could "engraft ideals, the thought of a great cause, of injured humanity, of fairness to his opponent, so that in the strain of competition, these higher motives control, [then the athlete] is being trained for a citizenship which will be strong, but peaceable, generous, magnanimous."[23]

When read one way, James's identification of sport as "the moral equivalent of war" revealed the heart of the sporting republic's creed. Aggression represented the most basic and most powerful human energy, responsible for the destruction of war; yet, sport also rendered the source of war—the aggressiveness of human nature and the need to dominate—"moral" by regulating and tempering warlike energies. Dyreson writes that while sport indeed lessened the chances for civil conflict and controlled the warlike impulses of the masses, it also, to a world which saw some wars as necessary, "kept the martial flame kindled and prepared the nation for what the global interventionists and jingoists insisted would be inevitable outbreaks of hostilities."[24]

Such concerns were consistent with American sentiments on the eve of the Spanish-American War. The patriotic propaganda of that war, according to historian Nina Silber, rested on "the foundation of the reunited, military patriotism of northerners and southerners, especially the white people of the two regions."[25] Northerner journalists and politicians, in particular, reflected the changing state of gender relations and the turbulent social order, and fashioned a new ideology that connected patriotism to the dominant sense of manhood that appealed to all regions. Cultural leaders who came of age and assumed power during the 1890s thought that aggressive athleticism was, in Silber's words, "manlier and offered a counter to the vigor of the new woman and angry worker."[26]

Militarism and aggressive athleticism met emotional needs and relaxed social tensions outside the urban bourgeoisie. The strenuous life and martial values were also championed by veterans of the Civil War; the sons and Daughters of the American Revolution; Boy Scouts organizers; antiimperialists; and, even occasionally, persons who called themselves "pacifists." During wars, social conflict was temporarily submerged in the rhetoric of national unity. But certainly, the bourgeoisie benefited much more from such conditions did than the working and immigrant masses, who regularly challenged the status quo of hierarchies and unequal social relationships. Preparedness advocates imagined that bourgeois society could remain intact, provided it was properly imbued with a rekindled martial spirit. They advocated moral reform within existing frameworks of bourgeois values and organized capitalist relations, rather than urging fundamental social change. Moreover, since war and sport were regarded as principally male-defining activities, preparedness advocates had no intention of including fit females in the American military machine.

The more public-minded militarists, like Brooks Adams and Alfred Thayer Mahan, urged war as a path to overseas economic expansion as well as moral revival. The most prominent militaristic spokesman in turn-of-the-century America was probably Oliver Wendell Holmes, whose speeches and correspondence were punctuated with bellicose statements. In a Memorial Day address at Harvard in 1895, Holmes proclaimed that "war's message is divine. . . . Some teacher of that kind we all need." Extolling the virtues of dangerous, manly sports like polo, Holmes estimated that "if once in a while a neck is broken, it is a price well paid for the breeding of a race fit for headship and command."[27] As Lears argues, the roots of the modern American empire were intertwined in economic interests and cultural crisis. He writes, "The desire for foreign markets drew strength from elite fears that America was becoming a sterile, stagnant nation," which clarifies how the acquisition of an empire "reinforced the self-confidence, the economic power, and the cultural authority of a bourgeoisie which felt threatened by internal decay and lower-class discontent."[28] During an age of "democratic" warfare, American elites realized that a major war would have to be fought by the masses *with their consent*.

These aims pervaded Major General Leonard Wood's article, "Heat Up the Melting Pot." Wood, the most outspoken preparedness leader, argued that if America were to become a "real" melting pot, its institutions must produce a "homogeneous mass which in cooling will not harden in layers which separate under pressure."[29] Fusing his Harvard Medical School training with his military experience as first commander of the Rough Riders, Wood had a moral perspective that held that martial discipline developed citizens physically and politically. Rigorous training taught immigrants and workers "appropriate" bourgeois habits of self-control and punctuality, respect for order, and an obligation to do national service; but it would also produce stronger physiques, and a people who thought "more in terms of the nation and less in those of the individual or the small community."[30] Wood's sentiments were representative of leading progressive intellectuals, who, according to historian Jean Quandt, relied on the appeal of local communities' sense of belonging, in efforts to foster a sense of national community, and its embodiment in institutions. The exigencies of a world war intensified this reform impulse, welcoming wartime national collectivism.[31]

The relationships among sport, physical training, and national preparedness had a precedent (which will be discussed in the next chapter).[32] "There is a rank due to the United States among nations," George Washington stated at America's inception, "which will be withheld, if not absolutely lost, by the reputation of weakness. If we desire to avoid insult, we must be able to repel it; if we desire to secure peace, one of the most powerful instruments of our rising prosperity, it must be known that we are at all times ready for war."[33] Placing Washington's call for a ready nation within a historical context that stretched back to ancient Greece, Major Palmer E. Pierce concluded that "history shows that a healthy state requires a healthy citizenry"; just as soon as "the inhabitants of a country begin to degenerate physically," he observed, "decay sets in all around and the existence of the state is endangered."[34]

What is important here is the way in which particular historical values were transmuted during the World War I period. Physical-education teachers and military officers brought the respectability of their establishments to the job of promoting American preparedness. Both groups were concerned that modern civilization had eroded Americans' sturdy impulses, and that future military success could be guaranteed only through national unity. Both believed the nation's moral and physical well-being depended on strict, disciplined programs that focused on athletic fitness.[35] From the 1914 outbreak of the war in Europe to the entry of the United States in the conflict in 1917, military officials and physical educators advocated sports to physically regenerate a nation on the brink of participation. Both camps invoked conceptions of citizenship that were rooted in the response to fundamental changes in American society and the threat of heretofore unprecedented global warfare. Although both groups strove toward similar ends, they occasionally differed over ideology, strategy, and goals. Proponents prophesied that standardized physical-education programs and military service would promote patriotism and respect for law among the nation's youth; temper the likelihood of class violence; and improve the health and physiques of American young men. This historic alliance was critical in raising public awareness about national preparedness, which ultimately affected America's entry into the war and the quality of its troops.[36]

PHYSICAL EDUCATORS' ROLE IN THE PREPAREDNESS DEBATE

The importance of the public school in bringing together the children of diverse ethnic strains and teaching them the responsibilities of U.S. citizenship had been recognized from the earliest days. What was new in the progressive period was heightened self-consciousness and a greater sense of urgency about these matters. But agreement that the schools played a vital role did not imply agreement about how they should go about it, or the spirit in which it should be undertaken. To a racialist like Elwood P. Cubberly, a well-known educational historian, the schools' task was "to imprint in their [the immigrants'] children, so far as can be done, the Anglo-Saxon conception of righteousness, law and order, and popular government; and to awaken in them a reverence for our democratic institutions and for those things in our national life which we as a people hold to be of abiding worth."[37] At the other extreme, John Dewey prescribed cosmopolitanism as the correct "nationalizing" policy for the public schools. It was the responsibility of the schools, he told the National Education Association in 1916, to "teach each [ethnic] factor to respect every other, and . . . to enlighten all as to the great contributions of every strain in our composite make-up."[38]

Physical educators assumed an increasingly prominent place in American academe during the first two decades of the twentieth century. The growing prominence of physical education as a legitimate discipline reflected the widening interest in athletics not only in higher education, but also at the high school level. *American Physical Education Review* surveys between 1905 and 1907 indicated that large numbers of high schools fielded major-sports teams (78 percent played football; 65 percent, baseball; and 58 percent, basketball).[39] Physical educators sought to broaden the objectives of their profession to accommodate them to the general aims of public schooling. The overwhelming trend of early-twentieth-century physical-education programs was away from gymnastics and toward athletic-sports instruction. This tendency reflected not only the growing popularity of men's intercollegiate sports, but also the new educational psychology of John Dewey (and others), who believed that children should learn from experience. This new approach to education openly encouraged extracurricular activities, use of playgrounds, special-education programs for the disabled, and closer school-community contacts.[40] Thus, by arguing that well-constructed physical-education programs promoted health, fitness, and wholesome leisure as well as social and moral attributes, Timothy O'Hanlon concludes, "physical educators contended that their subject contributed to the overriding goal of efficient citizenship."[41]

Although preparedness discussions were couched in male rhetoric and manliness metaphors, the majority of American physical educators were, in fact, women—nearly 80 percent of physical-education graduates in 1903 were female; and two-thirds of the public-school physical educators included in a 1905 survey were females.[42] Female physical educators thus played an important role in defining health in both disciplinary and preparedness terms. Unlike men's physical-fitness and athletic programs, which stressed competition and strength, women's programs, like Wellesley's (under the direction of Lucille E. Hill), instituted anthropometric exams to gather evidence about the compatibility, even symbiosis, of mental and physical education for women. Their notions of "able-bodied womanhood," according to historian Martha Verbugge, emphasized the degree of fitness necessary to fulfill one's duties in the modern world—a view shaped by their Victorian upbringing, their specialized training at the Boston Normal School of Gymnastics (under the direction of William Dudley Sargent), and their experiences as working women. The result, according to Verbugge, was "a mixture of unorthodox and conventional ideas, laced with some ambivalence."[43]

This mix of orthodoxy and conventional opinion represented a compromise between able-bodied womanhood (and fit motherhood) and masculine athleticism. Susan Cahn recognizes that female physical educators embraced conventional wisdom in that they warned that lack of exercise left women unfit for motherhood, but also counseled that overextension would dissipate female reproductive resources and, as a result, the race. In this traditional vein, most agreed that athletic games should be modified to suit society's refined sensibilities and the unique physiology of women. Early-twentieth-century physical educator Elizabeth R. Stoner believed that the purpose of physical education was to make students better mothers and fathers, citizens, and professionals, and to make them fit for industrial life. Vigorous exercise and athletics, Stoner thought, fostered "promptness of decision, courage, initiative, judgment, good sportsmanship, fairness, enthusiasm, leadership, and the sense of responsibility."[44] Stoner's peer, Ethel Perrin, added the "ability to respond to commands, originality, poise, resourcefulness, and self-appraisal."[45] Physical education, as the means to these ends, was nothing less than training in good citizenship—perfectly consistent with the male-preparedness pronouncements.

Female physical educators' statements might have reflected an accomodationist strategy. Male sports hegemony was never absolute, but had to be constantly negotiated as the "new woman" emerged early in the twentieth century. Middle-class women negotiated a feminine sporting identity within the collegiate physical-education environment, by consenting to the ideology of sports patriarchy, while simultaneously using the space allotted them to challenge the terms of their own subordination. The single-sex structure of separate male and female physical-education departments provided female physical educators with substantial freedom to promote their own views of fitness. They hedged their strategies so as not to challenge prevailing male-dominated social norms too radically, for to do so threatened their limited autonomy.[46] Cahn suggests that "strict adherence to middle-class standards of feminine behavior smooth[ed] the road to a secure position within academe, [while], at the same time, producing a generation of physically fit, socially acceptable young women who had been spared the harmful effects of masculine sport."[47] Lilian Drew, however, challenged orthodoxy when she concluded that most Americans understood that "strength and weakness both physical and mental" were not "definite attributes" of either men or women, but applied to both sexes. Drew and others, citing the fact that one-third of World War I draftees were declared physically unfit, aimed to debunk the myth that all women were weak and that men were, by their biological nature, strong. Despite certain gender differences, early-twentieth-century views from the physical education community were remarkably consistent with the goals and ideology of the broader preparedness movement.[48]

The custodianship of dominant American values during the early part of the twentieth century was a primary responsibility of the academic community.[49] Prior to U.S. military involvement in World War

I, Jesse Feiring Williams, Columbia University physical educator, expressed the growing anxiety that the nation lacked both the physical preparation and a "unity of expression, a definiteness of ideals," necessary for warfare. "As civilization has more and more deprived man of the need to fight," Williams wrote, it has subsequently provided "more time and attention to the games which are substitutes for war."[50] Williams's concerns were representative of a generation of physical educators who thought that organized sports would cultivate the positive and spiritual habits needed for the defense of the national spirit. Physical educators linked their professional aspirations to calls for the nationalization of American education. An *Outlook* writer indeed called for greater federal educational resources, comparable to those of other Western industrialized democracies; he emphasized the "evident need for the development of National unity and National resolution and National idealism in America."[51] Just as the German nation was made in the schools, he claimed, "the American Nation will be made in the schools."[52] In particular, Davenport believed that the nation should ensure the highest level of physical education for every boy and girl, and their mastery of nationalistic ideals. Many educators, like Charles Prosser, differentiated between inculcating patriotism and rationally addressing national needs. Prosser observed that "a super abundance of sentimental patriotism" that had little effect on daily conduct could not be taught by precept and song"; rather, it was best taught through ritual: "the repetition of acts" in "drill, discipline, and training."[53] Educators and school administrators believed that sports and athletics provided the surest solution. Physical education and sports, they claimed, offered lessons in social discipline and cooperation that were no less valuable for citizens in an industrial society than for future soldiers.

Physical educators sought to extend their expertise to students of all ages, classes, and athletic capabilities. Their emergent goals reflected the increased attention to socialization throughout professional circles in early-twentieth-century America. "If preparedness must be had," Dr. E. H. Arnold insisted, at a meeting of the American Physical Education Association in 1916, "it will prove inefficient unless it prepares the people as a whole, all the people, certainly both sexes."[54] Many physical educators, school administrators, and social commentators agreed, so long as school sports were made more accessible to all students, rather than to a select few.[55] Arnold's historical survey of school athletics and physical education confirmed, moreover, that most of the attention had been directed toward training college students, rather than toward the larger majority of primary- and secondary-school pupils. Given the fact that most students would never reach college, Arnold recognized that the great majority of children and youth were systematically neglected.

Therefore, the goal must be "the establishment of habits of physical activity in [the] people," so as to make them "fit for life."[56]

Many people openly questioned the national commitment to physical fitness and called for new strategies. Some wondered whether the existing system, modeled on "imported" German and Swedish gymnastic and calisthenic drills, was adequate for training a heterogeneous mass society. Allegheny College physical educator C. E. Hammett confessed that for "nearly a half century we have been forcing our youth to practice artificial movements, devoid of any element of pleasure"—these appeared to have been "scientific," but were "deplored" by the participants themselves.[57] Buoyed by scientific breakthroughs, spokesmen sought a "system of physical training that would be a genuine expression of the national character."[58] Educators found such a national athletic tradition in sports like basketball and football, in which "young men would voluntarily spend an hour and bathe themselves in sweat," but would also "develop heart and lungs, employ all the muscle groups," stimulate the sweat glands, and cleanse the system.[59] Enthusiasts like Hammett discovered that competitive sports developed courage, initiative, judgment, and force, which would be fundamental assets on the battlefield. An emergent, "distinctly *American* system of physical training," which combined physical prowess with character building, solved "the most difficult problem" of the physical educator: that of "interesting his pupils, and developing a race of virile young men."[60]

Astute observers noted the significance of the time frame necessary for developing a fit and fighting generation. Calls for national, government-subsidized programs proliferated during the years 1917–19. F. L. Kleeberger, of the University of California, thought that preparing a physically fit, athletic nation could be best promoted through the creation of a Department of Physical Education, which would coordinate its efforts with the Bureau of Education and the War Department. Physical training would be federally subsidized and nationally standardized. Kleeberger proposed a comprehensive physical-education program that would embrace "physical drill, free play, and highly organized athletics in the development of real physical efficiency in our entire citizenry."[61] Such a system would effectively meet the "fighting objectives" of health, morale, skill, strength, and endurance, but it would also stop Americans from being "a race of vicarious sportsmen."[62] Moreover, a system of "government gymnasia and athletic fields throughout the entire country would help to solve the problem of labor unrest," by providing a replacement for "the present poor man's club," and by providing mental, moral and physical development.[63] Paradoxically, such proposals embraced a form of government socialism as an antidote to working-class unrest.

As long as the debate about preparedness revolved around the issue of developing a physical, sporting nation, little dissent arose. However, as the issue became politicized, in regard to how colleges and high schools could best prepare young men for combat, physical educators broke ranks with the military establishment and its elite allies, who proposed compulsory military training. Thus the old nationalistic question of military training, dormant since the Civil War, came to the fore once again. Most educators and administrators believed that sports-infused physical-education programs offered a means of fostering preparedness without encouraging "lockstep militarism." Physical education and sports, they claimed, offered lessons in social discipline and cooperation that were no less valuable for citizens in an industrial society than for future soldiers.

At the 1918 National Education Association meeting, physical-education hawks urged the introduction of military drills into elementary schools. With the outbreak of war, physical-education programs in many schools and colleges were set aside for military training, in spite of opposition by the organized physical-education profession and some military leaders. Yet, military opinion on the matter was not uniform. Secretary of War Newton D. Baker, for instance, declared that military drills made little contribution to immediate military strength, and that vigorous, disciplined physical training (particularly sports and athletics) furnished excellent preparation for either civil or military usefulness. Most physical educators stuck to their guns and occasionally exploited such statements as Baker's to promote their cause for athletic preparedness.[64]

Taking their cues from Dudley Allen Sargent, the most influential physical educator in the land, opponents of military training feared that such instruction would produce sinister, "Prussian-style militarism," and suggested, alternatively, that physical education and athletics would usefully prepare young people for military attributes (as well as efficient citizenship), without encouraging a militaristic mentality.[65] A graduate of Bowdoin College and Yale Medical School, Sargent served as director of Harvard's Hemenway Gymnasium for 40 years, during which time he exerted a greater influence on the development of physical training in American colleges and schools than any other individual.[66] It was in the rigor of competitive games, not in the "tin soldierism" of the drill field, where boys developed courage and a spirit of competition and self-sacrifice. "What America needs," concluded Sargent, "is some way of providing more athletic students and fewer student athletes, some way of providing more soldierly schoolboys, instead of schoolboy soldiers."[67]

Some physical educators took more direct aim at what they perceived were the inherently undemocratic, authoritarian premises that underlaid military training. Edward Degroot believed that advocates of high-school military training were merely "misguided amateurs in the field of military science," who practiced a blatantly undemocratic art that "eliminated the weak and endeavor[ed] to make the strong stronger." "Let us give our boys a definite, scientific physical education," wrote Degroot, director of physical education for San Francisco's public schools; the processes of this education are inclusive, rather than exclusive, and aim to "bring up the average of health, vigor, skill and endurance—eliminating no one, no matter how weak."[68] Looking to the playgrounds, gymnasiums, and athletic fields, rather than to uniforms, arms, and rifle ranges, the nation that guaranteed a well-directed athletic life to its children "will not want for virile, patriotic defenders."[69]

Others sounded explicitly progressive tones. Making it clear that the progressive reform movement would not be threatened because of hyped wartime exigencies, Edward Devine proclaimed that "social and industrial justice is a live issue"—fundamental elements in national preparedness.[70] More than shrill patriotism, strong militaristic capabilities, and virile bodies, "our strength depends upon our intelligence, our physical and mental vigor, our standards of living, our social spirit."[71] Thus, in Devine's estimation militaristic proposals for soldier training that did not simultaneously embrace liberal education, social hygiene, industrial justice, and improved standards of living were not worthy of consideration.

Physical educators' spirited defense of inclusion, individual free will, and democracy was not, however, without its own contradictions. American physical educators were caught between a rock and a hard place since they were, at the time, trying to establish a degree of professional closure; they had not totally shaken off the more rigid and dogmatic elements of the old gymnastic systems (which were inclined toward militarism, and which, in the case of the Ling system, grew out of a specific military context); and they had not yet come fully to terms with sports in their emergent curriculum. In this sense, leading physical educators fell into the conundrum of trying to develop a pedagogically sound approach to preparedness—in accordance with Dewey's principles—in the face of sports' rising popularity in American culture, and in the face of national concerns for a high level of national fitness.

THE MILITARY'S CONTRIBUTION TO THE DEBATE

Early-twentieth-century discussions of military sports stressed the importance of building "physical manhood." One writer for *Harper's Weekly* maintained that the government's use of sports was designed to "turn sergeants and privates into all-round men," and that the spirit of sports in the military "meant more than merely improving the physique of the soldier."[72] The writer suggested that "Uncle Sam has not encouraged athletics for amusement"—sports brought together officers and enlisted men, "showing the *esprit de corps* which both feel toward manly pastimes."[73]

Army and Navy officers shrewdly turned to the language of progressivism to reinforce their arguments for reform and mobilization.[74] Maintaining close intellectual and political ties with elites with whom they shared a similar social outlook, military officers, like progressive educators, described the armed services as schools for American citizenship. Major General William Carter feared that not only had citizens' mental and physical readiness for combat declined, but that it had also become increasingly difficult to discipline young men due to the "decadence of respect of the rising generation for those in authority."[75] Henry L. Stimson echoed Carter's sentiments. Surveying the "failure" of the volunteer system throughout American history, Stimson insisted that only during a time of crisis is "the attention of the people concentrated upon the question of national defense"; otherwise, during peacetime, "our citizens have habitually paid no attention to even the most self-evident necessities of military policy."[76] Although Carter acknowledged that "Americans are warlike when aroused," he advocated new legislation that would require "instruction in the duties of citizenship," and mandatory militia service prior to the exercising of the right to vote, so as to qualify "the rising generations to better comprehend and rightly value the generous liberty vouchsafed to them by the Republic."[77]

A group of vocal and energetic officers promoted summer military camps as a way to produce needed citizen soldiers. They believed that universal military training, infused with a heavy dose of sports and athletics would not only train American young men in the "soldierly values" of obedience, citizenship and combat; it would also usefully restore order, unity, and patriotism to the country.[78] Class schisms would be bridged at training camp; the experience of military training "would build better men, physically as well as morally, and would refashion superior workers who were mature, obedient, and productive."[79] Preparedness advocates promoted sports training and competition as an essential means of creating a pattern of conduct, shaping a habit of success, and producing an unconscious but deep commitment to military victory.[80] Shortly after the war, Captain John Griffith cogently spoke to these aims. "Men look upon fighting as a game," Griffith wrote. "An assault is a big game; . . . practice on the range resolves itself into a contest between men, platoons, and companies. War is a game in which the individual may have to fight as an individual . . . or as a part of the machine."[81]

General Leonard Wood, heading pressure groups in support of defense legislation, and heading a model training camp at the Plattsburgh (N.Y.) Barracks, was the preparedness movement's major spokesman for universal military training (UMT). Wood and his allies believed that UMT would promote the work ethic, lower the crime rate, Americanize the immigrant, teach responsibility to the nation's youth, and bind together all classes of society into a common purpose. According to *The New Republic*, UMT would serve as an instrument of "social hygiene," a sort of "moral equivalent of war."[82] By the time of America's entry into World War I, military officers and their spokesmen had nearly two decades' experience in their advocacy of UMT—a cooperation that clearly revealed the degree to which military officers both shared the values of civilian reformers and sought to use the federal government to ameliorate the conflicts in American society.

Despite the sometimes contradictory alliances and the often dubious mass support, schools, colleges, the military, and patriotic leagues employed sports for the preparedness cause. This loose but formidable network, for instance, took the form of a "physical regeneration movement" launched by the National Security League, under the leadership of Walter Camp. The league worked through leaders in school athletics and various teacher associations to promote standardized nationwide exercise programs. Brought to national attention by Connecticut Congressman John Tilson, Camp's physical-regeneration plan was adopted by the Boy Scouts, the Girls' Patriotic League, and more than 300 mayors of major cities throughout the country.[83] The preparedness debate, the use of sports during the war, and the successful effort to integrate sports into the physical-education curriculum—these had the effect of solidifying and reinforcing the association between athletics and the conception of effective citizenship that had begun to emerge two decades earlier.[84] The widespread use of athletics during the war fueled the demand for standardized physical-education programs.[85] The ideological and strategic aims of physical educators, university administrators, military officials, popular intellectuals, and sporting enthusiasts fused around their near-consensual advocacy of football as the emergent national sporting pastime.

A VISION OF UNITY

World War I preparedness efforts produced a vision of an united national community, but in truth, national unity was a widely contested phenomenon. Prior to April 1917, American sentiment was overwhelmingly neutral and pacific. Even those persons who believed, in a vague way, that the United States had some interest in the European settlement were reassured by the knowledge that the Allies were bound to win. The ideological basis of American neutrality, in fact, rested on the total separation of American and European interests; and as historian Arthur Link recognized, no catastrophe occurred before April 1917 to shock Americans out of their complacency or compel them to seriously calculate the consequences of German domination of Europe.[86]

Nevertheless, a consensual version of American readiness was dramatized on the streets of New York on May 13, 1916, when a Citizens' Preparedness Parade featured representatives of all the trades and occupations in the city. For over one month, the *New York Times* devoted regular, high-profile news coverage and commentary to the impending celebration. In late April, Mayor John Purroy Mitchel issued a proclamation that called on all businesses to display the American flag during the parade. Prior to the event, 60,000 would-be marchers were refused entry due to stringent municipal limitations imposed on parades. Mrs. J. Borden Harriman and Mrs. Theodore Roosevelt, Jr., leaders of the battalion of Independent and Patriotic Women, responded to criticisms of the possibility that upwards of 20,000 women would march; the *New York Times* had characterized these women as "undeluded by the cowardly sentimentalities of pacifism, women who will teach their children that 'life is dear only as it is held cheap by the side of honor and of duty.'"[87] In a letter to the *Times* editor, Mrs. Harriman and Mrs. Roosevelt noted, "Surely it is better and far more benefiting the democratic ideals of this country, to make no distinction, and to have all women who wish to show their belief in preparedness march together on a basis of equality."[88]

The parade was more a public-relations event, staged by the New York elite to push a hesitant Congress to an aggressive stance, than an actual demonstration of the city's military resolve. The patriotic *New York Times* spoke on behalf of the "unmistakable demand of the people" for preparedness, and branded the antipreparedness faction as a "small minority" whose "evil influence wanes daily."[89] Billed as the "greatest civilian marching demonstration in the history of the world," the parade made good on its promoters' forecast, by marshaling 135,683 participants, and lasting 12 hours.[90] Despite earlier predictions that 10,000 to 20,000 women would take part, only 3,287 did so. The parade's 105,674 male marchers, and the more than 16,000 additional National Guardsmen and bandsmen, dramatized the gendered dimension of the early preparedness crusade. The following day, the *New York Times* devoted three full pages to the parade, and published a list of the participating organizations. In several enthusiastic editorials that heralded New York as the leader of patriotic preparedness, the *Times* shamelessly praised the city's efforts, and the example it set for other cities throughout the country.[91]

SUMMARY

During the progressive era, Dyreson argues, the idea of a vigorous, sporting republic played an important role in the revitalization of a middle-class culture, and in the adjustment of a bourgeois frame of reference to America's relationship to global rivalry and modern corporate capitalism. "A middle-class ideology of strenuosity, designed in part by an elite [national] leadership," he writes, "shaped political dialogue and expectations, reinvigorated the cult of civic virtue, and placed athletic physical culture in a central position in modern American life."[92] As such, the preparedness debate, in particular, provided a suitable forum for a wide range of individuals and groups to engage in the invention of an American sporting tradition. Harvard professor L. B. R. Briggs spoke to this tradition: "An athlete would be expected to accept, out of hand, the sporting challenge of old-fashioned warfare—to lead made cavalry charges, to match himself like a knight of old with every newcomer as man against man."[93] But unlike previous wars, World War I portended the unprecedented horrors of not just camp monotony, but of the machine gun and gas bomb. In this respect, Briggs surmised that "intercollegiate athletics are brought face to face with the problem that confronts America. . . . Like America, they will stand or fall according as they choose between luxury and simplicity, trickery and integrity, the senses and the spirit."[94] The comparisons between sports and war depended on the similarity with which they linked primal force to sophisticated management—in other words, on the tailoring of nature to the precepts of the new managerial society. It was this meld of natural, primal power with organization and rationality that William James identified as crucial to American culture, in his approval of sports as a "moral equivalent of war." As Mrozek ascertains, "In a society impatient with metaphysics, rationality and social control were the substitutes for contemplation; and for James, as for others, sports assumed a role in linking contemplation and action."[95]

American wartime "unity" was, in reality, enforced by repression, and not simply the result of the wartime rallying effect. The federal government quelled dissent; persecuted minorities and aliens; attacked socialists and labor organizations; coercively marketed war bonds; censored the media and personal speech; and arbitrarily arrested and imprisoned American citizens. All told, as many as 10,000 Americans faced imprisonment, suppression, deportation, or mob violence during the war. This sordid wartime history was presaged by President Wilson, who, prior to the war, stated that if Americans entered the war, "they'll forget there ever was such a thing as tolerance. To fight you must be brutal and ruthless, and the spirit of ruthless brutality will enter into the very fiber of our national life."[96] In this sense, the physical-preparedness crusade diverted public attention away from the repressive impulses inherent in modern wartime activities and to the more altruistic, humane promises of American sports. Ultimately, the preparedness debate created a critical context for the invention of a modern American sporting culture. Sports were, indeed, more than mere amusement; they were vital to a nation participating in an unprecedented, international military conflict.

EIGHT

THE WORLD WAR I AMERICAN MILITARY SPORTING EXPERIENCE

Between 1917 and 1919, the armed services made sports and athletic training a central component of military life. Millions of enlisted men participated in organized sports at domestic training camps and behind the front lines in France. On playing fields at home and in Europe, "narrow-chested clerks made three-base hits on the same ball teams with college athletes and lean-visaged philosophers learned how to use their fists," boasted *Scientific American*.[1] At Camp Devens, one could see Walter R. Agard, a former Amherst College Greek instructor, spar with light-heavyweight champion "Battling" Levinsky (aka Barney Lebrowitz). "Uncle Sam has created not only an army of soldiers," one writer observed, but "an army of athletes."[2] Sportswriter Albert Britt suggested that every high school and college construct memorial lists alongside the playing fields—these would bear the names of the soldier athletes who had made the ultimate sacrifice. "Let their memory be an inspiration," Britt declared, "to bodily fitness and clean, hard sportsmanship for every boy who comes after."[3]

This vision linking sports and the military was a newly invented early-twentieth-century tradition. The goals, ideology, and organization of the modern American military were profoundly transformed by the Spanish-American War experience. A younger, reformist generation of uniformed officers assumed a moral commitment to the soldiers' welfare and used sport initially to combat desertion, alcohol use, and the lure of prostitution. Immediately after the Spanish-American War, the Navy pursued, as one of its central departmental policies, "all proper means to preserve the health of the ship's crews."[4] As one officer explained, this new orientation represented more than merely a growing awareness of physical fitness, but the knowledge of how to achieve it: "There is no better way to make a good sailor," he explained, "and at the same time a loyal and true man to ship and country, than [through] these athletic contests."[5] Maintaining close intellectual and political ties with other preparedness advocates, civilian military officials embraced sport as the most efficient means to cultivate national vitality, citizen-

139

ship, and the martial spirit. Military training, infused with a heavy dose of sports would not only train American men in the soldierly values of obedience, citizenship, and combat, but would also usefully restore class schisms, social order, unity, and patriotism to the nation. In fact, military sport, historian Donald Mrozek observes, reaffirmed the Victorian concept of manliness by adding a supportive "encrusting" set of rhetoric, rituals, and symbols.[6]

Despite its relative brevity, the war was the most intense conflict the nation had ever fought. Between the declaration of war and the November 1918 armistice, the United States drafted nearly three million men, transported two million of them to Europe, and lost over 100,000 in combat. By 1918, the cost per soldier was almost seven times that of the Civil War in constant dollars. The war prompted the first significant use of the corporate form of organization by Washington, and the first use of direct federal aid to state and local governments—driving a vigorous fiscal-military process of government centralization and growth consonant with an increasingly complex American society and economy. The federal government regulated industry, imposed price controls, and intervened in labor disputes. Adjusted for inflation, annual per-capita spending during the war was nearly twice as high as in either the Civil War or World War II. Indeed, federal outlays soared from $713 million in 1916 to $1.95 billion in 1917; $12.7 billion in 1918 and $18.5 billion in 1919—a 2500 percent increase in less than three years.[7]

The success of military sport during World War I surpassed all expectations—the war experience accelerated the development of a national sports culture. As a visible, respected state institution, the military was ideally suited for popularizing the causes of physical vitality and the American sporting spirit. Millions of men were introduced to sports for the first time and became converts to the cult of strenuosity. Contrary to many prewar speculations, the war did not destroy America's sporting spirit, but, to the contrary, did much to legitimize it in the public mind, both at home and abroad.[8] Shortly after the war, all West Point cadets were obligated not only to engage in major sports, but also learn how to teach them. The mission of spreading American sport throughout Europe culminated dramatically in the Inter-Allied Games of 1919. Never before had so much information about a sports event reached so many publications in so many countries. The War Camp Community Service recreation programs, initiated during the war, multiplied thereafter, and focused national attention on government-funded sports for the masses. The war experience brought sports into high-school and college curriculums. Between 1919 and 1921, 17 states passed physical-education legislation. More important, the military legitimized boxing (illegal in most states before the war) and football (restricted primarily to the collegiate scene) as bona-fide American spectator sports.[9]

NINETEENTH-CENTURY VIEWS OF SPORT
AND MILITARY PREPAREDNESS

The American armed forces had traditionally tolerated sports as useful diversions from the rigors of military life. In 1777, George Washington urged his officers to promote exercise and vigorous amusements among the troops. As an heir to Protestant suspicions of play, as a believer in republican self-restraint, and as a leader of the revolutionary struggle, Washington insisted that recreations be *useful*. During the Civil War, soldiers, on holiday reprieves, competed in baseball, boxing, wrestling, horse racing, shooting matches, and foot races.[10] Some battalions held gala sports days. Troops embraced the young game of baseball with particular enthusiasm, playing both previously arranged and pickup games. According to baseball lore, a game between two New York infantry squads at Hilton Head, South Carolina, supposedly attracted 40,000 spectators, but in truth, the game's attendance figures were probably closer to several thousand. Nevertheless, the game, and many other such exhibitions, popularized the New York game, sparking a postwar explosion which made the sport the national pastime.[11]

Camp and field programs rewarded toughness, punished squeamishness, and created working conditions that freed up distinct periods of leisure time. Boxing became the other sport of choice. In 1861, American men rushed to war with vivid memories of the Thomas Sayers-John Heenan prizefight, and, within a military context, began to make explicit connections between boxing and warfare.[12] Elliott Gorn astutely captures the ring's symbolism behind Civil War battle lines. "Just as the ring brought momentary symbolic order to the chaos of working-class streets," Gorn writes, "so the drama of fistfighting between equals presented a poignant if fleeting alternative to the ghastliness of battle."[13] Sports like boxing became more than just the "moral equivalent to war"—they supplanted it because, according to Gorn, "the violence of play offered meaning denied by the anarchy of war."[14]

The young, inexperienced U.S. military establishment, in the years immediately following the Civil War, did not embrace sports and amusements in any serious way until the 1890s. During these years, the military was fighting the Indian wars in the West. Men stationed at remote posts relaxed through improvised amusements such as conversation, card playing, and drinking. The diary entries of Private B. C. Goodin (C Troop, First Cavalry), stationed at Fort Grant, Arizona, illuminate how he was on a mounted pass for half a day, and spent the rest of his off-duty time reading in his quarters, strolling, playing cribbage, singing and dancing, attending an entertainment in the post chapel, and playing jokes on his comrades in the barracks. But daily mounted drills, saber exercises, revolver practice, and line skirmishes exacted a heavy physical toll on the enlisted men. Most cavalrymen were avid horse racers and often staged competitions against rival companies, civilians, and Indians. In regions where wild game was plentiful, the men sometimes went on extended hunting trips, and a few were ardent anglers. In some companies, athletically minded officers organized baseball games, track-and-field contests, and boxing matches. But, as the historian of the nineteenth-century U.S. regular Army explains, "few post commanders were personally interested in promoting an athletic program"; without any sort of servicewide athletic policy, "organized sports were engaged in as much as a method of gambling as for the enjoyment of the game."[15]

During the 1890s, attitudes toward sports shifted from a toleration of them as diversions to tentative experimentation, as the fledgling American military integrated athletics into the daily regimen of soldiers and sailors to bolster military fitness.[16] As the new century neared, military-sports advocates turned to the strenuous lifestyle. In 1890, Lieutenant C. D. Parkhurst began a series of essays on "The Practical Education of the Soldier," claiming that physical training should precede all specifically military activities, with the exception of battle itself. Parkhurst argued that exercise in the gymnasium and on the playing fields, fusing vitality, traditional deference, and republican virtue, would bring the soldier to a level of "quick and unthinking obedience to orders."[17] Lieutenant Colonel A. A. Woodhull claimed that the James Corbett–John L. Sullivan prizefight demonstrated the importance of speed and agility, and suggested that boxing elevated "primitive force" that harnessed athleticism to military ends.[18] Like their progressive physical-educator peers, military officials believed that cutting-edge physical-fitness programs would achieve specific, desirable results, underscoring, in the words of Mrozek, sport's "entry into the duty-day and into the obligation of 'service' of the American soldier."[19]

The growth of military sports was closely tied to its introduction into the military academies during the 1890s.[20] Prior to 1890, athletics at American military academies were obstructed by stringent restrictions, dismissive official attitudes, and a fundamental lack of functional organization. During these dark ages, for instance, tennis had to be played by cadets in dress coats, and a cadet was punished for having two buttons of his coat unbuttoned while he was playing baseball! The first Army-Navy football game, played on December 1, 1890, was the important watershed in military athletic history. On that memorable day, an impromptu gridiron was roped off on the West Point quadrangle. The Midshipmen's quarterback used nautical terms for signals, like "clear deck for action," while the Cadets employed military commands such as "right front into double line."[21] By 1895, the military academy's sports program had become competitive with established eastern colleges like Harvard, Yale, and Brown. Renowned sports authority Caspar Whitney proclaimed his unabashed admiration for the West Point and Annapolis football programs, just six years after their initiation, when he wrote that "no other institution in the United States more thoroughly demonstrates the *mens sana in corpore sano* in college sport than these two." Army Captain Richmond Davis received letters—from Alaska, Cuba, Puerto Rico, and the Philippines—about the annual Army-Navy game, which elevated the brotherhood of both services to a fuller appreciation of the good old song: "May the services united ne'er sever; But hold to their colors so true; The Army and Navy forever; Three cheers for the Red, White, and Blue." Several years later, sportswriter Arthur Ruhl commended the Army-Navy game as a pleasant occasion, when "these strong and eager young men might meet and receive this greeting of each other's courage and resource and pluck, and not have to wait for it until those sterner games when they shall have to fight together."[22]

The military academy's sports program was buttressed by a mandatory system of physical training conceived by Lieutenant H. J. Koehler, physical director at West Point for 17 years. Koehler's program developed muscular fitness, and, more important, produced a heroic spirit. For 45 minutes each day, cadets systematically performed a battery of stretching and strengthening exercises. In all, by the turn of the century, just a decade after the legitimization of sports at the service academies, one-half of the cadets took active part in at least one sport; and the other half were enthusiastic spectators and rooters. In 1902 the *Army and Navy Journal* asserted that companies that excelled in athletics would also excel in military duty. Cavalry officer Edward L. King cited the "marvelous results" that the Eleventh Cavalry Regiment obtained when officers added athletics to military instruction. Recruits changed, according to King, from being "soft and awkward" into men who were "rugged, hardy, active, and tough as nails."[23]

The popularity of military baseball, between the Spanish War and World War I, owed much to the deepening inroads of the game at West Point, where the basic attitude apropos of baseball had changed from one in which authorities regarded games as an amusement, in which the outcome mattered little, to one in which a "must-win spirit" was instilled.[24] As the battle fleet continued to expand, so, too did baseball at the Naval Academy. Under the aegis of the Navy Athletic Association, the academy fielded a varsity baseball team along with teams in fencing, football, and rowing. Beginning in 1901, the highlight of each baseball season at Annapolis was the final game, with West Point (staged, alternatively, at each academy)—the series was dominated by the Annapolis team. Under the tutelage of professional coaches, Annapolis not only won most of its games with West Point; it also proved its mettle against leading college teams.[25]

Military veterans sometimes worked to spread their newfound sporting gospel and combative exercise programs in civilian society. During the 1890s, for instance, General George A. Wingate promoted military

training in New York City's public schools—an effort which culminated
in the creation of the New York Public Schools Athletic League in the
early years of the twentieth century.[26] With 100,000 members, the league
claimed to be the "largest athletic body in the world." The league's transformation of Wingate's military-training program won it more recruits
when musket swinging, marching, and fencing were supplanted by running, jumping, basketball, and a wide range of other athletic activities.
The Illustrated Sporting News speculated that "the patriotic idea will not
be in the least minimized" by such a change.[27] Through athletics, the
students would acquire basic combative virtues; and the influence of
the military would intermix with civilian leadership.

During the first decade of the twentieth century, the American armed
forces moved from tentative experimentation with sports to an unquali-
fied acceptance of them as essential elements of a soldier's responsibility. A new generation of West Point and Annapolis graduates chafed at
the prospect of suppressing labor disputes and fighting Indians, and
campaigned for a modern, national military. Despite its brevity, the
Spanish-American War established the United States as an imperial
power, whose newly acquired colonies in the Philippines, Guam, Puerto
Rico, and Cuba prompted ambitious political and military leaders to
double the size of the American armed forces.[28] The new military professionals worked to combat the endemic rate of desertions, and widespread vice among enlisted troops; and, in general, to make military life
more attractive. Organized sports were central components in this
mission.

Military officials assured doubters that sports and fitness activities
made good military sense in developing needed physical endurance.[29]
Early-twentieth-century discussions of military sports stressed the importance of building physical manhood. A writer for *Harper's Weekly*
maintained that governmental sports sponsorship was designed to "turn
sergeants and privates into all-round men," and that the spirit of military sports "meant more than merely improving the physique of the
soldier."[30] The writer suggested that "Uncle Sam has not encouraged
athletics for amusement," but for the way in which it produced the esprit
de corps among both officers and enlisted men—a "rebuilding process
which begins when the soldier puts on the blue or khaki."[31]

Despite the growing importance of physical fitness in military circles, its spread was highly erratic. Major R. L. Bullard, superintendent
of athletics at Fort Snelling, estimated that the military's use of athletics
and physical training in 1905 was "unsystematic, irregular and uncertain in the extreme."[32] Standards varied from post to post, and were
dependent on initiatives of particular officers; spectatorship overshadowed mass participation. Lieutenant Colonel Charles Richard thought
that physical training should be systematized throughout the year.
According to him, officers needed to arrange monthly schedules as their

"tastes dictate or their stations afford."[33] Lieutenant Edmund L. Butts, the leading advocate of military sports prior to World War I, declared that athletics "should not be made a fad, but a part of [a] soldier's training, and should be properly subordinated to the more important and practical duties of a soldier's life."[34]

WORLD WAR I AND THE MATURATION OF MILITARY SPORT

The military moved to systematic application of sports during the 1916 border crisis sparked by the Mexican Revolution. Anticipating a full-scale war, the United States twice invaded Mexico, and twice more mobilized the National Guard along the border.[35] Without recreational facilities, there was nothing to compete with the saloons and red-light districts patronized by the 100,000 American troops. When reports of widespread venereal disease reached Washington, D.C., early in 1917, War Secretary Newton Baker sent Raymond Fosdick, of the Rockefeller Foundation, to investigate the situation.[36] Fosdick's report confirmed the brass's worst suspicions. Promptly thereafter, he was appointed head of the War Department's Commission of Training Camp Activities, which coordinated activities of other welfare organizations, such as the YMCA, the Knights of Columbus, and the Jewish Welfare Board, to ensure a wholesome environment for the enlisted men. Secretary Baker later admitted that military athletics were "an attempt to occupy the minds of the soldiers and to keep their bodies busy with wholesome, healthful, and attractive things, . . . to free [the body] from temptations which come to those who are idle."[37]

Shortly after the April 6, 1917 declaration of war, General John J. Pershing summoned YMCA experts for managing Army cantonments. The YMCA combated vices with sports and leisure activities.[38] A YMCA worker noted that "whether men found themselves in populous cantonments or in lonely guard posts, in [a] city or in [a] forest lumber camp," the Y's "right to service was unquestioned."[39] About 75 percent of American troops spent time in one of 32 training camps managed by the YMCA. The Y's war efforts were organized by Dr. John McCurdy, of the YMCA College at Springfield, a leader in the field of physical education, who had been chairman of the National Commission on Secondary Education and was a former editor of the *American Physical Education Review*.[40] As the official representative, in France, of the War Department's Commission on Training Camp Activities, McCurdy also undertook, in September 1917, the duties of YMCA athletic director for the American Expeditionary Forces (AEF). Shortly thereafter, McCurdy hired Dr. James Naismith, a Kansas University physical educator, the inventor of basketball, and a former National Guard chaplain, to head the Y's Hygiene Department. Naismith prepared literature and lectures, infused with Christian principles, on the importance of clean living, social hygiene, fighting efficiency, and the sporting spirit. National organizations, like the American Library Association and the Recreation Association of America, along with churches, social clubs, and fraternal lodges, supported the Y's mission with patriotic fervor.[41]

The YMCA assigned physical-fitness directors to each of the 32 military camps to coordinate the Y's sports mission. The directors sought to develop the abilities of average soldiers, rather than polishing the skills of star athletes.[42] Comprehensive sporting programs were established, featuring intercompany and barracks baseball and basketball leagues. YMCA sponsorship of athletic programs emphasized activities of military significance, including cross-country runs, obstacle races, and military dispatch relays—all done in military uniform.[43] According to an official spokesman, the first important promotional event for military mass athletics was a pentathlon held on Memorial Day in 1917, at an officers' training camp at Fort Niagara; 25 men from each company— 375 in all—competed in the standing broad jump, relay races, medicine-ball throwing, 100-yard dashes, and a tug-of-war. This spectacle awakened thousands of mostly college men to the value of mass athletics. The Y's muscular Christian mission was enthusiastically endorsed by the military brass and a host of sports commentators as well.[44]

Many observers feared that U.S. involvement in the European war would wreak disaster on the American sports scene. Collegiate and professional athletics, the argument ran, would fall into entropy, as promising stars would be whisked off to the European front to fight the Huns. Such doomsday prognoses ultimately foundered after the successful incorporation of sports in the military. During the summer of 1917, War Secretary Baker publicized his support of military sports in numerous newspaper and magazine articles. When approached by Verne Lacy, chairman of the Western Association of the AAU, regarding the track-and-field championships scheduled for St. Louis in August 1917, Baker demonstrated his support by granting furlough privileges to athletes participating in an event whose proceeds went to the Red Cross.[45] In October, the War Department and the YMCA radioed the result of the World Series, between Chicago and New York, to the enlisted men in Honolulu, Manila, the Panama Canal zone, Paris, Koblenz, Vladivostok, and Constantinople—an endeavor repeated in 1918 and 1919.[46] Baker, like many other contemporaries, understood the vital connections between sport and Americanism.

The official actions of the military brass were bolstered by confident appeals in the popular media. When some colleges and universities considered discontinuing athletics, due to the War, Washington and Jefferson College football coach Sol Metzger presented evidence that indicated that not only did athletes exceed the regular student body in military enlistments, but that athletic programs usefully trained students for the war effort. Metzger wrote in the *New York Times*, "I regard participating in athletics now the patriotic duty of the student, in that training and preparation make him of far greater value to the country than if he did not have them."[47] Optimistic predictions by sports insiders, like Princeton professor Dr. Joseph Raycroft, did much to bolster public confidence in the compatibility of sports and military involvement. Quoted in *The Sporting Goods Trade Journal*, Raycroft estimated that "there will be more real and widespread athletic activity in this country during the next twelve months [1917–18] than ever before in our lifetime."[48]

Equally assuring to the American sports public were the efforts of Walter Camp. The dean of American football believed strongly in the complementary value of sport in military preparation, a belief that underlay his Naval Training Station athletic program, designed to teach sailors discipline, teamwork, fellowship, leadership, physical fitness, and toughness.[49] Standardized rules for boxing and wrestling were central components of Camp's naval-training regimen. A *New York Times* sportswriter noted that "Uncle Sam's army of stay-at-homes is behind the army of gone-to-war and has organized a system of athletics which is far better systematized than the athletics of the leading eastern universities since the date of the war's beginning."[50] Moreover, in addition to organizing a physical-fitness program for President Wilson's cabinet, which Camp supervised behind the Treasury building every morning, the single most popular event of Camp's wartime sporting activism was the development of his "daily dozen" exercise routine for all Americans concerned about keeping physically fit.[51]

In early March of 1918, two weeks before Germany's mighty spring offensive, the idea of sports for improving fighting efficiency had made sufficient progress, among officers and enlisted men, to warrant a comprehensive proposal written by the commander in chief of U.S. forces, regarding compulsory mass athletics in the Army. Mass athletics were designed to raise the physical efficiency of troops who could neither jump over six-foot-wide trenches, nor run 220 yards in 30 seconds; and who led the commander to assert that "such men could neither catch a Hun nor get away from one."[52] Clearly, an army of athletes had to be made. Led by Luther Gulick, a spirited campaign recruited 1,600 men, who were subsequently trained at the YMCA Training Schools at Springfield and Chicago; and by September, 300 new physical directors had sailed to France.[53] To improve physical efficiency among enlisted men, the YMCA appropriated over $300,000 worth of athletic goods.[54] In a short time, the Y had created an athletic structure which catered to the exigencies of various military regions. Ports of entry, SOS areas, aviation camps, training camps, combat zones, convalescent camps, and leave areas featured mass games, calisthenics, competitive sports, and boxing instruction.[55]

Organized athletic activities were designed to train enlisted men in the survival skills needed for life on the front. Combative exercises, particularly wrestling maneuvers, trained recruits for hand-to-hand combat. Baseball-throwing fundamentals were emphasized in grenade-tossing exercises. Scaling, balancing, jumping, and vaulting exercises incorporated gymnastic skills into daily trench maneuvers and basic survival skills for frontline combat. The greatest attention, however, was given to boxing as training for bayonet fighting.[56] Prior to 1917, boxing was mostly illegal in the United States; and "then came the war to dwarf the miniature battles of the squared circle," wrote *Outing* correspondent Thomas Foster. The result, he contended, was that "the duels of the fighters and their promoters became absurdly small alongside the greater duel and four-ounce gloves were puny weapons as compared with bayonets."[57] Before the American military intervened in Europe, a U.S. sergeant had been teaching Canadian recruits the use of the bayonet, and discovered that the essential movements of feet and hands in bayonet fighting are the same as those of boxing. After 1917, according to Foster, "Uncle Sam dragged the padded gloves out of discard and hastied them on the hands of boys that they may better cope with the Boche when they meet him with steel against steel."[58] For this effort, the military quickly assigned professional boxers, like Mike Gibbons, Johnny Kilbane, Benny Leonard, Packy McFarland, and "Battling" Levinsky, as instructors at training camps, under the direction of the Commission on Training Camp Activities. Boxing not only trained soldiers in hand-to-hand combat; it effectively relieved the monotony of military drilling. American soldiers learned to use the steel and, at the same time, became avid converts to what would become a principal spectator sport at home after the war.[59]

Official integration of sport into military training sparked a wave of team-athletic competition. Not surprisingly, the principal organized sports were baseball, football, and basketball—the big three American sports on the domestic front. Baseball, the national pastime, caught on like wildfire in every place where American troops were stationed on the French front. The *New York Times* marveled that the widespread enthusiasm for baseball in the military marked "a Utopia in athletic endeavor that pioneers in physical education have dreamed of, but never believed would be realized"—particularly, the way in which "every bare space behind the battle lines in France will be converted into a baseball diamond." In early March, the *New York Times* announced the spring training for "Uncle Sam's League"—"greater by far than all the major and minor leagues, together with the semiprofessional and amateur baseball organizations" in the United States, this baseball league was "vaster than any athletic movement in the history of sport," numbering over two million players.[60]

Equally impressive strides were made on the football field. Initially bypassed because of the considerable expenses needed for outfitting teams with pads and helmets, football was quickly recognized as a popular sport among soldiers and sailors, many of whom were former collegiate players and coaches. Service football found favorable opportunities for colleges and intracamp teams to battle in major stadiums. The game quickly proved an unexpected success during the 1917 season, when training-camp teams proved competitive with college football teams. *Outing* magazine noted that never before had so many American men played football. "In every army cantonment," the editor wrote, "footballs were as thick as pumpkins in an autumn cornfield."[61] Sport historian James Mennell suggests that service football popularized the collegiate game significantly. For those athletically inclined, service football was more accessible than the select collegiate game. And the nonplaying soldiers experienced the music, color, drama, and spirit of the game, previously limited to the collegiate crowd.[62] By the war's end, a *New York Times* sports journalist was confident that "football owes more to the war in the way of the spread of the spirit of the game than it does to ten or twenty years of development in the period before the war."[63]

Between February 1918 and June 1919, American soldiers followed service sports through the pages of *Stars and Stripes*, a weekly newspaper whose circulation grew from 30,000 to more than 526,000. Created as an internal organ of propaganda "to stimulate a healthy morale among troops of the A.E.F. by giving them the news of the War and of America attractively and interestingly presented," *Stars and Stripes* became the best-known army newspaper in history.[64] Next to *Stars and Stripes*, the *Sporting News* was the most popular publication among the AEF. Its editor, Taylor Spink, persuaded baseball's American League to buy copies at a reduced rate and send them to the troops at the league's expense. Moreover, the U.S. postmaster allowed civilian readers to merely put a one-cent stamp on their copies if they wanted the paper delivered to overseas soldiers.[65] *Stars and Stripes* accepted the fact that any worthy American newspaper must have a respectable sports page. The editors soon realized that the American sporting experience could help the soldier relate to the war pressures. As an early editorial claimed, "the 'game of war' should hold no terrors for the average American soldier already trained in sports—the familiar experience of the playing field was a framework for war experiences."[66]

Occasionally, *Stars and Stripes* contributors waxed poetic on the nationalistic character of American sport. During the spring-training season of 1918, a soldier penned the following doggerel:

> He's tossed the horsehide far away to plug the hand grenade
> What matter if on muddy grounds this game of war is played?
> He'll last through extra innings and he'll hit as well as pitch
> His smoking Texas Leaguers'll make the Fritzies seek the ditch!"[67]

With less poetic, but equally assured, conviction, Walter Camp assessed the importance of athletics in American military preparation:

> Our boxing was made the basis of bayonet fighting and our baseball arms were adept in learning to throw the grenade. The men who had gone into the opposing football line when their signal came went "over the top" with that same abandon. Those who had made a stand on the last five-yard line in the grim determination of the gridiron field faced the scrimmage of war with the same do-or-die fortitude. Those who had raced on the cinder track and thrown their last efforts into the sprint at the finish were just as "game" when the pathway was a Flanders field or a Chateau Thierry line. The man who took the big chance on the motor track took the greater chances in the air with the same spirit. The man whose nerves had been tested with "two men on," "one out," and "a run to tie and two to win," stood smiling when the line was thin.[68]

Just as Camp praised athletics for preparing American soldiers for victories on foreign soil, other commentators, like Frank Kleeberger, of the University of California-Berkeley, interpreted German "brutality and unsportsmanlike conduct" as a function of a deficient national system of physical training.

POSTWAR DEVELOPMENTS

Shortly after the armistice, the U.S. military converted Europeans to the athletic cause, which bolstered a maturing national sporting tradition. Although a vibrant sporting scene had existed in Europe for many centuries, American sports had steadily won the hearts and minds of Europeans during the war. United States military personnel saw themselves as international missionaries of the American sporting life. "Thanks to the American doughboy, and his confreres, the marine and the blue jacket, sport, the world over, is about to have its greatest revival," wrote sportswriter Edwin A. Goewey, early in 1919.[69] Noting that baseball had always "followed the flag" to places in Latin America and the Far East, Goewey surmised that it took "the big war" to introduce the game throughout Europe. The widespread popularity of American sport in Europe, accordingly, signaled "a new era for sport," reflecting the "increased interest and general feeling of good will toward the people of this country."[70] The lesson for postwar America, according to Goewey, was that, if subsidized and promoted by government, sport "would greatly improve in general health, and more splendid, more contented, and more democratic citizenship. Nothing does more for true democracy than sport, in which men of all ranks mingle and become brothers in effort and interest."[71]

Fletcher Brockman, a YMCA spokesman, made the case in even more explicit political terms. Speaking to the Physical Directors' Society in

Detroit, Brockman said that "to teach half a billion people the true meaning of democracy and train them in its wise use" was the "supreme and urgent task before the world today." Under the able tutelage of Western capitalist societies, particularly the United States, Eastern European and Far Eastern countries could successfully be brought within the respectable, democratic fold, through YMCA-sponsored athletic programs. As an antidote to the wave of "radical democracy" emanating from Petrograd like a "cloud of poisonous gas," association athletics provided the "practical outworking of some of the most difficult problems in democracy."[72]

At no point were the American athletic missionaries' efforts more dramatically successful at converting the unbelievers to sports than during the Inter-Allied Games. The games were designed to provide "constructive and interesting bodily activity" for soldiers who were awaiting return to the States.[73] Military and YMCA officials feared that peace would provoke "moral temptations" and "disorderly physical expressions" among enlisted men.[74] A grand, military Olympiad would be a safety valve and a reinforcement of the military sporting message.

The YMCA handled the logistical details. Led by Elwood Brown, who capably pioneered the Far Eastern Games (designed to promote better relations among Chinese, Japanese, and Filipinos),[75] the Y procured huge amounts of athletic gear; prepared rule books and other printed material; secured pageantry specialists, grounds and prizes; and organized the elimination-contest schedules. With the full cooperation of the YMCA, the Army invited the military commanders of 29 nations, colonies, and dependencies to participate in "keen rivalry, a free field, and fair play"—the ends for which the Allied forces had fought the war. American Olympic gold-medal winner Jim Thorpe described the Games as "one of the most worthwhile experiments the world had ever seen"; he praised Brown as one ideally suited to lead the way, saying Brown was "equipped with a knowledge of the reaction of various races in athletic competition, as perhaps no other man."[76] The YMCA agreed to build a monumental structure, the Pershing Stadium, which would accommodate 40,000 spectators, and would be presented to the French people as a token of American goodwill. Situated in the Bois de Vincennes (on the outskirts of Paris), where French knights, since the time of Henry of Navarre, had contended, the site, donated by the French government, was ideally located. The YMCA appropriated one million francs for the preparation of the site and for general operating expenses. On June 22, the stadium was officially dedicated by distinguished guests from all the Allied nations, military delegations, and numerous eloquent speakers who promoted the cause of international sport. Before a standing-room-only crowd of 90,000, Edward G. Carter, the YMCA's chief secretary, proclaimed that the larger meaning of the AEF championships at the Inter-Allied Games "lies not in a few hundred final competitors, but in the hundreds of thousands of soldiers of average skill who unconsciously have established play for play's sake, and sport as the possession of all."[77]

The democratic rhetoric of international sports was not entirely invented, for, in fact, the AEF elimination contests, held between January and June 1919—in football, basketball, boxing, wrestling, baseball, golf, shooting, soccer, swimming, tennis, and track and field—constituted the most extensive athletic program hitherto executed under one management.[78] The AEF championships in football and boxing were a huge success. According to a YMCA spokesman, "no season in the history of sport ever developed better matched teams or more exciting contests" than the preliminary American football games held to decide the supremacy of the Second Army. The finals, won by the Seventh Division, were watched by the Army with all the interest ever called forth by a Yale-Harvard game or a world's championship series—75,000 officers and other personnel participated in football. Thousands of enlisted men competed in the boxing elimination bouts. The majority of the finalists had been professionals before the war. "To witness or take part in a boxing match was, next to a good feed and baseball, the most enjoyment in the Army," Frederick Harris observed, citing the total of more than six million spectators as evidence enough for his assertion. Much of the credit for the success of the boxing contests derived from the active involvement of American welfare organizations, like the Knights of Columbus, the Jewish Welfare Board, and the Red Cross.[79]

American athletes took the Games very seriously. During the rainy French spring, soldier-athletes trained in 150 airplane hangars. The 400′× 150′ facilities were ample enough for football scrimmages, a dozen simultaneous basketball games, and about twice that number for volleyball practice.[80] American and European newspapers dutifully popularized the forthcoming Games. During the week preceding the Games, for instance, the *New York Herald* published 31 items on them, for a total of more than 19,000 words; the *Chicago Tribune* printed 90 items consisting of over 26,000 words; and the *London Daily Mail* featured 69 articles containing over 10,000 words. French newspapers followed suit. Once the Games began, the U.S. government's Committee on Public Information headed the effort to transmit news daily, by wireless, to the United States, Great Britain, Czechoslovakia, and to places throughout the Balkans.[81]

On opening day, 30,000 spectators rose to their feet during the military parade, which was headed by the Garde Republicaine Band, and followed by representatives of the most famous fighting contingents of the war. Tattered regimental flags, many stained with the blood of battles long antedating those of the Great War; national ensigns of all participating nations; uniforms, for example, of the Chasseurs Alpins, Zouaves, Tirailleurs, Italians, Serbians; and the presence of thousands of spectators in uniform—all these were reminders of the worldwide character of the long and bitter struggle now brought to a victorious close. Pershing Stadium was presented by the YMCA, in the name of the Army, to the French people. Commemorating the event, a bronze inscription outside the stadium expressed the hope that "the cherished bonds of friendship between France and America, forged anew on the common field of battle may be tempered and made enduring on the friendly field of sport."[82] Indeed, the partisan Games Committee interpreted the contests in unmistakably ideological terms—namely, to show how "wholeheartedly the nations that had striven shoulder to shoulder on the battlefield could turn to friendly rivalry in the stadium," one advocate claimed.[83] The Games effectively spread the cause of the sporting life to countries that "came into being in the travail of world war and which in the future will take part in the improvement of athletics."[84]

Throughout the two weeks of athletic festivities, nearly 1,500 athletes representing 18 Allied nations or dominions participated in the Games. The United States was the least handicapped of the nations competing, since most of the best American athletes had remained alive after the war and could therefore compete. The U.S. squad laid claim to 12 firsts and 7 seconds in the 24 separate events. The AEF proudly excelled in the rifle and pistol competitions, and took firsts in baseball, basketball, boxing, equestrian contests, swimming, the tug-of-war, and catch-as-catch-can wrestling. American F. C. Thompson, a former baseball player, surpassed all other competitors with a remarkable 246-foot grenade toss.[85]

Between September 1919 and April 1922, the spirit of sports among American enlisted men was kept alive among the American forces in Germany (AFG). This history was documented by a YMCA publication, *Athletic Bulletin*, of which 37 issues were published. The *Bulletin* reported that more than three million men saw or participated in sports at Koblenz. Soldiers participated in baseball, boxing, basketball, football, soccer, rugby, golf, track and field, swimming, tennis, and mass games.[86]

One November day in 1921, the cultural bonds established between France and the United States during the Allied war effort took ritualistic form. The fusion of sport, nationalism, and the military found dramatic expression for 75,000 spectators who flocked to New Haven, Connecticut, to watch Yale host Princeton in football. "For the first time in the history of Big Three football," the *New York Times* reported, "the greatest acclaim of the day was not for the hero of the game," but for another hero of "other and distant battlefields." Just before the opening kickoff, Marshal Ferdinand Foch, commander of the Allied forces in World War I, gallantly strolled into the stadium and then across the gridiron, while a roaring crowd greeted him. Foch's appearance was no less than a "triumphal procession," according to one journalist, who compared it to Lafayette's tour of America.[87] Foch's visit coincided with an elaborate melting-pot pageantry in New York, amid front-page rumors of Bolshevist demonstrations in America. Athletics, Americanization, and the brotherhood of Western democracies proved potent antidotes for a nation in the throes of economic and social transformation.

SUMMARY

The American sporting tradition was profoundly transformed by the military's widespread incorporation of sports into the war effort. The testimonies of militant preparedness advocates were validated: World War I revealed the utility of physical education to the armed services, and to the masses of Americans—many of whom had never been adequately exposed to athletic activity. "We should hang our heads in shame," because of the ill-prepared state of the nation's prewar citizenry, claimed Dr. Thomas Storey, head of the United States Interdepartmental Social Hygiene Board.[88] Citing statistics that revealed that one-third of military recruits were physically "unfit," and that even larger numbers of people were ignorant of protective hygiene, Storey applauded the war effort for heightening national consciousness about physical education. Physical education that begins in infancy and continues throughout life, Storey maintained, constituted the "necessary preparation for citizenship, whether that citizenship serves in peace or in war."[89] Riding the postwar patriotic fervor, many physical educators linked mass athletic activity with the democratic ideal. Thousands of schools nationwide were converted to the cult of strenuosity, and during the 1920s, municipalities increased expenditures sixfold. The war effort also powerfully legitimized the cause of college athletics, which, though national in scope, were not without lingering, trenchant critics—many of whom suggested abolishing collegiate sports. An *Outing* editor reviewed the role of college athletes in the war cause to suggest that the "problem" was not one of "too much athletics, but too little," convincing many former critics to "turn right about face."[90] Certainly, on one level at least, the sporting experience was becoming more widely accessible to the American public.

Some sports fared particularly well after the war. Boxing was the most widely publicized postwar sport. Before the war, boxing had had limited public appeal, due to the fact that it remained illegal in many states; but by 1920, state legislatures began to reverse the sport's prohibition. Although the battle for Sunday baseball probably garnered more newspaper space during 1919, the baseball controversy was only a skirmish as compared to the fight against the rising popularity of boxing. The rebuke by the religious establishment and influential groups of middle-class respectability were met by fierce resistance from the Army, the Navy, the American Legion, and the civilian board of boxing. Even conservative newspapers like the *New York Times* weighed in on the side of boxing by characterizing the opponents of boxing as a "half a century behind the times."[91] Thus, boxing became a huge commercial success during the 1920s, and New York regained its position as the national center of boxing—major bouts staged in Madison Square Garden became big social events that attracted celebrities, politicians, and thousands of avid women boxing spectators.[92]

In sum, the period between the Spanish-American War and World War I proved to be a ripe context for the invention and perfection of a distinctly American sporting tradition. Indeed, the two conflicts marked fundamental watersheds in the development of a sports-oriented military establishment. Several contemporary intellectuals explained the importance of war in modern society: "War is the health of the State," Randolph Bourne declared in 1919.[93] A wartime nation attains "a uniformity of feeling, a hierarchy of values culminating at the undisputed apex of the State ideal," and to such depths that, according to Bourne, distinctions between society and the individual are all but eliminated.[94] War and military service became powerful mechanisms, Eric Hobsbawm writes, for "inculcating proper civic behavior, and, not least, for turning the inhabitant of a village into the patriotic citizen of a nation."[95]

These civics lessons were not lost on the majority of Americans, who overwhelmingly acknowledged the legitimacy of military institutions. For them, the military's enthusiasm for organized sports was cause enough for popular acceptance and appreciation. For the unconverted ones, powerful commentaries emphasized the way in which military athletics transformed the morality of modern sports. Respected Protestant sports advocates like Luther Gulick acknowledged that physical prowess and competitiveness, which were previously associated with "lower-class immorality and crass professionalism," had been recently harnessed by the military for "more powerful social devotions" and patriotic ends.[96] Such views were popularized by a bevy of respected journalists and social commentators. A feature writer for *National Geographic* concurred: Noting the paradox that the "maddest" war ever fought had "turn[ed] the world to simple, wholesome play," the writer characterized sports as forming a "gazetteer of the habits and histories of their peoples." Writing from the Allied vantage point, he concluded that countries adopted national pastimes and modified them so as "to foster and fortify the peoples who play them."[97] Sports both "fortified" American participants and enabled the U.S. military to create an "army of athletes."

EPILOGUE

In 1927, sportswriter John Tunis penned a searing critique of what he characterized as "The Great American Sports Myth." Debunking what had become accepted wisdom for the previous half century—that competitive sport built character and strengthened the bond between nations and individuals—he indicted his fellow journalists for exaggerating and sentimentalizing the "promise" of American sport. "The best hope for a saner and more sensible outlook on sports," Tunis wrote in *Harper's Magazine*, "is to be found in the fact that if The Great Sports Myth grows but a little more it will defeat itself. It will fall from sheer topheaviness." Explaining this, he said that "there is a limit even to the credulity of a public brought up from childhood to believe in this fairy tale."[1] Neither an outsider nor a stranger to the world of sport, Tunis, a former Harvard athlete, a *New York Evening Post* writer, and one of the nation's finest writers of sports books for boys (his works were parables about athletes who faced moral dilemmas), wrote as one who refused to be deluded any longer by America's athletic infatuation.[2]

During the 1930s, Tunis waged an unceasing crusade against what he perceived to be the excesses and delusions of the national sporting culture. Like his colleague, Paul Gallico, who wrote his own *Farewell to Sports* in 1938, Tunis lamented how Americans were no longer interested in sports for sports' sake or exhibited true sportsmanship, but were, instead, obsessed with winning at any cost. "The sports and athletics that we get, then," he polemicized in *The Nation*, "are not only the sports we deserve; they are the sports that a materialistic civilization would naturally bring in its train."[3] The root of most evil, Tunis and several of his peers believed, was the failed and poisonous toxin of amateurism.

Amateurism was merely a subterfuge: Tunis proclaimed the distinction between amateurism and professionalism was "nebulous," and had, by the late 1920s, been growing "illogical," "impractical," and "more of a fiction."[4] Not only did he propose the abolition of amateurism, by suggesting that athletes should be openly paid wages "approximating their market value"; he connected criticisms of amateurism to the larger body politic. "If we can't adopt a realistic attitude toward such an inconsequential thing as [amateur] football," Tunis wrote in the midst of the Great Depression, "how can we as a nation hope to be realistic toward war or government or economics or any great problem of the moment?" Tunis's provocative, controversial article in *American Mercury* was overwhelmingly ridiculed by journalists and commentators throughout the country as "aimless wanderings," "literary mush," a "diatribe," "vitriolic," "sensationalistic," and "maliciousness."[5] In the 1990s, such criticisms about the abolition of the amateur code were still being voiced.

The demise of classical amateurism did not destroy American sport, as early-twentieth-century commentators, such as Caspar Whitney, had predicted.[6] In fact, the opposite occurred. With the demise of "pure" amateurism, Americans, if anything, grew increasingly fond of big-time, commercialized sport. By 1920, despite comments about the cash nexus and the impending doom, both professional and amateur sport had been transformed from primarily localized, occasional activities into nationally organized, commercial spectacles. Rooted in the material, social, and political realities of that era, sports dramatized many fundamental ideas in American society. Sports provided a common, readily accessible language that united, for example, Maine potato farmers, Seattle longshoremen, and Detroit autoworkers. The lexicon of sports pervaded the barbershop, the barroom, the church, and the public school. During the 1920s (America's golden age of sports), popular commentators praised the decade's esteemed sports giants—Babe Ruth, Bill Tilden, Knute Rockne, Red Grange, and the original Celtics—as exemplars of everything that was good in the country.

While commentators provided the mediating stories and myths, fans enjoyed the fun of watching and analyzing good athletic contests. In 1924, a *Nation* editor delineated this two-way infatuation. He said that "if we are as political a people as we are believed to be, our thoughts and energies should be concentrated" on the candidates and issues of the 1924 presidential campaign." Yet "judging from the newspapers and conversations," he observed, "the people are more occupied" with the World Series; the polo match between the Americans and British; the Davis Cup in tennis; and the Firpo-Wills prizefight. "We shall have to wait until election day to learn the fate of La Follette, Davis, and Coolidge," the editor wrote, with obvious remorse, but whatever the verdict, "we may say already—and with entire confidence—that the popular vote has been cast in favor of sports. It has been seated on the American throne."[7]

Paul Gallico, one of the nation's leading sportswriters during the 1920s, explained the popular love affair with the "golden people of the golden decade": "In those days in those times, we drugged ourselves with such romantic chronicles. We had just emerged from a serious war and now wanted no more reality but only escape. . . . Sports and sports stories and sports characters who were almost magical in their performance provided much of that escape."[8] Acknowledging his own complicity as a writer who created "great American fairy tale[s]," Gallico placed himself within the category of the "Gee-Whizzers"—ballyhooing romantics—who were, at heart, "sucker[s] for the theology of the good guys and the bad guys."[9] In short, they were guilty of sustaining the *illusion* that sports actually mattered.

Prior to the severe Great Depression, which shattered the nation's belief in the inevitable promise of modernity and progress, Americans found solace in their stable sporting culture and its well-established athletic traditions. Millions of unemployed fans accepted the explanation of their hero, Babe Ruth, as to why he earned more money than President Herbert Hoover in 1932 (he had a "better year"), because he had been firmly enshrined as a bona-fide celebrity and role model, above reproach. After all, "the Babe" appeared to symbolize the Horatio Alger myth of one who rose from humble working-class origins to stardom through persistent, hard work—and a little luck. But unlike contemporary journalists who expose athletes' often less than savory private lives, sports journalists chose not to dwell on the Bambino's voracious off-field appetites for sex, booze, and gambling. To do so threatened to expose sport's well-crafted illusion.

The 1940s and 1950s ushered in American sports' last great golden age. Manly, patriotic, clean-living baseball players like Ted Williams, Joe DiMaggio, and Stan Musial left the game during their prime to fight the Great War. During the early 1950s, Bobby Thomson's shot "heard around the world"; Don Larsen's perfect game; the debuts of future icons Mickey Mantle and Willie Mays; and the retirements of legends Williams, DiMaggio, and Jackie Robinson—these, collectively, provided structure and coherence for that monumental epoch of American professional sports. During the patriotically charged World War II years, several prominent historians emphasized how sports both reflected America's superior institutions and preserved the nation's open, democratic character. Foster Rhea Dulles stressed the unique, "exceptional" nature of American society and praised the widespread accessibility of sports and leisure as a sure sign of how "democracy had come into its heritage."[10] Moreover, the "democratic" character of American sports was regularly extolled as a carrier of "the American way of life" to the free world during the early Cold War years of the 1950s.

Many people remain obsessed with this golden age. On July 11, 1995, during the pregame festivities of the 66th All-Star classic, U.S. Secretary of the Army Togo West, Jr., made a presentation to Joe DiMaggio, who missed three seasons due to Army service between 1943 and 1945. Following the presentation, a 120–member chorus sang patriotic songs and military jets flew over The Ballpark in Arlington, Texas, after which Lyle Lovett sang the national anthem. David Halberstam's immensely popular books, *Summer of '49* (1989) and *October 1964* (1994), sustain the mythical epoch. As Halberstam intimates, by 1964 baseball no longer had a *national* team like the New York Yankees of old. Rather, the racially and ethnically integrated 1964 St. Louis Cardinals included a star African-American outfielder named Curt Flood, who pioneered what became a movement to repeal American professional sports' reserve clause. Once the players gained free agency in 1974, it became increasingly difficult for writers and observers alike to ignore the commercial nature of American sports. Although they, despite sizable salaries, are no closer to owning the store than they were 100 years ago, players have increasingly become the scapegoats for the "fall" of American sports in the 1990s.

Sports golden ages are created in times of national crisis, as a way of affirming comfortable notions of society and popularizing idealized versions of history and culture. During the late-nineteenth-century period, cultural leaders used sports as national myth and drama to legitimize a social, political, and economic order that was fundamentally at odds with the existing liberal state that had existed for over a century. As large corporations led the country's activities at the national and international levels, a powerful, modern nation-state was celebrated as benefactor and protector of all classes, regions, and races. Sports traditions evoked the resilience of individualism, the work ethic, democracy, class conciliation; and, thereby, helped shape an emergent national identity on the world stage—an effort profoundly bolstered by American involvement in World War I.

Americans continue to engage the past for a sense of security in the present, and to raise hopes for a more tranquil future. As people in the post–Cold War era struggle to comprehend all the complexities of the New World Order—the global marketplace, corporate downsizing, the information superhighway, and the like—they draw on nostalgia (the longing for a happier and simpler past) to cope with their rapidly changing world. British historian David Lowenthal succinctly describes nostalgia as "memory with the pain removed. The pain is today."[11] Karl Marx discerned this trans-historical tendency in 1851 when he wrote:

> Men make their own history, but they do not make it just as they please; they do not make it under circumstances chosen by themselves, but under circumstances directly encountered, given, and transmitted from the past . . . And just when they seem engaged in revolutionizing themselves and things, in creating something that has never yet existed, precisely in such periods of revolutionary crisis they anxiously conjure up the spirits of the past to their service and borrow from them names, battle-cries, and costumes in order to present the new scene of world history in this time-honored disguise and borrowed language.[12]

There is abundant evidence to suggest that Americans continue to celebrate and participate in the national sporting traditions created at the turn of the century. Baseball is still the acclaimed national pastime, despite the fact that, in the 1980s and 1990s, professional football has eclipsed it as the most popular sport. The Olympics foster the idealism of sports for sports' sake, even though the 1994 Games were dominated by the tabloidesque Tonya Harding–Nancy Kerrigan scandal. High-school and playground sports thrive in every community. College football is, arguably, the second-leading spectator sport (next to pro football). And, basketball, the truest American invention, is currently in the midst of the most popular, and most thoroughly commercialized, developmental phase of any sport in history.

Still, widespread laments about the future of professional sports persist. Such doubts reflect both the considerable staying power of the amateur ethos and the contemporary crises that bedevil both the sports world and the overall American society. Although fans conjure up the spirits of past sports stars, to allay the unsettling difficulties of the present, such nostalgic exercises will, too, eventually lose credibility. "Generation X" will only be able to remember the more pristine moments that date from the late 1970s and early 1980s.

The American sports culture of the near future will be mediated by advanced computerized digital technologies. The computer simulation games now available re-create the strategic dimensions and sensory experience of actual sports events. Fans can also subscribe to on-line computer services that provide statistics, late-breaking scores, injury reports, and assorted other news about the sports world. Several cutting-edge computer companies have designed virtual-reality sports games. In the near future, sports-on-demand video and computer services will enable customers to use their remote-control clickers to access games, customized statistics, special interview shows, marketing-oriented displays of sports paraphernalia, simulated games, and a variety of live games that reach specific league divisional and geographical areas. In an incisive article about the direction of electronic sports, Donald Katz asks: "Will computer-based technologies someday offer sportslike entertainment so enthralling and convenient and highly customized that games created from bits of the best of real sports and bits of the best sports fantasies render live games obsolete?"[13]

Maybe so. It's too early to speculate; but one thing is more certain: Just as people from years past interpreted their culture through the prism of sports, so, too, will other generations invent their own traditions, memories, and associations for a new American sporting imagination.

NOTES

PREFACE

1. Every Olympic sport is ultimately controlled by its own "amateur" international federation. For a compelling exposé of the world of big-time international sports, see Vyv Simson and Andrew Jennings, *Dishonoured Games: Corruption, Money and Greed at the Olympics* (London: 1992).

2. Donald Katz, *Just Do It: The Nike Spirit in the Corporate World* (New York: 1994), 17.

3. Ibid.; see also, the excellent chapter titled "Barcelona."

4. Ibid., 17.

5. Ibid., 16.

6. Ibid., 44.

7. Lipsyte, "The Emasculation of Sports," *New York Times Magazine*, April 2, 1995.

8. Fox, *Big Leagues: Professional Baseball, Football, and Basketball in the National Memory* (New York: 1994), 417.

9. Leonard Koppett, *Sports Illusion, Sports Reality: A Reporter's View of Sports, Journalism, and Society* (Boston: 1981), 179–80. Also, see George Sage's chapter "The Big Business of College Sport," in his *Power and Ideology in American Sport* (Champaign, Ill. 1990).

10. Koppett, *Sports Illusion, Sports Reality*, 179–80.

11. Ibid.

CHAPTER ONE

1. Michael Oviard, *Sporting with the Gods: The Rhetoric of Play and Game in American* Culture (New York: 1990), 11; Elliott J. Gorn, "Sports Through the Nineteenth Century," in Mary Kupiec Cayton, Gorn, and Peter W. Williams, eds., *Encyclopedia of American Social History* (New York: 1993), vol. 3, 1636.

2. Ibid.

3. John Nauright, "Nostalgia and the Use of the Sporting Past in Periods of Hegemonic Crisis" (Paper presented to the North American Society for Sport History, Long Beach, California, May 26–29, 1995). For a concise survey of the development of sports coverage in national magazines, see Frank Luther Mott's

classic *A History of American Magazines*, 5 vols. (Cambridge: 1938–68), vol. 4, 369–380; Mott, *American Journalism: A History of Newspapers in the United States Through 250 Years, 1690–1940* (New York, 1941); and John R. Betts, "Sporting Journalism in Nineteenth-Century America," *American Quarterly* 5 (1953), 39–56.

4. Walter Camp, "The Broad Folk Highway of American Sport," *American Scandinavian Review* 9 (1921), 257.

5. David Waldstreicher, "Rites of Rebellion, Rites of Assent: Celebrations, Print Culture, and the Origins of American Nationalism," *Journal of American History* 82 (1995), 61. Also, see Eric Foner, *Tom Paine and Revolutionary America* (New York: 1976); and Sean Wilentz, *Chants Democratic: New York City and the Rise of the American Working-Class, 1788–1850* (New York: 1984).

6. Elliott J. Gorn, The Manly Art: Bare-Knuckle Prizefighting in America (Ithaca, N.Y.: 1986), 159.

7. Ibid., 56–68.

8. See George B. Kirsch's introduction to *Sports in North America: A Documentary History*, vol. 4 (Gulf Breeze, Fla., 1995); see also, Benjamin G. Rader, *American Sports: From the Ages of Folk Games to the Age of Televised Sports* (Englewood Cliffs, N.J., 1990); and E. Gorn and W. Goldstein, *A Brief History of American Sports* (New York, 1994).

9. Eric Hobsbawm, "Mass Producing Traditions: Europe, 1870–1914," in Hobsbawm and T. Ranger, eds., *The Invention of Tradition* (Cambridge, Eng., 1983), 299. See John Betts, *America's Sporting Heritage, 1850–1950* (Reading, Mass., 1974), 109–11, 156–59. The most recent work on the early years of tennis is E. Digby Baltzell, *Sporting Gentlemen: Men's Tennis from the Age of Honor to the Cult of the Superstar* (New York, 1995).

10. See John Tebbel and Mary Ellen Zuckerman, *The Magazine in America, 1741–1990* (New York, 1991).

11. Waldstreicher, "Rites of Rebellion, Rites of Assent," 49, 50.

12. Nauright, "Nostalgia and the Use of the Sporting Past."

13. Alan Dawley, *Struggles for Justice: Social Responsibility and the Liberal State* (Cambridge, Mass., 1991). See also Wilbur Zelinsky, *Nation into State: The Shifting Symbolic Foundations of American Nationalism* (Chapel Hill, N.C., 1988); Michael Kammen, *Mystic Chords of Memory: The Transformation of Tradition in American Culture* (New York, 1991); John Bodnar, *Remaking America: Public Memory, Commemoration, and Patriotism in the Twentieth Century* (Princeton, N.J., 1991); and David Glassberg, *American Historical Pageantry: The Uses of Tradition in the Early Twentieth Century* (Chapel Hill, N.C., 1990).

14. See Mike Davis, "Why the U.S. Working Class is Different," *New Left Review* 123 (1980); Sean Wilentz, "Against Exceptionalism: Class Consciousness and the American Labor Movement, 1790–1920," *International Labor and Working Class History* 26 (1984), 1–24; David Montgomery, "Labor and the Republic in Industrial America: 1860–1920," *Mouvement Sociale* 111 (1980); Montgomery, *The Fall of the House of Labor: The Workplace, the State, and American Labor Activism, 1865–1925* (New York, 1987); Richard Judd, *Socialist Cities: Municipal Politics and the Grass Roots of American Socialism* (Albany, N.Y. 1990); and Paul Buhle, *Marxism in the United States: Remapping the History of the American Left* (London, 1987).

15. Dawley, *Struggles for Justice*; and Martin J. Sklar, *The Corporate Recon-*

struction of American Capitalism: The Market, the Law, and Politics (New York, 1988).

16. Bodnar, *Remaking America*, 36; and Sklar, *The Corporate Reconstruction of American Capitalism, 1890–1916:*, 13–14, 39.

17. Robert Wiebe, *The Search for Order, 1877–1920* (New York, 1967), 76–110.

18. See Alan Trachtenberg, *The Incorporation of America: Culture and Society in the Gilded Age* (New York, 1982), esp. 179–81; and Philip Gleason, "American Identity and Americanization," in Stephan Thernstrom, ed., *Harvard Encyclopedia of American Ethnic Groups* (Cambridge, 1980), 31–58.

19. Nina Silber, *The Promise of Reunion: Northerners and the South, 1865–1900* (Chapel Hill, N.C., 1993), 160–61.

20. Ibid., 166. For more on the late-nineteenth-century patriotic upsurge, see Merle Curti's classic book, *The Roots of American Loyalty* (New York, 1946), esp. 173–99; and Wallace Evans Davies, *Patriotism on Parade: The Story of Veterans' and Hereditary Organizations in America, 1783–1900* (Cambridge, Mass., 1955).

21. For a succinct discussion of the melting-pot concept as it applied to ethnicity in American identity between 1860 and 1924, see Gleason, "American Identity and Americanization," 38–39.

22. Hobsbawm, *The Invention of Tradition*, 279–80.

23. Tom Nairn, *The Break-Up of Britain: Crisis and Neo-Nationalism* (London, 1977), 354.

24. Merle Curti, *The Roots of American Loyalty* (New York: 1943), 173–99.

25. Herman Hagerdorn, ed. *The Works of Theodore Roosevelt*, 20 vols. (New York, 1926), vol. 19, 301–6.

26. Edward Bellamy, *Edward Bellamy Speaks: Again* (Kansas City, 1937), quoted in Curti, *Roots of American Loyalty*, 211.

27. Ibid., p. xx. The development of an American national ethos is well documented in the American Studies literature. For an overview, see Sacvan Bercovitch, *Rites of Assent: Transformations in the Symbolic Construction of America* (New York, 1992), 29–67. See also, Eric Hobsbawm, "Afterword: Working Classes and Nations," in Dirk Hoerder, ed., *Labor Migration in the Atlantic Economies: The European and North American Working Classes During the Period of Industrialization* (Westport, Conn., 1985).

28. Kammen, *Mystic Chords of Memory*, 408.

29. For a thorough overview of the first two decades of the new social history, see Oliver Zunz, "The Synthesis of Social Change: Reflections on American Social History," in Zunz, ed., *Reliving the Past: The Worlds of Social History* (Chapel Hill, N.C., 1985), 53–114. Earlier critiques of social history's failure to explicate the broader dimensions of social change (including the role of nations) included Eric Hobsbawm, "From Social History to the History of Society," *Daedalus* 100 (1971); Eugene Genovese and Elizabeth Fox Genovese, "The Political Crisis of Social History," *Journal of Social History* 10 (1976); Tony Judt, "A Clown in Regal Purple: Social History and the Historians," *History Workshop* 7 (197), 66–94; and James A. Henretta, "Social History as Lived and Written," *American Historical Review* 84 (1979), 1293–1322.

30. See John Higham, "The Future of American History," *Journal of American History* 80 (1994), 1300. He perceptively surveys the changing historio-

graphical landscape (1289–99), and encourages historians to regain a national focus on a culture permeated by the energies of differentiation, by investigating three basic issues. First, he notes that assimilation is a "legitimate, sometimes desirable, and often inescapable pathway in a heterogeneous but nonetheless cohesive culture." Second, below conspicuous expressions of patriotism and Americanism lie "unarticulated feelings of belonging, of being at home, that inhere in mundane rituals, routines, manners, and memories." And third, historians would be reminded to revisit and appreciate social classes as national segments. Higham writes, "Classes are primarily constituent segments of American society," and during the course of time, they "become rivals for national honor with their own distinctive inflections of a national culture" (1306–7). A national focus can enable historians to see class relations and differences as a national configuration.

31. With a few noteworthy exceptions—namely, Eugene Genovese's pioneering *Roll, Jordan, Roll*, published in 1974—few historians used the concept before the early 1980s. Those who did use the term used it as a more nuanced, dialectical alternative to the widely popular concept of social control, which implied that dominant groups somehow got their own way. For a helpful review of this earlier orientation, see Gareth Stedman Jones, "Class Expression versus Social Control: A Critique of Recent Trends in the Social History of 'Leisure,'" *History Workshop* 4 (1977), 162–70.

32. Harvey J. Kaye surveys the development of Gramscian hegemony theory, and its use by the British Marxist historians, in *The Educaiton of Desire: Marxists and the Writing of History* (New York, 1992). For examples of Gramsci's writing, see *Selections from the Prison Notebooks*, ed. Q. Hoare and G. Smith (New York, 1971); and Geoff Eley, "Reading Gramsci in English: Observations on the Reception of Antonio Gramsci in the English-Speaking World, 1957–82," *European Historical Quarterly* 14 (1984), 441–78. And for a thorough review of the ways in which American scholars have used the Gramscian framework, see Mark Hulsether, "Evolving Approaches to U.S. Culture in the American Studies Movement: Consensus, Pluralism, and Contestation for Cultural Hegemony," *Canadian Review of American Studies* 23 (1993), 1–55

33. Stuart Hall, "The Toad in the Garden: Thatcherism Among the Theorists," in Cary Nelson and Lawrence Grossberg, eds., *Marxism and the Interpretation of Cultures* (Urbana, Ill., 1988), 44–45, 53.

34 See Steven W. Pope, "Cultural Hegemony," *The Encyclopedia of Social History*, ed. Peter N. Stearns (New York, 1993), 181–83.

It has become equally chic in recent years to assert that the concept has now become overused and passé—particularly because, in Nauright's words, it keeps us focused on the "structural" level and consequently, "does not go far enough in explaining how a person experiences life and changes identity." Representing this emergent sensibility, sports sociologist Richard Gruneau makes a legitimate criticism: that neo-Gramscians (like myself) have been insufficiently concerned "with the precise ways in which particular sporting structures and beliefs have the effect of materializing a logic of social distinction in various sport styles and practices and in their accompanying constitution of the body." Gruneau's legitimate concerns notwithstanding, I demur by suggesting that overtheorizing is not essential to the historian's calling. Although I agree with sports historian Alan Metcalfe's concern that we need to clearly define our use of theoretical terms, I disagree with his assertion that "if we [historians] are to use theoretical terms in the history we write, they must be integrated into the actual writing of the essay, [and] they must be central to it." He contradicts himself earlier in his paper by stating that "historians may use theory to inform and guide their work but the object is not to test nor develop theory," but, rather, "to enhance our understanding of past societies." Metcalfe, "A Response to John Nauright: Thoughts on the Production, Nature, and Use of History" [Paper presented to the North American Society for Sport History, Long Beach, Calif., May 27, 1995]). To allay any criticisms (by Metcalfe or others) about the true nature of historical scholarship, I have avoided the perils of doing "historical sociology." Toward this end, I have consciously avoided employing overly theoretical concepts and jargon throughout this book. Thus, I confine any minimalist theorizing to this brief discussion. See Nauright, "Nostalgia and the Use of the Sporting Past"; Gruneau, "Sport and 'Espirit de Corps': Notes on Power, Culture and the Politics of the Body," in Fernand Landry, et al., *Sport: The Third Millennium* (Sainte-Foy, Quebec, 1991), 178.

35. Alan Ingham and Stephen Hardy, "Sport Through the Lens of Raymond Williams," in Ingham and J. Loy, eds., *Sport and Social Development* (Champaign, Ill., 1994), 1–19.

36. Antonio Gramsci, *Prison Notebooks*, 5.

37. Ibid.

38. Hobsbawm, The Invention of Tradition, 6.

39. Williams, *Marxism and Literature* (Oxford, 1977), 115.

40. Ibid.

41. John R. Gillis, "Memory and Identity: The History of a Relationship," in Gillis, ed., *Commemoration: The Politics of National Identity* (Princeton, 1994), 1–7.

42. Hobsbawm, *The Invention of Tradition*, 1–9, 263–307. See also, his chapter titled "Waving Flags: Nations and Nationalism," in *The Age of Empire*, 142–64; and *Nations and Nationalism Since 1780*.

43. Benedict Anderson, *Imagined Communities: Reflections on the Origins and Spread of Nationalism* (London, 1983), 12–13; and Etienne Balibar, "The Nation Form: History and Ideology," *Fernand Braudel Center Review* 13 (1990).

44. Nairn, *The Break-up of Britain*, 332–41, reprinted in Hutchinson and Smith, eds., *Nationalism*, 70–71.

45. Ibid.

46. Thomas Bender, "Wholes and Parts: The Need for Synthesis in American History," *Journal of American History* 73 (1986), 126.

47. Richard Gruneau, "Modernization or Hegemony: Two Views on Sport and Social Development," in Jean Harvey and Hart Cantelon, eds., *Not Just a Game* (Ottawa, 1988), 21–22. Like Gruneau, whose major work is *Class, Sports and Social Development* (Amherst, 1983), John Hargreaves has produced a similar analysis of British sport in *Sport, Power and Culture: A Social and Historical Analysis of Popular Sports in Britain* (New York, 1986).

48. See Stephen Hardy, "Entrepreneurs, Structures, and the Sportgeist: Old Tensions in a Modern Industry," in Donald Kyle and Gary Stark, eds., *Sport History and Sport Mythology* (College Station, Tex., 1990); and "'Adopted By All the Leading Clubs': Sporting Goods and the Shaping of Leisure, 1800–1900,"

in Richard Butsch, ed., *For Fun and Profit: The Transformation of Leisure into Consumption* (Philadelphia, 1990), 71–101.

49. I am indebted to Stephen Hardy for helping me tie together these themes in this particular manner.

CHAPTER TWO

1. Robert Lipsyte, "Why Sports Don't Matter Anymore," *New York Times Magazine*, April 2, 1995, 51.

2. Ibid., 52, 56.

3. Ibid., 53.

4. Quotes are taken from Warren Goldstein, *Playing for Keeps: A History of Early Baseball* (Ithaca, N.Y., 1989), 1; and Stephen Fox, *Big Leagues: Professional Baseball, Football, and Basketball in National Memory* (New York, 1994), 92.

5. Goldstein, *Playing for Keeps*, 125–26.

6. Ted Vincent, *Mudville's Revenge: The Rise and Fall of American Sport* (New York, 1981), 4.

7. Jennie Holliman, *American Sports, 1785–1835* (Durham, N.C., 1931), 154. For overviews of colonial and early-American sports, see William J. Baker, *Sports in the Western World* (Urbana, Ill., 1988), 82–114; Benjamin G. Rader, *American Sports: From the Age of Folk Games to the Age of Spectators*, 2d ed. (Englewood Cliffs, N.J., 1990); Elliott J. Gorn and Warren Goldstein, *A Brief History of American Sports* (New York, 1993), 3–46; and Hans Peter Wagner, *Puritan Attitudes toward Recreation in Early Seventeenth Century New England* (Frankfurt, Ger., 1982).

8. Gerald Redmond, *The Caledonian Games in Nineteenth-Century America* (Rutherford, N.J., 1971); Vincent, *Mudville's Revenge*; and George Moss, "The Long Distance Runners of Ante-Bellum America," *Journal of Popular Culture* 8 (1977), 370–82.

9. *New York Herald*, May 5, 1845.

10. Gorn and Goldstein, *A Brief History of American Sports*, 55–75. Gorn has written extensively on the working-class bachelor subculture. See his seminal work, *The Manly Art: Bare-Knuckle Prizefighting in America* (Ithaca, N.Y., 1986), and his articles, including: "'Gouge and Bite, Pull Hair and Scratch': The Social Significance of Fighting in the Southern Backcountry," *American Historical Review* 90 (1985), 18–43; and "'Good-Bye Boys, I Die a True American': Homicide, Nativism, and Working-Class Culture in Antebellum America," *Journal of American History* 74 (1987), 388–410. For recent perspectives on the burgeoning field of the history of American masculinity, see Mark C. Carnes and Clyde Griffen, eds., *Meanings of Manhood: Constructions of Masculinity in Victorian America* (Chicago, 1990); and E. Anthony Rotundo, *American Manhood: Transformations in Masculinity from the Revolution to the Modern Era* (New York, 1993).

11. Ronald A. Smith, *Sports and Freedom: The Rise of Big-Time College Athletics* (New York, 1990), 33–34.

12. Adelman, *A Sporting Time*, 196.

13. Smith, *Sports and Freedom*, 106; and Seymour R. Church, *Base Ball: The*

History, Statistics and Romance of the American National Game from Its Inception to the Present Time (Princeton, N.J., 1902), 27–28.

14. Smith, *Sports and Freedom*, 169.

15. For a detailed study of the mid-nineteenth century invention of the amateur myth, see David C. Young, *The Olympic Myth of Greek Amateur Athletics* (Chicago, 1984); and Young, "How the Amateurs Won the Olympics," in Wendy J. Raschke, ed., *The Archaeology of the Olympics: The Olympics and Other Festivals in Antiquity* (Madison, Wis., 1988). Allen Guttmann examines this ideology, in a broader historical context, in "The Belated Birth and Threatened Death of Fair Play," *Yale Review* 74 (1985), 525–37.

16. Paul Weiss, quoted in Smith, *Sports and Freedom*, 167.

17. Smith, *Sports and Freedom*, 13–25.

18. Walter Camp, *Walter Camp's Book of College Sports*, 1–2.

19. Ibid.

20. Vincent, *Mudville's Revenge*, 62.

21. Ibid., 69.

22. Ibid.

23. John Lucas, "The Hegemonic Role of the American Amateur Athletic Union 1888–1914: James Edward Sullivan as Prime Mover," *International Journal of the History of Sport* 11 (1994), 359; and Arnold W. Flath, *A History of Relations Between the National Collegiate Athletic Association and the Amateur Athletic Union of the United States, 1905–1963* (Champaign, Ill., 1964), 7–25.

24. Clarence Deming, "Athletics in College Life," *Outlook* 80 (1905), 570; and Stephen Fox, *Big Leagues: Professional Baseball, Football, and Basketball in National Memory* (New York, 1994), 237.

25. Camp, quoted in Fox, *Big Leagues*, 237; and Smith, *Sports and Freedom*, 171.

26. *The White Mountain Echo*, August 20, 1904.

27. Ibid.

28. Henry Beach Needham, "The College Athlete: His Amateur Code: Its Evasion and Administration," *McClure's Magazine* 25 (1905), 262.

29. Ibid.

30. Deming, "Athletics in College Life," 572.

31. Ibid.

32. Ibid.

33. The rise of the professional coach was the other major force in the early movement to adopt the professional model in American intercollegiate athletics. Although Yale's crew team introduced the pro coach as early as 1864, it became clear, with Bill Reid's tenure as Harvard football coach in 1905, that the professional model produced victories and national prestige. See Smith, *Sports and Freedom*, chap. 11, and Smith, ed., *Big-Time Football at Harvard, 1905: The Diary of Coach Bill Reid* (Urbana, Ill., 1994).

34. Smith, *Sports and Freedom*, 172.

35. Ibid.

36. Ralph D. Paine, "The Spirit of School and College Sport," *Century* 71 (1905), 116.

37. John Hargreaves, *Sport, Power and Culture: A Social and Historical Analysis of Popular Sports in Britain* (New York, 1986).

38. Eric Hobsbawm and Terence Ranger, eds., *The Invention of Tradition* (Cambridge, Eng., 1983), 288–89; Richard Holt, *Sport and the British: A Modern History* (London, 1989), 103–7.

39. Hobsbawm and Ranger, *The Invention of Tradition*, 291.

40. Ibid.

41. *The Nation* 128 (1929), 121.

42. *National Cyclopedia of American Biography* (1898–   ), 284; *Dictionary of American Biography* (1928–1937) vol. 21, 704–5.

43. Caspar Whitney, "A Sporting Pilgrimmage," *Harper's Weekly* 38 (1894), 398–99.

44. Whitney, *A Sporting Pilgrimmage* (New York, 1895), 166–67.

45. Ibid.

46. Ibid.

47. Young, "How the Amateurs Won the Olympics," 59.

48. A biography of Sullivan has not been written, due, in large measure, to the fact that his papers were destroyed in a fire at the AAU headquarters in 1904. See *Dictionary of American Biography*, vol. 18; John Lucas, *The Modern Olympic Games* (New York, 1980), 64–73; and Stephen H. Hardy, "Entrepreneurs, Structures, and the Sportgeist: Old Tensions in a Modern Industry," in Donald Kyle and Gary Stark, eds., *Essays in Sport History and Sport Mythology* (College Station, Tex., 1990), 64–69.

49. Hardy, "Entrepreneurs, Structures, and the Sportgeist," 66.

50. Ibid.

51. James B. Connolly, "The Capitalization of Amateur Athletics," *Metropolitan Magazine* (July 1910), 443–54.

52. Ibid.

53. Ibid., 448.

54. Ibid.

55. Ibid.

56. Andrew Ross, *No Respect: Intellectuals and Popular Culture* (New York, 1989), 5.

57. Adelman, *A Sporting Time*, 244, 285; Hardy, "Entrepreneurs." For the authoritative discussion of modern sports, see Allen Guttmann, *From Ritual to Record: The Nature of Modern Sports* (New York, 1978).

58. "Report of the Committee on Definition of an Amateur," *American Physical Education Review* 20 (1915), 68.

59. W. P. Bowen, "Some Current Athletic Problems," *American Physical Education Review* 20 (1915), 62–63.

60. Ibid.

61. Hobsbawm, *The Invention of Tradition*, 299–300.

CHAPTER THREE

1. Pierre de Coubertin, *The Olympic Idea: Discourses and Essays*, ed. Carl Diem (Stuttgart, 1967).

2. Coubertin's life and role in international sports is skillfully presented in John J. MacAloon, *This Great Symbol: Pierre de Coubertin and the Origin of the Modern Olympic Games* (Chicago, 1981); John Lucas, *The Modern Olympic Games*

(New York, 1980), 13–27; and Alan Tomlinson, "De Coubertin and the Modern Olympics," in Tomlinson and G. Whannel, eds., *Five-Ring Circus: Money, Power and Politics at the Olympic Games* (London, 1984), 84–97. The best selection of Coubertin's writings translated into English may be found in *The Olympic Idea: Discourses and Essays*, ed. Carl Diem (Stuttgart, 1967).

Simultaneous with Courbertin's efforts, which led to the 1894 Paris conference, various English cultural leaders proposed a Pan-Anglican Festival for the sake of revitalizing the British empire through popular spectacles. See R. P. P. Rowe, "The Proposed Pan-Anglican Festival," *Fortnightly* 58 (July 1892), 38–49; Henry A. Blake, "The Pan-Britannic Olympiad," *Fortnightly* 59 (February 1893), 288–90; J. Astley Cooper, "The Pan-Britannic Gathering," *Nineteenth Century* 34 (July 1893), 82–93; and Cooper, "Americans and the Pan-Britannic Movement," *Nineteenth Century* 38 (September 1895), 426–41.

The revival of the Olympics is well documented. The most recent survey is Allen Guttmann, *The Olympics: A History of the Modern Games* (Urbana, 1992).

3. Tomlinson, "De Coubertin and the Modern Olympics," in *Five-Ring Circus*, 84.

4. Percy Gardner, *New Chapters on Greek History* (London, 1892). David Young scrutinizes the writings of Mahaffy and Gardner, and scathingly exposes their falsehoods and shortcomings, in *The Olympic Myth of Greek Amateur Athletics* (Chicago, 1984); also see "How the Amateurs Won the Olympics," in Wendy J. Raschke, ed., *The Archaeology of the Olympics: The Olympics and Other Festivals in Antiquity* (Madison, 1988); and Gerald Redmond, "Pseudo-Olympics of the 19th Century," in Jeffrey O. Seagrave and Donald Chu, eds., *The Olympic Games in Transition* (Champaign, Ill., 1988), 78–79.

5. Tomlinson, "De Coubertin and the Modern Olympics," 85.

6. Ibid.

7. Ibid.

8. Young, "How the Amateurs Won the Olympics," 66.

9. Paul Shorey, "Can We Revive the Olympic Games," *Forum* 19 (1895), 317.

10. G. T. Ferris, "The Olympian Games," *St. Nicholas* 23 (1896), 508.

11. Rufus Richardson, "The New Olympian Games," *Scribner's Magazine* 20 (1896), 267, 270.

12. Richardson, "The New Olympian Games," 282; for a similar perspective, see Coubertin, "The Olympic Games of 1896," *Century* 31 (1896), 46, 51. Other early representative statements include Albert Shaw, "The Re-Establishment of Olympic Games: How International Sports Promote Peace Among Nations," *Review of Reviews* 19 (1894), 643–46; and George Horton, "Revival of Olympian Games," *North American Review* 162 (1896), 266–73.

13. Ibid.

14. Richard Gruneau and Hart Cantelon, "Capitalism, Commercialism, and the Olympics," in Seagrave and Chu, eds., *The Olympic Games in Transition*, 348–49.

15. For an instructive statement, see John MacAloon, "An Observer's View of Sport Sociology," *Sociology of Sport Journal* 4 (1987), 114; and John Hargreaves, "Olympism and Nationalism: Some Preliminary Considerations," *International Review for Sociology of Sport* 27 (1992), 119–34.

16. The first collegiate international track-and-field meet took place on

July 16, 1894, in London, where Oxford won five events and Yale won three, with one tie. For an overview of nineteenth-century American track and field, see Ronald A. Smith, *Sports and Freedom: The Rise of Big-Time College Athletics* (New York, 1988), 99–117.

17. Robertson, "The Olympic Games, By a Competitor and Prize Winner," *Fortnightly Review* 65 (June 1896).

18. Caspar Whitney, "Amateur Sport," *Outing* 36 (1900), 677; "American Triumphs in the Olympic Games," *American Review of Reviews* 33 (1906), 664.

19. Mark Dyreson has explained these philosophical goals, in much more detail, in "America's Athletic Missionaries: Political Performance, Olympic Spectacle and the Quest for an American National Culture, 1896–1912," *Olympika* 1 (1992), 70–91.

20. *Atlanta Constitution.*

21. *New York Times*, July 12, 15, and 23, 1900; "Americans Win at Paris," *Chicago Tribune*, July 16, 1900, 8; George Orton, "The Paris Athletic Games," Outing 36 (1900), 690–95; and John Lucas, "The Hegemonic Rule of the American Amateur Athletic Union 1888–1914: James Edward Sullivan as Prime Mover," *International Journal of the History of Sport* 11 (1994), 362.

22. William F. Slocum, "The World's Fair as an Educative Force," *Outlook* 77 (1904), 793–804. Robert K. Barney tells the story of how the 1904 Games were shifted from Chicago to St. Louis, in "Born From Dilemma: America Awakens to the Modern Olympic Games, 1901–1903," *Olympika* 1 (1992), 92–135.

23. For additional information about the anthropology contests, see Lew Carlson, "Giant Patagonians and Hairy Ainu: Anthropology Days at the 1904 St. Louis Olympics," *Journal of American Culture* 12 (1989), 19–26; and Matti Goksyr, "'One Certainly Expected a Great Deal More from the Savages': The Anthropology Days in St. Louis, 1904 and their Aftermath," *International Journal of the History of Sport* 7 (1990).

24. W. J. McGee, "Professor W. J. M'Gee," *World's Fair Bulletin* 4(August 1903), 29.

25. Robert Rydell, *All the World's a Fair: Visions of Empire at American International Expositions, 1876–1916* (Chicago, 1984).

26. Rydell, *World of Fairs: The Century-of-Progress Expositions* (Chicago, 1993), 15–37.

27. Allen Guttmann, *The Games Must Go On: Avery Brundage and the Olympic Movement* (New York, 1984), 20; and "A Novel Athletic Contest," *World's Fair Bulletin* 5 (1904), 50.

28. Baker, *Sport in the Western World*, 196.

29. Dyreson, "The Playing Fields of Progress: American Athletic Nationalism and the 1904 St. Louis Olympics," *Gateway Heritage* (Fall 1993), 10, lists the following supplemental competitions: schoolboy track meets; YMCA national championships; collegiate football games; baseball and basketball games; German (Turner) mass gymnastics; golf, boxing, lacrosse, swimming, bicycling, and rowing; and the first-ever football game between two American Indian schools, Haskell and Carlisle. See also, Guttmann, *The Olympics*, 21.

30. James Sullivan, *Spalding's Almanac for 1905* (New York, 1905), p. 161.

31. Coubertin quoted in Guttmann, *The Olympics*, 26.

32. Henry Adams, *The Education of Henry Adams: An Autobiography* (1918), reprint ed. (Cambridge, Mass., 1961), 466–67.

33. Ibid.

34. Dyreson, "The Playing Field of Progress," 4; see also David R. Francis, ed., *The Universal Exposition of 1904* (St. Louis, 1913), 539; Sullivan, ed., *Spalding's Almanac for 1905* (New York, 1905), 161; James B. Connolly, "The Capitalization of Amateur Athletics," *Metropolitan Magazine* (July 1910), 450; and Coubertin, quoted in Guttmann, *The Olympics*, 26.

35. "U.S. Representative to Olympic Games," *New York Times*, March 10, 1906, 8.

36. Ibid.

37. See John Lucas, "American Involvement in the Athens Olympian Games," *Stadion* 6 (1980), 217–228.

38. See, for instance, *New York Times*, May 4, 6, 1906; *Literary Digest* 32 (May 12, 1906), 712–13; and *Harper's Weekly* 50 (June 2, 1906), 774–75.

39. "The Olympic Games," *The Nation* 82 (1906), 467.

40. Coubertin, quoted in Guttmann, *The Olympics*, 28.

41. *New York Times*, July 12, 1908, 10; "Wants Congress to Aid Athletes," *New York Times*, February 20, 1907, 9; and Connolly, "The Capitalization of Amateur Athletics," 454.

42. Useful documentation of the 1908 Games can be found in Weyand, 79–104; Kanin, 34–35; George R. Matthews, "The Controversial Olympic Games of 1908 As Viewed by the *New York Times* and the *Times* (London)," *Journal of Sport History* 7 (Summer 1980), 40–53; Lucas, "American Involvement," 55–63; Michael Morris Killanin and John Rodda, eds., *The Olympic Games: 80 Years of People, Events and Records* (London, 1976). chap. 4; William O. Johnson, *All That Glitters Is Not Gold: The Olympic Games* (NY, 1972), 127–29. See also, John Lowerson, "Sport and National Decay: The British and the Olympic Games Before 1914," in N. Muller and J. K. Ruhl, eds., *Olympic Scientific Congress 1984 Official Report* (Niederhausen, 1985), 384. See also, Richard Holt, *Sport and the British: A Modern History* (New York: Oxford University Press, 1989), 274.

43. David Cannadine, "The Context, Performance and Meaning of Ritual: the British Monarchy and the 'Invention of Tradition,' c.1820–1977," in Hobsbawm and Ranger, eds., *The Invention of Tradition*, 108.

44. Cannadine, "The Context," 133.

45. Cannadine, "The Context," 121–22; *Times* (London), July 14, 1908, 10. See also, Nadjeda Lekarska, "Olympic Ceremonial," in Killanin and Rodda, *The Olympic Games*, 157–58.

46. During the opening ceremony for the 1906 Athens Games, U.S. coach Matt Halpin expressed only the highest adulation for being in the presence of the Greek monarch. Leading the American contingent before the royal box, Halpin dipped the flag, upon which "the King staked me to a smile that made me feel that I belonged . . ." At the concluding awards ceremony, Halpin rallied the American team together and led three deafening cheers in honor of the king. Three weeks later, the *New York Times* reported that even Roosevelt had sent the highest commendations to the king for his "impartiality and hospitality." Halpin is quoted in Johnson, *All That Glitters*, 126; *New York Times*, May 3, 1906, 4 and May 26, 1906, 9.

47. *New York Times*, July 24, 1908, 7; cf. *Times* (London), July 24, 1908, 6; and cf. Caspar Whitney, "The Viewpoint," *Outing* 53 (1908), 244–45.

Not until after the 1912 Stockholm Games would efforts be initiated to standardize rules, given the fact that each national federation had slightly different scoring standards. See Sir Theodore A. Cook (British Olympic Association member), *The Olympic Games* (London: Archibald Constable and Co., 1908), 97–98, for a post–London Games British perspective. William H. Sloane recognized the potential pitfalls of cheating and poor judging, and was influential in pushing for reform; see his journal article, "The Olympic Idea," *Century* 84 (June 1912).

48. Caspar Whitney, "The View-Point," *Outing* 52 (1908), 761, 766.

49. Ibid.

50. Ibid.

51. Ibid.

52. Ibid.

53. The American squad dominated the track-and-field competition, winning 15 gold medals, 12 silver, and 11 bronze (out of a total of 47 track-and-field medals. In all, the U.S. received a total of 47 medals against a total of 145 British medals. David Wallechinsky, *The Complete Book of the Olympics* (New York, 1984), xii.

54. Arthur Ruhl, "The Men Who Set the Marks," *Outing* 52 (1908), 389.

55. James B. Connolly, "The Sheperd's Bush Greeks," *Collier's* 41 (September 5, 1908), 12–13; Finley Peter Dunne, "When Greek Meets Greek," *New York Times*, July 19, 1908; and "British Incompetency Ruins Olympic Games," *New York Evening Call*, July 18, 1908, 2.

56. "Thousands Cheer Victors of the Olympic Games," *New York Times*, August 30, 1908, 1.

57. *New York Evening Call*, August 8, 12, 1908.

58. Ibid.

59. Ibid.

60. John MacAloon, "Sociation and Sociability in Political Celebrations," in *Celebrations: Studies in Festivity and Ritual*, ed., Victor Turner (Washington, D.C., 1982), 268.

61. Edward Bayard Moss, "America's Olympic Argonauts," *Harper's Weekly* 56 (July 6, 1912), 11.

62. Moss, "America's Athletic Missionaries," *Harper's Weekly* 56 (July 27, 1912), 8.

63. "Race Questions at the Olympic," *The Independent* 73 (July 25, 1912), 214.

64. Thompson, "Race Questions at the Olympics," *The Independent* 73 (July 25, 1912), 15; Thompson's comments are from the *New York Times*, August 25, 1912, sec. V, 10; and "More Remarks on our Athletic Supremacy," *Literary Digest* 45 (1912).

65. Dunne, "Mr. Dooley on the Olympic Games," *American Magazine* 66 (1908), 617.

66. "Race Questions at the Olympic," *The Independent*, 215.

67. Ibid.

68. Charles E. Woodruff, "The Failure of Americans as Athletes," *North*

American Review 186 (1907), 204; Woodruff, "Why the Native American Does So Badly at the Olympic Games," *Current Literature* 53 (1912), 182–84.

69. "Olympic Champions Cheered and Dined," *New York Times*, August 25, 1912, 4.

70. Ibid.

71. Arnold W. Flath, *A History of Relations Between the National Collegiate Athletic Association and the American Athletic Union, 1905–1963* (Champaign, 1964), 40.

72. Baker, *Sport in the Western World*, 207.

73. *New York Times*, January 28 and 29, 1913.

74. "Amateur Athletics: A Poll of the Press," *Outlook* 103 (1913), 344.

75. "The Amateur," *Outlook* 103 (1913), 293–94.

76. "Amateur Athletics," 345.

77. Ibid.

78. "Amateur Athletics," 345.

79. "Thorpe's Case Discussed," *New York Times*, January 29, 1913, 10.

80. "Amateur Athletics," 347.

81. "Thorpe's Case Discussed," *New York Times*, January 29, 1913, 10.

82. "Accuses Our Athletes: Correspondent of London *Times* Alleges Trickiness at Stockholm," *New York Times*, August 30, 1912, 4.

83. "The Two Athletic Standards," *The Nation*, August 22, 1912, 163.

84. Ibid.

85. Dunne, "Dooley on the Supremacy of the English," *New York Times*, July 28, 1912.

86. Kanin, *A Political History of the Olympic Games*, 38.

87. Coubertin quoted in Baker, *Sports in the Western World*, 207.

88. Ibid.

89. "U.S. Vessels Likely to Carry Athletes," *New York Times*, May 23, 1920, sec. 8, 4; and Roy Lewis, "Our 'Scintillating Stars' at Antwerp," *Outing* 77 (1920), 162–65. For a thorough discussion of the 1920 U.S. participation, see John Lucas, "American Preparations for the First Post–World War Olympic Games, 1919–1920," *Journal of Sport History* 10 (Summer 1983), 30–44.

90. "To Finance Trip of Olympic Team," *New York Times*, May 17, 1920, 11.

91. Arthur L. Drew, "The Seventh Olympiad: An Interpretation," *Playground* 14 (1920), 164–65.

92. *Report of the American Olympic Committee, Seventh Olympic Games, Antwerp, Belgium, 1920* (New York, 1920), 17; for more information on the military's involvement, see *Report*, 84–112.

93. Weeks is quoted in John Lucas, "American Preparations for the First Post–World War Olympic Games, 1919–1920," *Journal of Sport History* 10 (1983), 35.

The military transport conditions were far from ideal. See "U.S. Athletes Return Angry at Committee," *New York Tribune*, September 5, 1920, 16; and "Olympians Return, Condemn Officials," *New York Times*, September 12, 1920, 21.

94. *New York Times*, August 8, 1920, 19.

95. *New York Times*, September 12, 1920, 21.

96. "General Statement of the American Olympic Committee," *Report of the American Olympic Committee*, 33; *New York Times*, August 14, 1920, 9; and Flath, *A History of Relations*, 46–49.

97. *New York Times*, May 14, 1921, 12.

98. Newton Fuessle, "America's Boss-Ridden Athletics," *Outlook* 130 (1922), 642, 644. Also, see "Colonel Thompson Defends the AAU and Replies to 'America's Boss-Ridden Athletics,'" *Outlook* 131 (1922), 723–25.

99. Fuessle, "Americas Boss-Ridden Athletics," 130.

100. Ibid.

101. Coubertin, *The Olympic Idea: Discourses and Essays*, ed. Carl Diem (Stuttgart, 1967), 56.

CHAPTER FOUR

1. For a perspective review of the scholarly literature on baseball history, see Larry R. Gerlach, "Not Quite Ready for Prime Time: Baseball History, 1983–1993," *Journal of Sport History* 21 (1994), 103–37.

2. Stephen Fox, *Big Leagues: Professional Baseball, Football and Basketball in National Memory* (New York, 1994), 209; and Warren Goldstein, *Playing for Keeps: A History of Early Baseball* (Ithaca, 1989).

3. Fox Butterfield, "Cooperstown? Hoboken? Try New York City," *New York Times*, October 4, 1990, B14.

4. Ibid.

5. Goldstein, *Playing for Keeps*; and Elliott J. Gorn and Warren Goldstein, *A Brief History of American Sports* (New York, 1993), 77–97.

6. Melvin L. Adelman, *A Sporting Time: New York City and the Rise of Modern Athletics, 1820–70* (Urbana, 1986), 109–11.

7. Ibid., 111.

8. The best monographs on the origins of baseball are Goldstein, *Playing for Keeps*; Adelman, *A Sporting Time*; George B. Kirsch, *The Creation of American Team Sports: Baseball and Cricket, 1838–72* (Urbana, Ill., 1989); and Ted Vincent, *Mudville's Revenge: The Rise and Fall of American Sport* (New York, 1981). The first major scholarly work was Harold Seymour, *Baseball: The Early Years* (New York, 1960), followed by David Q. Voigt, *American Baseball: From Gentlemen's Sport to the Commissioner System* (Norman, Okla., 1966).

9. Adelman, *A Sporting Time*, 116.

10. Steven M. Gelber, "Working at Playing: The Culture of the Work Place and the Rise of Baseball," *Journal of Social History* 16 (1983), 3–20.

11. Ibid.; Adelman, *A Sporting Time*; and Adelman, "Baseball, Business and the Work Place: Gelber's Thesis Reexamined," *Journal of Social History* 23 (1989), 285–302.

12. Adelman, *A Sporting Time*, 150–74.

13. John R. Betts, *America's Sporting Heritage, 1850–1950* (Reading, Mass., 1974), 93.

14. John Bale charts this process in British sport in his *Sports Geography* (London, 1989).

15. Cited in R. Terry Furst, "Conflicting Images of Organized Baseball in the 19th Century Sport Press," *Canadian Journal of the History of Sport* 21 (1990), 1.

16. Ibid.

17. Quotes cited in Betts, *America's Sporting Heritage*, 93.

18. Ibid.

19. Ibid.

20. Gunther Barth, *City People: The Rise of Modern City Culture in Nine-teenth-Century America* (New York, 1980), 165–67. See the editorial about "baseballese"—the slang associated with baseball journalism early in the twentieth century—in "English and Baseball," *The Nation* 97 (August 21, 1913), 161.

21. Goldstein, *Playing for Keeps*, 151. See also Vincent, *Mudville's Revenge*, 87–122.

22. Ibid.

23. Ibid.

24. Robert F. Burk, *Never Just a Game: Players, Owners, and American Baseball to 1920* (Chapel Hill, N.C., 1994), 1–49.

25. Burk, *Never Just a Game*, 50–51.

26. Leonard Koppett, *Sports Illusion, Sports Reality: A Reporter's View of Sports, Journalism and Society* (Boston, 1981), 36–37.

27. Ibid.

28. John F. Rooney, Jr. and Richard Pillsbury, *Atlas of American Sport* (New York, 1992), 33. See also Rooney's pioneering work, *A Geography of American Sport: From Cabin Creek to Anaheim* (Reading, Mass., 1974).

29. Albert G. Spalding, *Baseball: America's Game* (New York, 1911),

30. Burk, *Never Just a Game*, 236–37.

31. J. M. Ward, "Is the Ballplayer Chattel?," *Lippincott's*, August 1887, 310.

32. Burk, *Never Just a Game*, 243.

33. Warren Goldstein, "Sports in the Twentieth Century," in Mary Kupiec Cayton et al., *Encyclopedia of American Social History* (New York, 1993), vol. 3, 1641. For more on the players' rebellion, see Vincent, *Mudville's Revenge*, 180–221; Seymour, *Baseball*, 104–15 (on the reserve clause), and 221–39; Leo Lowenfish, *Imperfect Diamond*, 35–36; and Burk, *Never Just a Game*, chap. 5.

34. Goldstein, *Playing For Keeps*, 153–54.

35. Seymour, *Baseball*, 239; and Goldstein, "Sports in the Twentieth Century," 1643.

36. M. Cready Sykes, "The Most Perfect Thing in America," *Everybody's Magazine* 25 (1911), 439–46.

37. Ibid.

38. Ibid.

39. Burk, *Never Just a* Game, 111–113; Goldstein, *Playing for Keeps*, 152–53.

40. Quote from Seymour, *Baseball*, 230–32.

41. Gerald Astor, *The Baseball Hall of Fame 50th Anniversary Book* (New York, 1988), 29, cited in Burk, *Never Just a Game*, 107.

42. Burk, *Never Just a Game*, 107.

43. Fullerton, cited in Seymour, *Baseball*, 112–13.

44. Ibid.

45. Stephen Hardy, "'Adopted by All the Leading Clubs': Sporting Goods and the Shaping of Leisure, 1800–1900," in Richard Butsch, ed., *For Fun and Profit: The Transformation of Leisure into Consumption* (Philadelphia, 1990), 72; and see his earlier essay, "Entrepreneurs, Organizations, and the Sport Mar-

ketplace: Subjects in Search of Historians," *Journal of Sport History* 13 (Spring 1986), 14–33. John Clarke and Charles Critcher note that a similar process has occurred, over the last two centuries, throughout much of the leisure domain. Though informal pastimes remained a central part of ordinary peoples' lives, "the major forms of organized leisure were outside the control of those who enjoyed them"; and though controlling bodies could not ignore their consumers, "the essential relationship was that of provider and customer." See Clarke and Critcher, *The Devil Makes Work: Leisure in Capitalist Britain* (Urbana, Ill., 1985), 70.

46. John Wilson, "Cleaning Up the Game: Perspectives on the Evolution of Professional Sports," in Eric Dunning and Chris Rojek, eds., *Sport and Leisure in the Civilizing Process: Critiques and Counter Critique* (Toronto, 1992), 89.

47. Ibid., 82–93.

48. Cyrus R. K. Patell, "Baseball and the Cultural Logic of American Individualism," *Prospects* 18 (1993), 423.

49. "Henry Chadwick," *Dictionary of American Biography*, vol. 3, ed. Allen Johnson (New York, 1929), 587; L. J. DeBekker, "The Father of the Game," *Harper's Weekly* 51 (June 8, 1907), 838; Henry Chadwick, *The American Game of Baseball* (Philadelphia, 1889); Chadwick, "Old Time Baseball," *Outing* 39 (1901), 422. For a perceptive overview of Chadwick's significance, see Stephen Hardy, "Entrepreneurs, Structures, and the Sportgeist: Old Tensions in a Modern Industry," in Donald Kyle and Gary Stark, eds., *Sport History and Sport Mythology* (College Station, Tex., 1990), 55–59.

50. Seymour, *Baseball*, 9.

51. Peter Levine, *A. G. Spalding and the Rise of Baseball: The Promise of American Sport* (New York, 1985), xiii.

52. Curiously, Doubleday's 1893 obituary makes no mention of the alleged game. The vast body of correspondence and testimony, including the alleged Abner Graves letter, was destroyed in a fire at the American Sports Publishing Company office in 1911.

53. The definitive, partisan account of the investigation was published by Spalding, *Baseball*, 17–26, (quotes on cricket: 6, 9). The first authoritative study that interrogated the commission's findings was Robert W. Henderson, *Ball, Bat and Bishop: The Origin of Ball Games* (New York, 1947), chaps. 23–24. For an excellent overview of the Doubleday myth, see James A. Vlasich, *A Legend for the Legendary: The Origin of the Baseball Hall of Fame* (Bowling Green, Ohio, 1990), 5–23; 225–31.

54. Gould, "The Creation Myths of Cooperstown," 29.

55. Ibid., 33.

56. Ibid.

57. Benjamin G. Rader, *American Sports: From the Age of Folk Games to the Age of Televised Sports*, 2d ed. (Englewood Cliffs, N.J., 1990), 152.

58. Vlasich, *A Legend for the Legendary*.

59. Spalding, *Baseball*, 4–5.

60. Ibid.

61. Henry S. Curtis, "Baseball," *Journal of Education* 83 (1916), 466.

62. Editorial: "Know Baseball, Know the American," *American Magazine* 76 (1913), 94.

63. Dean A. Sullivan, "Faces in the Crowd: A Statistical Portrait of Baseball Spectators in Cincinnati, 1886–1888," *Journal of Sport History* 17 (1990), 354–65.

64. Riess, "Baseball Myths, Baseball Reality, and the Social Functions of Baseball in Progressive America," *Stadion* 3 (1977), 273–311.

65. These insights derive from John Ehrenreich, "Socialism, Nationalism, and Capitalist Development," *Review of Radical Political Economics* 15 (1983), 1–42.

66. Peter Levine, *Ellis Island to Ebbets Field: Sport and the American Jewish Experience* (New York, 1992), 88.

67. Ibid., 98.

68. Hugh Fullerton is quoted in Riess, *Touching Base*, 25; also, see Riess, *City Games: The Evolution of American Urban Society and the Rise of Sports* (Urbana, 1989), esp. 93–123.

69. Bill Brown, "Waging Baseball, Playing War: Games of American Imperialism," *Cultural Critique* 17 (1990), 51–78; Michael Hunt, *Ideology and U.S. Foreign Policy* (New Haven, 1987); see also Donald Mrozek's discussion of the way sports metaphors make war more comprehensible to the American public, in his "The Interplay of Metaphor and Practice in the U.S. Defense Establishment's Use of Sport, 1940–1950," *Journal of American Culture* 7 (1984), 54–59.

70. Spalding, *Baseball*, 14.

71. Brown, "Waging Baseball, Playing War," 65. J. A. Mangan explores similar issues from the British perspective in *The Games Ethic and Imperialism: Aspects of the Diffusion of an Ideal* (Middlesex, Eng., 1986).

72. The best overview of the 1888 World Tour is in Levine, *A. G. Spalding and the Rise of Baseball.*

73. John J. McGraw, "Americans in Manila Turned Out in Great Crowds to Welcome Giants and White Sox," *New York Times*, January 25, 1914, sec. IV, 1.

74. Ibid.

75. Ibid.

76. Ringgold Wilmer Lardner, *The Homecoming of Charles A. Comiskey, John J. McGraw, and James J. Callahan* (Chicago, 1914).

77. George C. Rable, "Patriotism, Platitudes and Politics: Baseball and the American Presidency," *Presidential Studies Quarterly* 19 (1989), 363–72.

78. Seymour, *Baseball: The Golden Age*, 20, 244–46; and Alexander, *Our Game*, 108–9.

79. Quotes cited in Richard Crepeau, *Baseball: America's Diamond Mind, 1919–41* (Orlando: University Presses of Florida, 1980), 68–69.

80. Richter is quoted in Crepeau, 69; "The Baseball Strain," *New York Times*, September 22, 1924, 18. and for the reaction to Harding's death, see "Sportsmen Honor Harding's Memory," *New York Times*, August 11, 1923.

81. *New York Times*, October 2, 1924, I, 18, quoted in Rable, "Patriotism, Platitudes, and Politics," 367.

82. Betts, *America's Sporting Heritage*, 252.

83. Ibid., 272.

84. Richard Vidmer, "National League Extols 50th Year," *New York Times*, February 3, 1926, 18.

85. Ibid.

86. Ibid.

87. Seymour, *Baseball*, 49. Without footnotes, the source of this anecdote is not clear.

88. Simeon Strunsky, "The Game," *Atlantic Monthly* 114 (1914), 249–50.

89. Morris R. Cohen, "Baseball," *The Dial* 67 (July 26, 1919), 57.

90. Raymond Williams, "Base and Superstructure in Marxist Cultural Theory." *New Left Review* 82 (1973).

91. Colin D. Howell, "Baseball, Class and Community in the Maritime Provinces, 1870–1914," *Historie Sociale* 22 (1989), 265–86, esp. 286. Howell develops this in more elaborate form in his *Northern Sandlots: A Social History of Maritime Baseball* (Toronto, 1995).

92. David Q. Voigt, "Getting Right with Baseball," in Alvin Hall, ed., *Cooperstown Symposium on Baseball* (Westport, Conn., 1991), 26.

93. Roger Kahn, *Games We Used to Play: A Lover's Quarrel with the World of Sport* (New York, 1992), 28.

94. Edward Pessen, "Life, Baseball and Intellectuals," *Reviews in American History* 20 (1992), 112.

95. A. Bartlett Giamatti, *Take Time for Paradise: Americans and Their Games* (New York, 1989), 83.

96. Ibid.

97. Giamatti, "Baseball and the American Character," in David Gallen, ed., *The Baseball Chronicles* (New York, 1991), 356.

98. Michael Novak, *The Joy of Sports* (New York, 1976).

99. Allen Guttmann, *From Ritual to Record: The Nature of Modern Sports* (New York, 1978), 91–116.

100. Ibid.

101. The contextual overview comes from Alan Dawley, *Struggles for Justice: Social Responsibility and the Liberal State* (Cambridge, 1991).

102. Riess, "Baseball Myths, Baseball Reality, and the Social Functions of Baseball in Progressive America," *Stadion* 3 (1977), 309.

103. Riess, *Touching Base*, 103.

104. Nicholas Dawidoff, "Field of Kitsch," *New Republic*, August 17–24, 1992, 22.

105. Hofstra University, for instance, recently hosted a major conference commemorating the 100th birthday of Babe Ruth, which was underwritten by a host of major league teams, museums, and private and municipal foundations. The conference had both critical scholarly and nostalgic papers, and featured keynote addresses by the New York and Baltimore mayors, university officials, a production of the Broadway musical *Damn Yankees*, and the recollections of various Hall of Famers.

106. James Wolcott, "Romancing the Diamond," *The New Yorker*, September 19, 1994, 105–7. Gerlach's critique was presented, as part of a panel discussion on Burns's "Baseball," at the North American Society for Sport History's Twenty-third Annual Convention, 1995.

107. James Wolcott, "Baseball," *New Yorker* 70 (Sept. 19, 1994), 106.

108. See Goldstein, "Field of Schemes," *The Nation*, March 1, 1993, 273–75.

109. Patell, "Baseball and the Cultural Logic of American Individualism," 436–37; Guttmann, *A Whole New Ball Game: An Interpretation of American Sports*

(Chapel Hill, N.C., 1988), 69; and Jack Sands and Peter Gammons, *Coming Apart at the Seams* (New York, 1993).

110. Lewis Lapham, "Field of Dreams," *Harper's* 283 (April 1991), 11–12.

111. Ibid. (Pritchett quoted by Lapham)

CHAPTER FIVE

1. Richard Harding Davis, "The Thanksgiving Game," *Harper's Weekly* 37 (1893), 1170.

2. Ibid., 1171.

3. Ibid.

4. Finley Peter Dunne, "Mr. Dooley on Thanksgiving," *Harper's Weekly* 44 (1900), 1133. Dunne exerted considerable influence on national opinion during his career as a regional and national humorist (from 1893 to 1926).

One year earlier, in a tone strikingly similar to Davis's, a YMCA publication noted that "no longer do families in the land peaceably assemble around the festive board to eat the Thanksgiving turkey and render thanks for the blessings that have been showered upon them"; rather, the general public cry is, "'Onward to New York! We must see the great match." See "Editorial," *Young Men's Era* 18 (1892), 1012. See also, the *New York Herald*, November 30, 1893, 6.

5. Edwin H. Cady, "The Sort of Sacred, Sometimes Ritual," in David L. Vanderwerken and Spencer K. Wertz, eds., *Sport Inside Out: Readings in Literature and Philosophy* (Fort Worth, 1985), 312–13.

6. Ibid.

7. Nancy B. Bouchier makes a similar argument in her interesting case study of Ingersoll and Woodstock, Ontario—"'The 24th of May is the Queen's Birthday': Civic Holidays and the Rise of Amateurism in Nineteenth-Century Canadian Towns," *International Journal of the History of Sport* 10 (1993), 159–92.

8. Donald Mrozek, *Sport and American Mentality, 1880–1910* (Knoxville, 1983).

9. Eric Hobsbawm, "Mass-Producing Traditions: Europe, 1870–1914," in Hobsbawm and Terence Ranger, eds., *The Invention of Tradition* (Cambridge, Eng., 1983), 291–98.

10. Two excellent discussions of national rituals are Wilbur Zelinsky, *Nation Into State: The Shifting Symbolic Foundations of American Nationalism* (Chapel Hill, 1988); and James O. Robertson, *American Myth, American Reality* (New York, 1980). See C. H. Rockwell, "A New England Thanksgiving Day Forty Years Ago," *Harper's Weekly* 38 (1894), 1139, for a useful rendition of a representative antebellum Thanksgiving Day.

11. Robertson, *American Myth, American Reality*, 11.

12. Ibid, 15–18, 44–53—these pages illuminate the Thanksgiving story better than any other source with which I am familiar.

13. Janet Siskind, "The Invention of Thanksgiving: A Ritual of American Nationality," *Critique of Anthropology* 12 (1992), 176.

14. Elliott J. Gorn and Warren Goldstein, *A Brief History of American Sports* (New York, 1993), 47–97; and Warren H. Wilson, "College Department," *Young Men's Era* 18 (1892), 1554. Not all Protestants converted to the cult of football. In 1892, North Carolina Methodists launched a fierce campaign against

a fledgling football program at Trinity College (now Duke University) in the pages of the *Raleigh Christian Advocate*. Comparing the morals of intercollegiate football to those of "the blood-curdling games of the [Roman] Colosseum," the *Advocate* added that the game smacked of professionalism and "unduly excites and cultivates the *animal*." Methodist critics not only ousted Trinity's muscular Christian president; they also effectively banned the game for a quarter of a century. To be sure, the South held no monopoly on moral crusades against college football. The game drew the wrath of western pietists for involving drinking, gambling, brutal, and dissipative tendencies. See, for instance, Jim L. Sumner, "John Franklin Crowell, Methodism, and the Football Controversy at Trinity College, 1887–1894," *Journal of Sport History* 17 (1990), 13; and Hal D. Sear, "The Moral Threat of Intercollegiate Sports: An 1893 Poll of Ten College Presidents, and the End of the 'Champion Football Team of the Great West,'" *Journal of Sport History* 19 (1992), 211–26.

15. Andrei Markovits, "The 'Other American Exceptionalism': Why is There No Soccer in the United States?" *International Journal of the History of Sport* 7 (1990), 130–64.

16. Hobsbawm, "Mass-Producing Traditions," 297.

17. *New York Herald*, November 27, 1885.

18. Ibid., November 25, 1887. Allen L. Sack provocatively explains Yale's unrivaled early football dominance over Harvard as reflecting the *nouveau riche* character of Yale; whereas, Harvard represented old money, and Boston Brahmins who were much less interested in athletic spectacles. See Sack, "Yale 29–Harvard 4: The Professionalization of College Football," *Quest* 19 (1973), 24–34. An in-depth history of this rivalry can be found in Thomas G. Bergin, *The Game: The Harvard-Yale Football Rivalry, 1875–1983* (New Haven, 1984).

19. New York Herald, November 25, 1887.

20. Godkin, "The Athletic Craze," *The Nation* 57 (1893), 423.

21. Lewis, "The Intercollegiate Football Spectacle," 203–4. Harvard initiated the stadium-building boom of the early twentieth century. For more on this development, see Lawrence Perry, "The Stadium and College Athletics," *Scribner's Magazine* 56 (1914), 571–86.

22. James A. Leroy, "As the Middle Western Universities View It," *Outing* 36 (1900), 196–97.

23. "Sports and Athletics," *Literary Digest* 76 (January 13, 1926), 64; and George Sage, *Power and Ideology in American Sport* (Champaign, Ill., 1992), 95–98.

24. Michael Oriard, *Reading Football: How the Popular Press Created an American Spectacle* (Chapel Hill, 1993), esp. 61–89; quote is on 93. See also, William Nugent, "The Sports Section," *American Mercury* 16 (1929), 337; and John R. Betts, "Sporting Journalism in 19th Century America," *American Quarterly* 5 (1953), 54.

25. Oriard, 93.

26. Ibid.

27. Davis, "Richard Carr's Baby," *St. Nicholas* 14 (1886), 50–53.

28. Camp, "Intercollegiate Football in America," *St. Nicholas* 17 (1889); and Camp, "A Historic Game of Football," *Youth's Companion* 74 (1900), 625–26.

29. Oriard, *Reading Football*, 121.

30. Abbott, "College Athletic Conferences and American Regions," *Journal of American Studies* 24 (1990), 211–21; Reed, "The Big Game," *The Independent* 88 (1916).

31. Arnold W. Flath, *A History of Relations Between the National Collegiate Athletic Association and the Amateur Athletic Union of the United States, 1905–1963* (Champaign, 1964).

32. *Chicago Daily Tribune*, November 28, 1919.

33. *Nashville American* November 26, 30, and December 2, 1894.

34. Andrew Doyle, "'Causes Won, Not Lost': College Football and the Modernization of the American South," *International Journal of the History of Sport* 11 (1994), 240–41. See also, Robert A. Orsi, "Parades, Holidays, and Public Rituals," in Mary Kupiec Cayton, Elliott J. Gorn, and Peter W. Williams, eds., *Encyclopedia of American Social History* (New York, 1992), vol. 3, 1915.

35. J. Steven Picou, "Football," in Charles Reagan Wilson and William Ferris, eds., *Encyclopedia of Southern Culture* (Chapel Hill, 1989), 1221–24; Edward L. Ayers, *The Promise of the New South: Life After Reconstruction* (New York, 1992), 313–16; Doyle, "Causes Won, Not Lost"; and Paul K. Conkin, *Gone With the Ivy: A Biography of Vanderbilt University* (Knoxville, Tenn., 1985), 135–41.

36. John Egerton, *The Americanization of Dixie: The Southernization of America* (New York, 1974); and Michael Novak, *The Joy of Sports: End Zones, Bases, Baskets, Balls, and the Consecration of the American Spirit* (New York, 1976)

37. Doyle, "'Causes Won, Not Lost,'" 247.

38. Murray Sperber, *Shake Down the Thunder: The Creation of Notre Dame Football* (New York, 1993).

39. Hal A. Lawson and Alan G. Ingham, "Conflicting Ideologies Concerning the University and Intercollegiate Athletics: Harper and Hutchins at Chicago, 1892–1940," *Journal of Sport History* 7 (1980), 37–67; quote is on 42.

40. Robin Lester, "Michigan-Chicago 1905: The First Greatest Game of the Century," *Journal of Sport History* 18 (1991), 267–73.

41. "Berkeley Item," *The Examiner* (San Francisco) March 18, 1892.

42. John Craig, "Football on the Pacific Slope," *Outing* 22 (1893), 448–59; Roberta J. Park, "From Football to Rugby and Back, 1906–1919: The University of California-Stanford University Response to the 'Football Crisis of 1905,'" *Journal of Sport History* 11 (1984), 5–40; and *The Examiner*, November 25–December 1, 1919.

43. Joseph Lee, "Football in the War," *Playground* 10 (1916), 323.

44. Raymond G. Gettell, "The Value of Football," *American Physical Education Review* 22 (1917), 140–41: and George E. Johnson, "The Fighting Instict—Its Place in Life," *Survey* 35 (1915), 245–48.

45. *Puck*, December 19, 1914, 5.

46. Johnson, 248.

47. Bruce, "The Psychology of Football," 541.

48. Ibid.

49. For more on the early days of this rivalry, see Park Benjamin, "Public Football vs. Naval Education: In Defense of the Naval Academy," *The Independent* 55 (1903), 2777–79.

50. Arthur Ruhl, "The Army-and-Navy Game," *Outing Magazine* 49 (1907), 305–6, 308.

51. *New York Times*, November 23, 1919, sec. III, 1.

52. *NYT* November 30, 1919, sec. X, 1–2.

53. *New York Times*, November 28, 1926, sec. X, 2.

54. Ibid.

55. Oriard, *Reading Football*.

56. Warren Goldstein, *Playing for Keeps: An Early History of Baseball* (Ithaca, 1989).

57. Benjamin G. Rader, *American Sports: From the Age of Folk Games to the Age of Televised Sport*, 2d ed. (Englewood Cliffs, N.J., 1990), 107.

58. Arthur Twining Hadley, "Wealth and Democracy in American Colleges," *Harper's Monthly* 93 (1906), 452.

59. Thorstein Veblen, *Theory of the Leisure Class: An Economic Study of Institutions* (New York, 1899).

60. Mrozek, *Sport and American Mentality*, 103.

61. Oriard, *Reading Football*, 17–18.

62. Ibid., 121.

63. Ibid.

64. "The Fall War Game," *Outlook*, November 2, 1927, 269.

65. Raymond G. Gettell, "The Value of Football," *American Physical Education Review* 22 (1917), 138–42.

66. Joseph Hamblin Sears, "Football: Sport and Training," *North American Review* 153 (1891), 750–53.

67. Ibid.; Oriard notes how crusading journalists, ministers, and educators read football in moral, ethical, and, occasionally, theological terms—*Reading Football*, 169–75.

68. Ibid.

69. The early-twentieth-century reform of college football has attracted considerable scholarly attention. See Smith, *Sports and Freedom*; Smith, "Harvard and Columbia and a Reconsideration of the 1905–06 Football Crisis," *Journal of Sport History* 8 (1981), 5–19; G. Lewis, "Theodore Roosevelt's Role in the 1905 Football Controversy," *Research Quarterly* 40 (1969), 717–24; and John Hammond Moore, "Football's Ugly Decades, 1893–1913," *Smithsonian Journal of History* 2 (1967), 49–63.

70. "How Football Fosters Fair Play and Clean Living," *Literary Digest* (October 31, 1925), 57–58.

71. Sol Metzger, "Boys, Parents, and Football," *St. Nicholas* 48 (1920), 69.

72. Oriard, *Reading Football*, 37–42; see also, his excellent overview of Camp's writing, 42–56.

73. Briggs, "Intercollegiate Athletics and the War," *Atlantic Monthly* 122 (1918), 303–9.

74. Ibid.

75. Caspar Whitney, "Amateur Sport," *Harper's Weekly* 37 (November 4, 1893).

76. Ibid.

77. Oriard, *Reading Football*, 158.

78. Oriard, *Reading Football*, 161–62.

79. Ibid., 229.

80. Leigh Eric Schmidt, "The Commercialization of the Calendar: American Holidays and the Culture of Consumption, 1870–1930," *Journal of Ameri-*

can History 78 (1991), 887–916; and Michael Kazin and Steven J. Ross, "America's Labor Day: The Dilemma of a Worker's Celebration," *Journal of American History* 78 (1992), 1294–1323.

81. Tristam Potter Coffin and Hennig Cohen, eds., *The Folklore of American Holidays* (Detroit, 1987), 347; and Theodore C. Humphrey and Lin T. Humphrey, eds., *"We Gather Together: Food and Festival in American Life"* (Ann Arbor, 1988).

CHAPTER SIX

1. For a stimulating analysis of early American street theater, see David Waldstreicher, "Rites of Rebellion, Rites of Assent: Celebrations, Print Culture, and the Origins of American Nationalism," *Journal of American History* 82 (1995), 37–61.

2. Miller, "The Old-Fashioned Fourth of July: A Photographic Essay on Small-Town Celebrations prior to 1930," *South Dakota History* 17 (1987), 118–37.

3. "Independence Day," *New York Times*, July 4, 1877, 4. See John Berens, *Providence and Patriotism in Early America, 1640–1815* (Charlottesville, Va., 1978), 155; Wilbur Zelinsky, *Nation Into State: The Shifting Symbolic Foundations of American Nationalism* (Chapel Hill, 1988), 70; Daniel Boorstin, *The Americans: The National Experience* (New York, 1965), 383, 390; James O. Robertson, *American Myth, American Reality* (New York, 1980), 54–71; and Len Travers, "Hurrah for the Fourth: Patriotism, Politics, and Independence Day in Federalist Boston, 1783–1818," Essex Institute Historical Collections, 1989, 125, 129–61.

4. *New York Times*, July 4, 1877, 4.

5. See Susan Davis, *Parades and Power: Street Theater in Nineteenth Century Philadelphia* (Philadelphia, 1986); Sean Wilentz, *Chants Democratic: New York City and the Rise of the American Working Class, 1785–1850* (New York, 1984); Timothy J. Meagher, "'Why Should We Care for a Little Trouble or a Walk Through the Mud'?: St. Patrick's and Columbus Day Parades in Worcester, Massachusetts, 1845–1915," *New England Quarterly* 5f8 (1985), 5–26; Eugene Genovese, *Roll, Jordan, Roll: The World the Slaves Made* (New York, 1974); Leonard I. Sweet, "The Fourth of July and Black Americans in the Nineteenth Century: Northern Leadership Opinion Within the Context of the Black Experience," *Journal of Negro History* 61 (1976), 269.

6. This history is well documented in the following sources: Christopher HIll, *Society and Puritanism in Pre-Revolutionary England* (New York, 1967), chap. 5; Dennis Brailsford, *Sport and Society: Elizabeth to Anne* (London, 1969); Robert W. Malcolmson, *Popular Recreations in English Society, 1700–1850* (London, 1973); E. P. Thompson, "Time, Work Discipline and Industrial Capitalism," *Past and Present* 38 (1967), 56–97; Norbert Elias and Eric Dunning, "Folk Football in Medieval and Early Modern Britain," in Dunning, ed., *The Sociology of Sport* (London, 1971); Peter Burke, *Popular Culture in Early Modern Europe* (New York, 1978), 207–43.

7. *New York Times*, July 4, 1877.

8. Ibid., July 5, 1871, 8; also, see Scott Martin, "The Fourth of July in Southwestern Pennsylvania, 1800–1850," *Pittsburgh History* 75 (1992), 59.

9. Whitman is quoted in Benjamin G. Rader, *Baseball: A History of America's Game* (Urbana, 1992), xv.

10. For the early history of baseball, see Melvin L. Adelman, *A Sporting Time: New York City and the Rise of Modern Athletics, 1820–1870* (Urbana, 1986); Warren Goldstein, *Playing for Keeps: A History of Early Baseball* (Ithaca, 1989); and Stephen Fox, *Big Leagues: Professional Baseball, Football and Basketball in National Memory* (New York, 1994).

11. I offer my city of current residence, Portland, as a representative example of smaller American towns' Fourth celebrations. See "Harvard and Bowdoin at Base Ball," *Daily Eastern Argus*, July 6, 1864, 1; and Will Anderson, *Was Baseball Really Invented in Maine?* (Portland, 1991), 2–5. Historian David C. Smith has located about 40 box scores of games played in Maine prior to 1880; see his unpublished essay, "Backwoods Baseball: The Game in Maine, 1860–1880" (in the author's possession). During the early 1880s, the *Argus* began to include a weekly column, "Sporting Matters," which was a summary of major league standings with commentary. Coverage of the Portlanders in the New England League rivaled local papers' coverage of major league baseball.

12. Anderson, *Was Baseball Really Invented in Maine?*, 6, 10–20.

13. *Portland Sunday Times*, July 5, 1903, 2, 16.

14. Ibid.

15. Don Rickey, Jr., *Forty Miles a Day on Beans and Hay: The Enlisted Soldier Fighting the Indian Wars* (Norman, Okla., 1963), 204–5.

16. Albert G. Spalding, *Baseball: America's National Game* (New York, 1911), 4, 7; Edward Marshall, "The Psychology of Baseball," *New York Times*, November 13, 1910, sec. V, 13; and Donald Mrozek's treatment of this interview in his *Sport and American Mentality, 1880–1910* (Knoxville, 1983), 174–75.

17. Know Baseball, Know the American," *American Magazine* 76 (1913), 94.

18. Addington Bruce, "Baseball and the National Life," *Outlook* 101 (1913), 105; Simeon Strunsky, "The Game," *Atlantic Monthly* 114 (1914), 249–50."

19. George Earle Raiguel, "The Fourth of July That Rang Round the World: The Greatest Baseball Game Ever Played," *Ladies' Home Journal* 36 (July 1919), 118–19. Also see, "America Hailed at Fetes Abroad," *New York Times*, July 5, 1918; and "What London Thought of Its Fourth of July Baseball Game," *Literary Digest* 58 (August 10, 1918), 41. "The Fourth in England: The King at the American Baseball Match," *Living Age* 298 (1918), 494–96.

20. Ibid.

21. Ibid.

22. Ibid.

23. Raiguel, "The Fourth," 119.

24. The *Worcester Daily Press* is cited in Roy Rosenzweig, *Eight Hours For What We Will: Workers and Leisure in an Industrial City, 1879–1920* (New York, 1983), 71.

25. A. B. Riker, "Fourth of July Celebrations and the Interests of Ballot Reform," *North American Review* 164 (1897), 636–37.

26. Ibid.

27. "The Standardization of Holidays," *The Independent* 77 (1914), 546.

28. Typical of this cultural transformation is the history of Labor Day. By the early 1900s, rank-and-file union members had adopted a new view of the holiday, for which union-sponsored parades and picnics were only two of a myriad of available leisure activities. With the holiday's legitimacy having been established, most workers wanted the option of spending the day with friends and family, which symbolized newly won working-class power to resist the bosses at the workplace and enjoy the fruits of this resistance outside work. Local organizers infused their celebrations with a variety of leisure activities as enticement, including baseball games, boxing matches, pole-climbing contests, running races, and the like. See Michael Kazin and Steven J. Ross, "America's Labor Day: The Dilemma of a Workers' Celebration," *Journal of American History* 78 (1992), 1294–1323.

The history of working-class and radicals' participation in American sports has yet to be written. Instructive British and European analyses include Stephen G. Jones, *Sport, Politics and the Working Class: Organised Labour and Sport in Inter-War Britain* (Manchester, Eng., 1988); Chris Waters, *British Socialists and the Politics of Popular Culture* (Cambridge, Eng., 1990); Patrick Joyce, *Visions of the People: Industrial England and the Question of Class, 1848–1914* (Cambridge, Eng., 1990); and Abrams, *Workers' Culture in Imperial Germany*.

29. *New York Evening Call*, July 9, 1909.

30. Francis G. Couvares, *The Remaking of Pittsburgh: Class and Culture in an Industrializing City, 1877–1920* (Albany, N.Y., 1983), 65–73; and *Chicago Verbote*, July 1, 1876, 1.

31. "This is the Day to be Patriotic," *New York Evening Call*, July 4, 1908.

32. Ibid.

33. Abrams, *Workers' Culture in Imperial Germany*, 51–52.

34. "The Spirit of Play," *New York Evening Call*, July 6, 1913.

35. Ibid.

36. Ibid.

37. Ibid.

38. "Play for the People," *The Independent* 62 (1907), 514.

39. Gulick, "The New and More Glorious Fourth: A Method of Celebrating the National Holiday Which is Significant of its Origins," *World's Work* 18 (1909), 11784, 11787.

40. Ibid.

41. T. J. Jackson Lears, *No Place of Grace: Antimodernism and the Transformation of American Culture, 1880–1920* (New York, 1981), xvi.

42. Ibid.

43. Rosenzweig, *Eight Hours For What We Will*; Davis, *Parades and Power*; Couvares, *The Remaking of Pittsburgh*; and Christine Stansell, *City of Women: Sex and Class in New York, 1789–1860* (New York, 1986).

44. Quotes are cited in John R. Betts, *America's Sporting Heritage, 1850–1950* (Reading, Mass., 1974), 173–74.

45. Ibid.

46. Raymond W. Smilor, "Creating a National Festival: The Campaign for a Safe and Sane Fourth, 1903–1916," *Journal of American Culture* 2 (1980).

47. "The Week," *Outlook* 86 (1907), 354; "Prevention of Our Animal Holocaust," *The Indendent* 55 (1903), 2821–23. The seventh annual report of

the *Journal of American Medical Association*, entitled "Fourth of July Injuries and Tetanus," noted that "the killed and injured at the Battle of Bunker Hill were only 1,474 compared with 1,622 killed and injured while 'celebrating' the Fourth of July in 1909." Moreover, between 1903 and 1913, 39,808 people were reportedly killed or injured in Fourth celebrations; see *American City* 8 (1913), 653. The most informative overview of the movement, highlighting its goals, successes, and methods, is August H. Brunner, "Suggestions for Celebrating Independence Day," *Playground* 4 (1910), 1–20.

48. Lee F. Hanmer, "Celebrating the Fourth in Large Cities," *Playground* 4 (1910), 45–52.

49. Hardy, *How Boston Played*, 102.

50. Lee, quoted in Hardy, 103.

51. Hanmer, "Celebrating," 51.

52. Everett B. Mero, "Holidays as a Builder of Citizenship," *Mind and Body* 20 (1913), 209–13.

53. Mero, *American City* 9 (1913), 323–26.

54. *New York Times*, July 5, 1913, 1; and Mrs. Issac L. Rice, "The Child and the Fourth," The Forum 50 (1913), 38.

55. *Denni Hlastel*, June 15, 1913, translated in the Works Progress Administration's project, *The Chicago Foreign Language Press Survey*; and J. R. Hildebrand, "The Geography of Games: How the Sports of Nations Form a Gazetteer of the Habits and Histories of their Peoples," *National Geographic* 36 (August 1919), 121.

56. William Orr, "An American Holiday," *Atlantic Monthly* 103 (1909), 782–89.

57. Ibid.

58. Ibid.

59. Ibid.

60. *Chicago Daily Socialist*, July 5, 1910, 1–2, and June 25, 1910, 1.

61. Ibid.

62. This paragraph and the following one come from Steven W. Pope, "Patriotic Pastimes: Sporting Traditions and American Identity, 1876–1926" (Ph.D. diss., University of Maine, 1993), 39–41. The best biography of Johnson is Randy Roberts, *Papa Jack: Jack Johnson and the Era of White Hopes* (New York, 1983).

63. *New York Times*, July 4–5, 1910.

64. *Chicago Tribune*, July 3, 1910; "Johnson Wins the Great Fight," *Harper's Weekly* 54 (July 9, 1910), 8; Nat Fleischer, *The Heavyweight Championship: An Informal History of Heavyweight Boxing from 1719 to the Present Day* (New York, 1949); Reverdy C. Ransom, "The Reno Prize Fight," in *The Spirit of Freedom and Justice: Orations and Speeches* (Nashville, 1926), 123; and Stuart Mews, "Puritanicalism, Sport and Race: A Symbolic Crusade of 1911," in G. J. Cuming and Derek Baker, eds., *Popular Belief and Practice* (Cambridge, 1971), 303–31.

65. Leonard I. Sweet, "The Fourth of July and Black Americans in the Nineteenth Century: Northern Leadership Opinion Within the Context of the Black Experience," *Journal of Negro History* 61 (1976), quote on 269.

66. Ibid., 273–74.

67. "Johnson Gets Big Victory," *Chicago Daily Socialist*, July 5 and July 7, 1910.

68. Ibid.

69. I deal with sports during World War I, in considerable detail, in the next two chapters.

70. "The Day of Spiritual Union of the Free Peoples," *Literary Digest* 58 (July 13, 1918), 1–2.

71. "The Fourth of July as an International Holiday," *Current Opinion* 65 (August 1918), 1–2.

72. "Day-Long Pageant Pictures America United For War," *New York Times*, July 5, 1918, 1, 6.

73. Ibid.

74. Ibid. Such pageants provided immigrant Americans with an opportunity to reaffirm their loyalty within an otherwise intolerant nativistic social context. An editorial, for instance, in *The American Scandinavian Review* 6 (1918), 287–88, stated:

> Those of us who have always believed in retaining the spiritual bond between the immigrant and his mother country felt our faith justified by the splendid pageant on Fifth Avenue, where it seemed that the essence of all the beauty and color and poetry of the old nations was brought together to enrich America. May the spirit of that day stay with us! This country has already in a measure solved the problem of harmonizing different races. . . . Freedom of language, of creed, of family custom, of thought and speech has contributed to this result as much as, perhaps more than, the right to vote and the opportunity to earn a fair wage. There should be no tampering now with the policy of broad tolerance that has made us a happy and united nation.

75. "Huge Array of Athletes," *New York Times*, June 30, 1918, sec. II, 7.

76. "50,000 Athletes in Carnival of Sport," *New York Times*, July 5, 1918, 14; "Camp Grant Plans Big 4th, Then Overseas," and "Soldiers' Athletic Carnival to Mark Independence Day," *Chicago Tribune*, June 2, 1918; letter from Emil C. Wetten (chairman of the Soldiers' Athletic Carnival Organizing Committee), June 4, 1918, Fitzpatrick Papers, Chicago Historical Society; and *Portland Evening Express*, July 5, 1919, 2.

77. Louis Weinberg, "Celebrating Independence," *New Republic* 3 (1915), 278–79.

78. Ibid.

79. "City, State, U.S. Guards Ready to Foil Red Threat," "U.S. Keeps Eyes Peeled for Red Flares Today," "The Last Scramble Before the Great Drought," "Chicago Gulps its Final Cups Amid a Bedlam," *Chicago Tribune*, July 4, 1919, 1, 3, 13. In Chicago, two companies of the U.S. Fourteenth Infantry, state militia, police, and the entire personnel of the city's detective bureau were quartered throughout the city. In New York, all 11,000 members of the police and detective force were mobilized for continuous duty. Similar plans were initiated in Spokane, Oakland, Pittsburgh, Seattle, Boston, and Detroit.

80. Ibid.

81. The *New York Times*, astonishingly, published 66 separate items pertaining to the fight, between February and August 1919—see its *Index*, January-June 1919, 355–56, and July-December 1919, 329.

82. For a survey of the national coverage, see *Chicago Tribune*, July 5, 1919.

Indicative of the fight's importance in smaller cities, hundreds of Mainers listened to the round-by-round coverage at a Portland newspaper office, which, the following day, boasted that it had announced Dempsey's victory in less than one minute after Willard quit, in addition to having provided news of the event to thousands of telephone callers. See *Portland Evening Express-Advertiser*, July 5, 1919, 10.

83. *New York Times*, May 28, 1919, 13.

84. *New York Times*, August 20, 1926, 16.

85. Elliott Gorn, "The Manassa Mauler and the Fighting Marine: An Interpretation of the Dempsey-Tunney Fights," *Journal of American Studies* 19 (1985), 27–47.

86. Sammons, *Beyond the Ring*, 58.

87. *New York Times*, September 24, 1926, 1–9.

88. "Philadelphia Opens Sesquicentennial Today With 150 Guns;" "Coolidge Asks Support of Sesquicentennial," *New York Times*, May 31, 1926, 1, 4; "Track Stars Race Today for Titles," *New York Times*, July 5, 1926; "Seven Records Fall in U.S. Title Games," *New York Times*, July 6, 1926; and "The Sesquicentennial Exposition," *American Review of Reviews* 73 (1926), 496. The principal work on the Exposition is the official history written by E. L. Austin and Odell Hauser, *The Sesquicentennial International Exposition: A Record Based on Official Data and Departmental Records* (Philadelphia, 1929).

89. Waldstreicher, "Rites of Rebellion, Rites of Assent," 50–52.

90. Zelinsky, *Nation Into State*, 107–8; Robertson, *American Myth, American Reality*, 256.

91. Hardy, *How Boston Played*, 106. Hardy notes that the Boston playground movement was only partially successful, and that the "proof" was in the eyes of the beholder.

92. Abrams documents how similar efforts by middle-class German reformers (most notably, combating working-class drinking patterns during holiday celebrations) were a mixed, and contradictory, bag in *Workers' Culture in Imperial Germany*, 74–76, 85–86, 58.

93. Again, Portland's experience is instructive of this trend. In 1922, the *Portland Press Herald* devoted four full pages (roughly one-quarter of the total paper) to sports and commercialized leisure on the Fourth. Page five dealt solely with major league baseball; page six covered Benny Leonard's successful lightweight-title defense and other assorted national and regional sports news; and page seven reported on Maine sports events, including baseball, golf tournaments, and auto racing. Four years later, the standard local contests were conspicuously overshadowed by the proliferation of regional and national events—signaling an increasing national sporting-culture consciousness. An article about major league baseball played on the Fourth was accompanied by a syndicated column "Babe Ruth Says"; and the AAU track-and-field championships in Philadelphia and the extensive boxing results from Jamestown (N.Y.), Tampa, Havana, Everett (Wash.), and Billings (Mont.) were the featured items in the 1926 Portland coverage. Even the most noteworthy local baseball game, between the Kennebunkport Collegians and the Lawrence (Mass.) Harps had national implications, since the Kennebunkport team was managed by a former major league pitcher and Princeton coach, and was witnessed by a bevy of well-known vacationers, like Vice President Charles G. Dawes and noted novelist

Booth Tarkington. See the coverage in *Portland Press Herald*, July 5, 1922; and *Portland Evening Express*, July 6, 1926.

CHAPTER SEVEN

1. Root's statement accompanied a 340-page preparedness-movement jeremiad that was made public at the National Security League's Congress of Constructive Patriotism in January 1917; cited in Michael Pearlman, *To Make Democracy Safe for America: Patricians and Preparedness in the Progressive Era* (Urbana, Ill., 1984), 145.

2. Mark Dyreson, "Regulating the Body and the Body Politic: American Sport, Bourgeois Culture and the Language of Progress, 1880–1920," in S. W. Pope, ed., *The New American Sport History: Recent Approaches and Perspectives* (Urbana, 1996), 136. I have found Alan Dawley, *Struggles for Justice: Social Responsibility and the Liberal State* (Cambridge, Mass., 1991) particularly informative, esp., 184–90; and Stephen Skowronek, *Building a New American State, 1870–1920* (Cambridge, Mass., 1986), 47–84, 177–211, is also useful.

3. John Higham, *Strangers in the Land: Patterns of American Nativism, 1860–1925* (New York, 1963), 234–61; and Dawley, *Struggles for Justice*, 114–16.

4. Philip Gleason, "American Identity and Americanization," in Stephan Thernstrom, ed., *Harvard Encyclopedia of American Ethnic Groups* (Cambridge, 1980), 40; also, see Rivka Shpak Lissak, *Pluralism and Progressives: Hull House and the New Immigrants, 1890–1919* (Chicago, 1989), 17–23. For perspectives on working-class immigrants, see David Montgomery, "Nationalism, American Patriotism, and Class Consciousness among Immigrant Workers in the United States in the Epoch of World War I," in Dirk Hoerder, ed., *'Struggle a Hard Battle': Essays on Working Class Immigrants* (DeKalb, Ill.: 1986), 327–51.

5. Gayle Gullett, "Women Progressives and the Politics of Americanization in California, 1915–1920," *Pacific Historical Review* (1995), esp. 72–75; Anne Rhodes, "Americanization through Women's Organizations," *Immigrants in America Review* 2 (1916), 71–73; Virginia Shapiro, "Women, Citizenship, and Nationality: Immigration and Naturalization Policies in the United States," *Politics and Society* 13 (1984), 1–26; John F. McClymer, "Gender and the 'American Way of Life': Women in the Americanization Movement," *Journal of American Ethnic History* 10 (1991), 3–20.

6. Gullett, 75.

7. For the role of women during the war, see Blanche Wiesen Cook, "The Woman's Peace Party: Collaboration and Non-Cooperation," *Peace and Change* 1 (1972), 36–42; and Barbara Steinson, *American Women's Activism in World War I* (New York, 1982).

8. George W. Ehler, "Preparation, For Peace or War!" *Playground* 10 (1916), 172–78; Major Palmer E. Pierce, "College Athletics as Related to National Preparedness," *American Physical Education Review* 22 (1917), 132. F. L. Kleeberger claimed that only 24 percent of the 400,000 men who applied for enlistment were accepted by military officials; see "Athletics and the War Game," *School and Society* 7 (1918), 541.

9. H. W. Foster, "Physical Education vs. Degeneracy," *The Independent* 52 (1900), 1836–37.

10. Arthur A. Knoch, M.D., "How Does Physical Training Aid the School in Training its Pupils for Efficient Citizenship?" *American Physical Education Review* 19 (1914), 508. William Hemmingway, "Building Men—Not Champions," *Harper's Weekly* 57 (June 14, 1913), 11. John H. Finley, president of the University of the State of New York, highlighted Dr. Storey's physical-training institute in "In the Service of the State," *Survey* 37 (1917), 424–25.

11. Rittenhouse's statements in a *New York Times* article were presented in "Is American Stamina Failing?" *Literary Digest* 51 (1915), 705.

12. Susan Cahn, *Coming On Strong: Gender and Sexuality in 20th Century Women's Sport* (NY, 1994), 28–29.

13. Roosevelt, *The Winning of the West*, quoted in Thomas G. Dyer's very useful overview, *Theodore Roosevelt and the Idea of Race* (Baton Rouge, 1980), 42.

14. Ibid.

15. Oriard, *Sporting with the Gods: The Rhetoric of Play and Game in American Culture* (Cambridge, 1991), 19.

16. Ibid.

17. "War as Moral Medicine," *Atlantic Monthly* 86 (1900),735–38.

18. T. J. Jackson Lears, *No Place of Grace: Antimodernism and the Transformation of American Culture, 1880–1920* (New York, 1983), 108, 124; Higham, *Stangers in the Land*, and Michael H. Hunt, *Ideology and U.S. Foreign Policy* (New Haven, 1987).

19. William James, "The Moral Equivalent to War," originally published in *McClure's Magazine*, August 1910; quotes are, however, drawn from a reprinted version in John J. McDermott, ed., *The Writings of William James* (New York, 1967), 660–71.

20. Ibid.

21. Paul C. Phillips, "Relation of Athletic Sports to International Peace," *American Physical Education Review* 20 (1915), 143–47.

22. Ibid.

23. Ibid.

24. Mark Dyreson, *Inventing the Sporting Republic: American Sport, Political Culture, and the Olympic Experience, 1877–1919* (Urbana, 1997).

25. Nina Silber, *The Romance of Reunion: Northerners and the South, 1865–1900* (Chapel Hill, N.C., 1994), 195.

26. Ibid., 196.

27. Holmes is quoted in Peter Karsten, "Militarization and Rationalization in the United States, 1870–1914," in John R. Gillis, ed., *The Militarization of the Western World* (New Brunswick, N.J., 1989), 33.

28. Lears, *No Place of Grace*, 112, 116–77. See also, Walter LaFeber, *The New Empire: An Interpretation of American Expansion, 1860–1898* (Ithaca, N.Y., 1963); and Robert Cuff, *The War Industries Board: Business-Government Relations During World War I* (Baltimore, 1973).

29. Leonard Wood, "Heat Up the Melting Pot," *The Independent* 87 (1916), 15.

30. Ibid. Between December 1915 and May 1916, Wood, despite President Wilson's efforts to muzzle him, addressed audiences totaling more than 130,000 in over 100 separate speeches. For more on Wood, see Pearlman, *To Make Democracy Safe for America*. Pioneering statements calling for active fed-

eral support of military athletics (modeled along British lines) can be found in Edmund Butts, "Soldierly Bearing, Health and Athletics," *Outing* 43 (1904), 707–11 (quote is on 711); Captain Richmond P. Davis, "Athletics at the United States Military Academy," *Outing* 39 (1901–02), 384–91; and H. Irving Hancock, *Life at West Point: The Making of the American Army Officer: His Studies, Discipline, and Amusements* (New York, 1902).

31. Quandt, *From the Small Town to the Great Community: The Social Thought of Progressive Intellectuals* (New Brunswick, 1970).

32. See, for instance, Melvin Adelman, *A Sporting Time: New York City and the Rise of Modern Athletics* (Urbana, 1986), 270–81, for a survey of early discussions on sports and recreation as vehicles for physical well-being and as agents against physical degeneration. John Nauright addresses similar issues, from a British imperial perspective, in "Sport, Manhood, and Empire: British Responses to the New Zealand Rugby Tour of 1905," *International Journal of the History of Sport* 8 (1991), 239–55.

33. Washington quoted in Pierce, "College Athletics as Related to National Preparedness," 129–30.

34. Ibid.

35. Donald Mrozek, *Sport and American Mentality, 1880–1910* (Knoxville, 1983), 67–102. For a discussion of the military's place in twentieth-century America, see Skowronek, *Building a New American State*, 212–47; Paul Koistinen, "The Industrial-Military Complex in Historical Perspective: World War I," *Business History Review* 41 (1967), 378–93; Alan R. Millet and Peter Maslowski, *For the Common Defense: A Military History of the United States of America* (New York, 1984), 299–322; James Abrahamson, *America Arms for a New Century: The Making of a Great Military Power* (New York, 1981); John Whiteclay Chambers, II, "Conscripting for Colossus: The Progressive Era and the Origin of the Modern Military Draft in the United States in World War I," in Karsten, ed., *The Military in America*, 300. Chambers later published a monograph, *To Raise an Army: The Draft Comes to Modern America* (New York, 1987); esp. 73–102.

36. The best works that deal with sports and middle-class values include: Mrozek, *Sport and American Mentality*; Steven A. Riess, *City Games: The Evolution of American Urban Society and the Rise of Sports* (Urbana, Ill., 1989); Riess, *Touching Base: Professional Baseball and American Culture in the Progressive Period* (Westport, Conn., 1980); J. A. Mangan and James Walvin, eds., *Manliness and Morality: Middle-Class Masculinity in Britain and America, 1800–1940* (New York, 1987); Stephen Hardy, *How Boston Played: Recreation and Community, 1865–1915* (Boston, 1982); Peter Levine, *A. G. Spalding and the Rise of Baseball: The Promise of American Sport* (New York, 1985); and Dominick Cavallo, *Muscles and Morals: Organized Playgrounds and Urban Reform, 1880–1920* (Philadelphia, 1981).

37. Gleason, "American Identity and Americanization," 40.

38. Ibid.

39. J. H. McCurdy, "A Study of Characteristics of Physical Training in the Public Schools in the United States," *American Physical Education Review* 12 (1905), 210; and Guy S. Lowman, "The Regulation and Control of Sports in Secondary Schools in the United States," *American Physical Education Review* 14 (1907), 245.

40. Betty Spears and Richard Swanson, *History of Sport and Physical Activ-*

ity in the United States (Dubuque, Iowa, 1978), 174–86; Lawrence Cremin, *The Transformation of the School: Progressivism in American Education, 1876–1957* (New York, 1961); John Dewey, *The School and Society* (Chicago, 1899); and Dewey, *Experience and Education* (New York, 1938).

41. Timothy O'Hanlon, "Interscholastic Athletics, 1900–1940: Shaping Citizens for Unequal Roles in the Modern Industrial State," *Educational Theory* 30 (1980), 92; see also, Guy Lewis, "Adoption of the Sports Program, 1906–39: The Role of Accommodation in the Transformation of Physical Education," *Quest* 12 (1969).

42. Martha H. Verbugge, *Able-Bodied Womanhood: Personal Health and Social Change in Nineteenth-Century Boston* (New York, 1988), 163.

43. Ibid., 190.

44. Stoner quoted in Verbugge, 159.

45. Ibid., 184–85.

46. Steven W. Pope, "Negotiating the 'Folk Highway' of the Nation: Sport, Public Culture and American Identity, 1870–1940," *Journal of Social History* 27 (1993), 332.

47. Cahn, *Coming On Strong*, 29; and Verbugge, *Able-Bodied Womanhood*, 186.

48. Ibid.

49. Lawrence Veysey, *The Emergence of the American University* (Chicago, 1965).

50. Jesse Feiring Williams, "Proposals for Preparedness in Physical Education," *American Physical Education Review* 21 (1916), 452.

51. Frederick M. Davenport, "The Nationalizing of American Education," *Outlook* 116 (1917), 142–44.

52. Ibid.

53. Charles A. Prosser, "Education as Preparedness," *School and Society* 3 (1916), 796–807; quote is on 804–5. This general topic is discussed thoroughly in Timothy P. O'Hanlon, "School Sports as Social Training: The Case of Athletics and the Crisis of World War I," *Journal of Sport History* 9 (1982); and O'Hanlon, "Interscholastic Athletics, 1900–1940."

54. E. H. Arnold, "Preparedness," *American Physical Education Review* 21 (1916), 351–9.

55. Ronald Smith deals with these concerns in his *Sport and Freedom: The Rise of Big-Time College Athletics* (New York, 1988). For typical contemporary statements in this vein, see Alfred E. Stearns, "Athletics and the School," and C. A. Stewart, "Athletics and the College," in *Atlantic Monthly* 113 (1914), 148–60. Both Stearns and Stewart offered representative critiques of the spectatorship and specialization of collegiate sports, and cited the "moral laxity" that they believed was pervasive. Compare these prewar views with L. B. R. Briggs, "Intercollegiate Athletics and the War," *Atlantic* 122 (1918), 303–9.

Reflective of the growing acceptance of sports by editors of *The Nation*, see its editorial response to Briggs's article, "The War and College Athletics," *The Nation* 107 (1918), 244. And reflective of those who sought to democratize institutional athletics was Joseph E. Raycroft, "The Educational Value of Athletics in Schools and Colleges," *School and Society* 3 (1916), 295–300.

56. Arnold, 354, 356, 358. Arnold's position resembled one which sought to determine the suitability of collegiate sports for the nation's well-being. "If

[they are] mere costly luxuries of a small leisure class, let's fling them away," wrote Brown University President H. P. Faunce, in "Athletics for the Service of the Nation," *American Physical Education Review* 23 (1918), 137.

57. C. E. Hammett, "The Influence of Athletics Upon Physical Education in American Colleges," *Educational Review* 51 (1916), 355–59.

58. See Jesse Williams, "Proposals for Preparedness," 456, where he suggests that "formal exercises are to education what drugs are to medicine," and suggests new thinking and methods.

59. Hammett, "The Influence of Athletics."

60. Ibid.

61. F. L. Kleeberger, "Athletics and the War Game," *School and Society* 7 (1918), 541–55.

62. Ibid.

63. Ibid.

64. David Starr Jordan, "Military Training in American High Schools," *Advocates of Peace* 78 (1916), 266–67; Jordan, "Massachusetts Commission on Military Training," *School Review* 25 (1917), 168–76; Leonard Ayres, "Military Drill in High School," *School Review* 25 (1917), 161–76; and D. C. Bliss, "Military Training in the High Schools," *School Review* 25 (1917), 161–67. Frederick C. Camp provides an endoresement for high-school military training in "Physical Education and Military Drill: What Should Be Our Policy?" *School Review* 25 (1917), 537–46. See also, Deobold B. Van Dalen and Bruce L. Bennett, A World History of Physical Education: Cultural, Philosophical, and Comparative (Englewood Cliffs, N.J., 1971), 435–39.

65. D. C. Bliss, "Military Training in the High School," *American Physical Education Review*, 157–60, 161–67.

66. O'Hanlon, "Interscholastic Athletics," 95–96; and Bliss, "Military Training," 167. Sargent's position was published as "Military Drill in the Public Schools," *American Physical Education Review* 21 (1916), 429–32. For biographical information on Sargent, see the *Dictionary of American Biography*, vol. 16, 355–56; F. E. Leonard, *A Guide to the History of Physical Education* (New York, 1923); and R. Tait McKenzie, ed., *History of Physical Education* (1927). See also, *Dudley Allen Sargent: An Autobiography*, ed. Ledyard W. Sargent (Philadelphia, 1927), for rich personal perspectives on the early days of physical-education programs.

67. Sargent, "Military Drill in the Public Schools," *Selected Articles on Military Training in Schools and Colleges Including Military Camps*, 168–70. An even stronger dissenting viewpoint was articulated by Edward B. Degroot, director of physical education for the San Francisco public schools, in "Physical Education Versus Military Training in Secondary Schools," *American Physical Education Review* 22 (1917), 302–4.

In contrast, leading college and university presidents avidly supported military training and rigorous physical education. The athletic view of life, which led Cornell president Andrew Dickson White to stress the importance of physical and military education (the Reserve Officers' Training Corps), at times, consumed him. "I fully believe that today in the United States physical education and development is a more pressing necessity even than mental development," he announced in his inaugural address. White is quoted in Burton J. Bledstein, *The Culture of Professionalism: The Middle Class and the*

Development of Higher Education in America (New York, 1976), 152. According to Bledstein, White was in the vanguard of a later generation of presidents, including such men as Jacob Gould Schurman at Cornell; Arthur T. Hadley at Yale; and Woodrow Wilson at Princeton. They believed that military training and athletics hardened the moral character of students who were growing soft and lazy from the destructive effects of luxury and self-indulgence. Besides promoting "discipline, cleanliness and efficiency," many believed such rigorous training taught "order, system and punctuality" to Americans, who needed these attributes "more than any other people" (quoted in Bledstein, 152).

See also, Jacob G. Schurman, "Every College Should Introduce Military Training," *Everybody's Magazine* 32 (1915), 181; John G. Hibben, "The Colleges and the National Defense," *The Independent* 82 (1915), 532; and *New York Times*, January 24, 1915, pt. 3, 5. For an overview of universal military training at universities, see Michael Pearlman, "To Make the University Safe for Morality: Higher Education, Football and Military Training from the 1890s through the 1920s," *Canadian Review of American Studies* 12 (1981), 37-56.

68. Edward B. Degroot, "Physical Education Versus Military Training in Secondary Schools," *American Physical Education Review* 22 (1917), 302-3.

69. Ibid., 304.

70. Edward T. Devine, "Preparedness," *The Survey* 35 (1916), 732-34.

71. Ibid.

72. Day Allen Willey, "The Spirit of Sport in the Army," *Harper's Weekly* 50 (1906), 1100.

73. Ibid., 1101.

74. For an astute analysis of this tendency, see Joseph A. Schumpeter, *Imperialism and Social Classes* (New York, 1951).

75. Discipline and the Will," *New York Times*, November 1, 1915, 10; and U.S. Congress, Senate Military Affairs Committee, Hearings, Universal Military Training, 64th Cong., 2d sess., 1917, 785.

76. Henry L. Stimson, "The Basis for National Military Training," *Scribner's Magazine* 61 (1917), 408.

77. Major General William H. Carter, "Military Preparedness," *North American Review* 191 (1910), 641, 638.

78. John W. Chambers, *To Raise an Army: The Draft Comes to Modern America* (New York, 1987), 73-102.

79. Chambers, "Conscripting for Colossus," 301-2. Critics such as the socialist editor of *The Masses* charged that, although members of the elite (like Theodore Roosevelt) spoke of sharing pup tents with the working class, they had no intention of sharing their wealth with their less fortunate tentmates.

80. Mrozek, 38. This process, according to Mrozek, worked not through "a ritualistic appeal to sentiment but by the practical governance of behavior, introducing physical order and discipline into the actual experience of young men fated to serve their country as leaders."

81. Captain John L. Griffith, "The Value of Athletics as Part of Military Training," *American Physical Education Review* 24 (1919), 191-95.

82. Abrahamson, 116-17. O'Hanlon surveys the various state laws for mention of military drills and the debates surrounding such initiatives, in "School Sports as Social Training," 14-18.

83. See "Educators Adopt Security League's Great Physical Regeneration

Plan," *Chicago Tribune*, June 17, 1916. For the personnel of this coalition, which comprised educators, government officials, and their allies in civil society, see also, "Security League's 'Plattsburghs' for School Teachers Open This Week," *Chicago Tribune*, June 18, 1916. Camp described his own philosophy and activism in a number of articles. See, for instance, his "Our Government Plant," *Outlook* 117 (1917), 12–13; "Keeping the Nation Fit," *The Independent* 96 (1918), 400–1; and "What I Am Trying to Do," *World's Work* 46 (1923), 600–4.

84. Timothy O'Hanlon, "School Sports as Social Training: The Case of Athletics and the Crisis of World War I," *Journal of Sport History* 9 (1982), 24.

85. Between 1919 and 1925, 22 states passed some form of physical-education legislation—a dramatic increase over the previous two decades. See Thomas A. Storey, Willard S. Small, Elton G. Salisbury, "Recent Legislation for Physical Education," U.S. Bureau of Education, *Bulletin* 1 (1922) (Washington, D.C.: Government Printing Office, 5, 15, cited by O'Hanlon.

86. Arthur Link, *Woodrow Wilson and the Progressive Era, 1910–1917* (New York, 1954), 174. Link succinctly explains how American involvement in the European war conflicted with progressive sensibilities, 180–82.

87. *New York Times*, May 4, 1916, 10.

88. Ibid.

89. *New York Times*, May 7, 1916, sec. VII, 2.

90. May 13, 1; May 14, 1–3.

91. For representative preparedness editorials, see May 13, 14, and 23.

92. Dyreson, "Regulating the Body and the Body Politic," 137.

93. L. B. R. Briggs, "Intercollegiate Athletics and the War," *Atlantic Monthly* 122 (1918), 303.

94. Ibid., 309.

95. Mrozek, *Sport and American Mentality*, 229–30.

96. Wilson quoted in Bruce Porter, *War and the Rise of the State: The Military Foundations of Modern Politics* (New York, 1994), 272.

CHAPTER EIGHT

1. "How Uncle Sam Has Created an Army of Athletes." *Scientific American* 126 (1919), 114–15.

2. Ibid.

3. Albert Britt, "From Playing Field to Battle Field," *Outing* 73 (1919), 3. See William Haynes, "In Fighting Trim: Canada Teaching Her Soldiers to Play in Order to Fit Them for Fighting," *Outing* 69 (1916), 277–88, for a comparative example north of the border. Frederick Harris recorded 75 million "participations" in military sports between 1917 and 1919, in *Service With Fighting Men: An Account of the Work of the American Young Men's Christian Association in the World War* (New York, 1922), vol. 1, 320.

4. *New York Times*, March 8, 1903, 11.

5. Ibid.

6. Donald J. Mrozek, "The Habit of Victory: The American Military and the Cult of Manliness," in J. A. Mangan and James Walvin, eds., *Manliness and Morality: Middle Class Masculinity in Britain and America, 1800–1940* (New York, 1987), 222.

7. Bruce D. Porter, *War and the Rise of the State: The Military Foundations of Modern Politics* (New York, 1994), 269.

8. Mack Whelan, "Will the War Kill Athletics?: Ways in Which Army Life is Making Physical Fitness Faster Than Fighting Destroys It," *Outing* 68 (1916), 278–88. Guy Lewis was the first sports historian to argue that World War I led to widespread national sports interest in the 1920s, in "World War I and the Emergence of Sport for the Masses," *Maryland Historian* 2 (1973), 109–22. Timothy O'Hanlon took Lewis's thesis a step further by suggesting that the wartime emphasis on sports in military training stimulated postwar high-school sports and fitness programs—"School Sports as Social Training: The Case of Athletics and the Crisis of World War I," *Journal of Sport History* 9 (1982), 1–24.

9. Newton Fuessle, "America's Boss-Ridden Athletics," *Outlook* 130 (1922), 643.

10. John R. Betts, "Home Front, Battlefield and Sport During the Civil War," *Research Quarterly* 42 (1971), 113–32. Lawrence W. Fielding has ably documented this episode in American sports history, in three journal articles derived from his doctoral dissertation (Maryland, 1974): "Reflections From the Sport Mirror: Selected Treatments of Civil War Sport," *Journal of Sport History* 2 (1975), 132–44; "War and Trifles: Sport in the Shadow of Civil War Army Life," *Journal of Sport History* 4 (1977), 151–68; and "Gay and Happy Still: Holiday Sport in the Army of the Potomac," *Maryland Historian* 7 (1976), 19–32. Harold Seymour documents the place of baseball among Union troops, in *Baseball: The People's Game* (New York, 1991), 291–309.

11. Benjamin G. Rader, *Baseball: A History of America's Game* (Urbana, 1992), 13.

12. For an excellent, well-documented history of the nineteenth-century Army, see Edward M. Coffman's *The Old Army: A Portrait of the American Army in Peacetime, 1784–1898* (New York, 1986), esp. 215–86, 328–99; Elliott J. Gorn, *The Manly Art: Bare-Knuckle Prize Fighting in America* (Ithaca, N.Y., 1986), 160.

13. Gorn, *The Manly Art*, 164. For early, representative comments on the relationship between sports and militarism, see *Wilke's Spirit*, August 17, 1861; *New York Herald*, July 27, 1859; and *New York Times*, March 9, 1862.

14. Gorn, *The Manly Art*, 164.

15. Cited in Don Rickey, Jr., *Forty Miles a Day on Beans and Hay: The Enlisted Soldier Fighting the Indian Wars* (Norman, Okla., 1963), 186–88. This work is a thorough portrait of the U.S. regular Army on the frontier during the second half of the nineteenth century—particularly, in regard to the life of enlisted men.

16. Coffman, *The Old Army*, 359. Donald Mrozek sketches a cogent summary of the initial establishment of military sports during the late nineteenth century, in "Sport and the American Military: Diversion and Duty," *Research Quarterly* (Centennial Issue), 1985, 38–45.

17. C. D. Parkhurst, "The Practical Education of the Soldier," *Journal of the Military Service Institution of the United States* (1890), 946.

18. Quoted in Mrozek, *Sport and American Mentality*, 56.

19. Mrozek cites the War Department's Special Regulation no. 23: "Field Physical Training of the Soldier," (Washington, D.C., 1917), 7–10. See also, R. D. Evans, "Why Athletics Should be Fostered in the Navy," *The Illustrated Sporting News* 5 (1905), 5.

20. Nobody promoted this new approach more passionately than Edmund L. "Billy" Butts, the best all-around athlete in West Point's class of 1888; after graduation, he published articles in the *Journal of the Military Service, Outing,* and the *Army and Navy Journal,* wherein he maintained that athletic training would transform fighting men into "hardened veterans, upon whom the safety of the nation could depend." Such provocative sporting bombast earned him the respect of the Army, who dispatched Butts in the mid-1890s to various posts to initiate athletics and physical-training programs. See Seymour, *Baseball,* 297–98.

21. Fuessle, "America's Boss-Ridden Athletics," 642–43. Early football practices were limited. Only about 2 hours per week were allotted, during Cadets' "liberty time," for preseason practice. Typically, only 9 hours of actual preseason work preceded the first game; and only a total of 56 practice hours were spent during the entire football season. See Captain Richmond P. Davis, "Athletics at the United States Military Academy," *Outing* 39 (1901-02), 384–85; and H. Irving Hancock, *Life at West Point: The Making of the American Army Officer: His Studies, Discipline, and Amusements* (New York, 1902), 135–36.

22. Arthur Ruhl, "The Army-Navy Game," *Outing* 49 (1907), 314.

23. Davis, "Athletics at the United States Military Academy," 390–91; Hancock, *Life at West Point,* 77–81; 85–95; and King, quoted in Seymour, *Baseball,* 315–16. Military sports were not the sole preserve of the Army—naval ships were furnished with a wide variety of sporting goods; there were frequent summertime baseball games between naval teams. Further, regattas, swim meets, and boxing were immensely popular on Sunday evenings after the parade. Football men relished the opportunity of having their ship dock at New York during the fall. See, for instance, Martin E. Trench, "Athletics Among Enlisted Men in the Navy," *Outing* 39 (1902), 436–41. The early support for football in the Navy is cited in Park Benjamin, "Public Football vs. Naval Education: In Defense of the Naval Academy," *The Independent* 55 (1903), 2777–80.

24. Seymour, *Baseball,* 321.

25. Ibid., 314–15.

26. Luther H. Gulick is credited with founding the New York Public Schools Athletic League. As one of the pioneers of American athletics, he collaborated with James Naismith in devising basketball; headed the child-hygiene department at the Russell Sage Foundation; served on the American Olympic Committee and with the American Physical Education Association; and was called by the National War Council to make a survey of the American Expeditionary Forces and to write a report on proposals for physical training. See *Dictionary of American Biography,* vol. 8, 47–48; and *American Physical Education Review,* October 1918.

27. Quoted in Mrozek, *Sport and American Mentality,* 61.

28. Graham Cosmas, "Military Reform after the Spanish-American War: The Army Reorganization Fight of 1898–1899," *Military Affairs* 35 (1971), 12–17. In addition to the growth of regular forces, from 28,000 to nearly 60,000, the War Department also recruited more than 200,000 volunteers. Elihu Root, the secretary of war, encouraged Congress to create a permanent regular army— a decision enacted into law in the Reorganization Act of February 2, 1901. For an overview of the pivotal role played almost singlehandedly by Root during the first few years, see Russell F. Weigley, *History of the United States Army*

(Bloomington, 1984), 314–26. A useful contemporary assessment of Root's contributions can be found in William Harding Carter, "Elihu Root: His Services as Secretary of War," *North American Review* 178 (1908), 110–21.

29. Harrod, *Manning the New Navy*, 198; Lt. A. B. Donworth, "Gymnasium Training in the Army," *Journal of the Military Service Institution of the United States* 21 (1897), 508–14.

30. Day Allen Willey, "The Spirit of Sport in the Army," *Harper's Weekly* 50 (1906), 1100–1.

31. Ibid.

32. R. L. Bullard, "Athletics in the Army," *Journal of the Military Service Institions of the United States* 38 (1905), 399–404.

33. Charles Richard, "Suggestions for the Physical Training of Officers on the Active List of the Army," *JMSI* 44 (1909), 73–78.

34. Butts, quoted in Seymour, *Baseball*, 316.

35. See Karl Schmitt, *Mexico and the United States, 1821–1973* (New York, 1974).

36. See C. M. Cramer, *Newton D. Baker: A Biography* (New York, 1961); and M. J. Exner, "Prostitution in Its Relation to the Army on the Mexican Border," *Social Hygiene* 3 (1917).

37. Baker quoted in Seymour, *Baseball*, 331. Ronald Schaffer surveys the social purity crusades which arose in this context and which proliferated throughout the War Camp Community Service as well as behind the lines in France in his *America in the Great War: The Rise of the Welfare State* (New York, 1991), 98–108.

38. For an overview of early YMCA work see William J. Baker, "To Pray or to Play?: The YMCA Question in the United Kingdom and the United States, 1850–1900," *International Journal of the History of Sport* 11 (1994), 42–62.

39. Harris, *Service With Fighting Men*, 197–212.

40. Between June 1918 and April 1919, the YMCA handled in France alone over two million cigarettes, 32 million candy bars, 18 million cans of smoking tobacco, 50 million cigars, 60 million cans of jam, and 29 million packages of chewing gum. The Y distributed five million bound volumes of reading material, four million pieces of religious literature, two million magazines, 10 million newspapers, and 1 million copies of an approved songbook. Between August 1917 and April 1919, 90,000 movies were shown to audiences totaling 50 million men. And, between 1918 and 1919, the Y provided 2.25 million athletic items. See George W. Perkins, "Report on Activities of the Y.M.C.A. with the A.E.F.," 1919.

41. Edward Frank Allen, *Keeping Our Fighters Fit For War and After* (New York, 1918); a concise version of Allen's first chapter was published as "Athletics for the Army," in *Century* 96 (1918), 367–74.

42. Montrose J. Moses, "Training Soldiers to Play," *St. Nicholas* 45 (1918), 448–53.

43. George J. Fisher, "Physical Training in the Army," *American Physical Education Review* 23 (1918), 65–76.

44. Harris, *Service With Fighting Men*, vol. 1, 320–24.

45. "Baker Supports Games," *New York Times*, August 17, 1917, 10.

46. Ibid.; Edwin A. Goewey, "Flashing the Series to Our Boys in Uniform," *Baseball Magazine*, November 1919.

47. Sol Metzger, "Regards Athletics as Patriotic Duty," *New York Times*, July 22, 1917, sec. III, 4.

48. "Great Year Ahead in Army Athletics," *New York Times*, August 26, 1917, sec. III, 4.

49. Walter Camp, *Athletics All: Training, Organization and Play* (New York, 1927), 16, 67.

50. "Sport Flourishing in Naval Stations," and "Walter Camp Has Systematized Athletic Activities of the Nation's Soldiers," *New York Times*, February 3, 1918, sec. III, 8.

51. Camp, "Our Government Plant," *Outlook* 117 (1917), 12–13; and "Review of the Football Service and the All-America Team," *Collier's* 63 (1919), 13.

52. "Keeping the Nation Fit," *The Independent* 96 (1918), 400–1; and "What I Am Trying to Do," *World's Work* 46 (1923), 600–4.

53. Harris, vol. 2, 34–37.

54. Ibid., 30–32.

55. Katherine Mayo, *'That Damn Y': A Record of Overseas Service* (Boston, 1920), 256.

56. Retired University of Wisconsin professor Walter Agard, who served as an athletics and recreation noncom, told Edward Coffman that boxing was the only sport readily comprehended by most soldiers—many of whom had never competed in organized team sports; hence the "game" concept was novel. I wish to thank Coffman, who shared this insight with me in a letter (in my possession). For a representative how-to guide on military sports drills, see F. L. Kleeberger, "War Sports Embracing Grenade Throwing, Boxing, and Athletic Drills, Arranged in Accord with Military Procedure," *American Physical Education Review* 23 (1918), 383–98. Luther Gulick could not emphasize the tactical importance of bayonet fighting enough in a speech delivered to the American Physical Education Association, shortly after his return from the French front. Lamenting the lack of effective training, Gulick recommended that one hour a day be appropriated for bayonet practice. See his "Physical Fitness in the Fighting Armies," *American Physical Education Review* 24 (1919), 341–54, esp. 342–46.

57. Thomas Foster, "Why Our Soldiers Learn to Box," *Outing* 72 (1918), 114–16.

58. Ibid.

59. Ibid.

60. "2,000,000 Men Join Uncle Sam's League," *New York Times*, March 11, 1918, 8.

61. *Outing* 71 (1918), 279.

62. James Mennell, "The Service Football Program of World War I: Its Impact on the Popularity of the Game," *Journal of Sport History* 16 (1989), 259.

63. "War Football," *New York Times*, November 23, 1919, III, 1.

64. Alfred E. Cornebise, *The Stars and Stripes: Doughboy Journalism in World War I* (Westport, Conn., 1984), 3–6.

65. Seymour, *Baseball*, 333.

66. Cornebise, *The Stars and Stripes*. For a transatlantic discussion of British military-sports journalism, see John M. Osborne, "'To Keep the Life of the Nation on the Old Line': The Athletic News and the First World War," *Journal of Sport History* 14 (1987), 137–50.

67. Cornebise, *The Stars and Stripes*, 139–40.

68. Camp, "Industrial Athletics: How the Sports For Soldiers and Sailors Are Developing into Civilian Athletics," *Outlook* 122 (1919), 253.

69. Edwin A. Goewey, "Fewer Fans and More Athletes," *Leslie's Weekly*, February 1, 1919, 168; and for a complementary statement on the spread of American sports in Europe, due to the military efforts and the Inter-Allied Games in particular, see "Europe Welcomes American Athletes," *Leslie's Weekly*, September 6, 1919, 372.

70. Goewey, "Fewer Fans."

71. Ibid.

72. Fletcher S. Brockman, "Association Athletics as a Training in Democracy," *Physical Training* 17 (1919), 71–76. Special efforts were made to promote sports among the Asiatic and African troops serving in the Allied forces. The Chinese Labor Corps; the Indian troops serving the British Army; the Arabs; the Senegalese; the Tunisians; and other Indo-Chinese soldiers within the French troops—all these encountered Western team sports. For information about the spread of baseball in postwar Europe, see Seymour, *Baseball*, 346–63.

73. Major G. Wythe, Captain Joseph Mills Hanson, Captain C. V. Burger, eds., *The Inter-Allied Games, Paris, 22nd June to 6th July 1919* (Paris, 1919), 17–19.

74. Ibid. For additional information on the advent of the Inter-Allied Games, see Frederick W. Cozens and Florence Scovil Strumpf, *Sports in American Life* (Chicago, 1953), 198–203; and Dixon Wecter, *When Johnny Comes Marching Home* (Boston, 1944), 587–9.

75. For a partisan interpretation of the Far Eastern Games, as well as the internationalist role of the Y.M.C.A., see Elwood S. Brown, "Teaching the World to Play," *Outlook* 121 (1921), 689–93.

76. *Jim Thorpe's History of the Olympics*, 229–30.

77. Harris, *Service With Fighting Men*, v.2, 39–49.

78. Thorpe, 230. Harris calculated the participation "in all sports for the first five months of 1919" as over 31 million, in his *Service With Fighting Men*, v.2, 44.

79. Ibid., 46–7. For several months after the signing of the Armistice, the YMCA staged weekly bouts at the Cirque de Paris, which accommodated a standing crowd of 8,000, where pro boxers like Carpentier, Jeannette, McVey, battled and soldiers were admitted free of charge.

80. Edwin A. Goewey, "The Doughboys' Great Olympics," *Leslie's Weekly*, April 5, 1919, 487, 496.

81. *The Inter-Allied Games*, 154.

82. Ibid., 159–60. See also, W. D. Ball, "The Greatest Athletic Event in History," *Association Men*, March 1919, 536–37.

83. Ibid.

84. Ibid.

85. *The Inter-Allied Games*, 177.

86. See the final issue of *Athletic Bulletin*, May 1, 1922, 2.

87. *New York Times*, November 13, 1921, sec. VIII, 1; sec. VII, 2; sec. I, 23.

88. Thomas A. Storey, "War-Time Revelations in Physical Education," *American Physical Education Review* 25 (1920), 1–5, quote, 5.

89. Ibid.

90. "Field Sports," *Outing* 72 (1918), 54.

91. *New York Times*, May 28, 1919, 13.

92. See Jeffrey T. Sammons, *Beyond the Ring: The Role of Boxing in American Society* (Urbana, 1988); Gorn, "The Manassa Mauler and the Fighting Marine: An Interpretation of the Dempsey-Tunney Fights," *Journal of American Studies* 19 (1985), 20–42; Riess, *City Games: The Evolution of American Urban Society and the Rise of Sports* (Urbana, 1989), 175–80, 206–8.

93. Randolph Bourne, "War as the Health of the State," in James Oppenheim, ed., *Untimely Papers*, reprinted in *The Annals of America* (Chicago, 1968), vol. 14, 135–39.

94. Ibid.

95. Hobsbawm, *The Age of Empire*, 304–305.

96. Gulick, "Physical Fitness for the Fighting Armies," 350–51, 348–49.

97. J. R. Hildebrand, "The Geography of Games: How the Sports of Nations Form a Gazetteer of the Habits and Histories of Their Peoples," *National Geographic* 36 (1919), 89–144; quotes are on 89 and 91.

EPILOGUE

1. John Tunis, "The Great Sports Myth," *Harper's Magazine* 156 (1927), 431; and Tunis, "The Great God Football," *Harper's Magazine* 157 (1928), 742–52.

2. For additional information about his life and work, see his autobiography, *A Measure of Independence* (New York, 1964).

3. Tunis, "American Sports and American Life," *The Nation* 130 (June 25, 1930), 730; and "The Amateur Sports Racket," *The New Republic* 63 (May 28, 1930), 34–36.

4. Tunis, "More Pay for College Football Stars," *American Mercury* 39 (1936), 268.

5. Tunis, "Who Cares About Amateur Sport?" *American Mercury* 40 (1937), 91–93.

6. See, for instance, Caspar, Whitney, "Expediency in Sport," *Outlook* 117 (September 19, 1917), 96–97.

7. "Sport is Elected," *The Nation* 119 (1924), 278.

8. Paul Gallico, *The Golden People* (New York, 1965), 27–28. See also, his collected essays in *Farewell to Sport* (New York, 1938).

9. Gallico, *Farewell to Sport*, 10.

10. Foster Rhea Dulles, *Amercia Learns to Play: A History of Popular Recreation, 1607-1940* (New York, 1940).

11. Lowenthal, *The Past is a Foreign Country* (Cambridge, Eng., 1985), 8. I am indebted to John Nauright's perceptive work, "Nostalgia and the Use of the Sporting Past in Periods of Hegemonic Crisis" (Paper presented at the 1995 North American Society for Sport History conference, May 27–29 (Long Beach, CA.

12. Karl Marx, "The Eighteenth Brumaire of Louis Bonaparte," (1851), excerpted from David McLellan, ed., *Karl Marx: Selected Writings* (New York, 1977), 300.

13. Donald Katz, "Welcome to the Electronic Arena," *Sports Illustrated*, July 6, 1995, 59–77 (quote is on 62).

INDEX